Provincial Politics in the French Revolution

Paul R. Hanson

Provincial Politics

in the French Revolution

Caen and Limoges, 1789–1794

LOUISIANA STATE UNIVERSITY PRESS
Baton Rouge and London

Copyright © 1989 by Louisiana State University Press
All rights reserved
Manufactured in the United States of America
First printing
98 97 96 95 94 93 92 91 90 89   5 4 3 2 1

Designer: Patricia Douglas Crowder
Typeface: Linotron 202 Sabon
Typesetter: G & S Typesetters, Inc.
Printer: Thomson-Shore, Inc.
Binder: John H. Dekker & Sons, Inc.

Library of Congress Cataloging-in-Publication Data

Hanson, Paul R., 1952–
    Provincial politics in the French Revolution : Caen and Limoges,
  1789–1794 / Paul R. Hanson.
        p.   cm.
    Bibliography: p.
    Includes index.
    ISBN 0-8071-1520-7 (alk. paper)
      1. Caen (France)—Politics and government.   2. Limoges (France)—
  Politics and government.   3. France—History—Revolution,
  1789–1794.   I. Title.
  DC195.C2H36   1989
  944'.22—dc20
                                                                89-8156
                                                                  CIP

The paper in this book meets the guidelines for permanence and durability of the Committee
on Production Guidelines for Book Longevity of the Council on Library Resources. ∞

For Betsy, Timothy, and Christopher

Contents

Preface   xiii
Acknowledgments   xvii
Abbreviations   xix

Introduction   1
One Local Economy and Social Structure   16
Two Revolutionary Politics Take Shape, 1789–1792   31
Three Crisis in National Politics, 1792–1793   70
Four The Provinces Respond: June, 1793   101
Five Repression and Reorganization   159
Six Behind the Scenes: A Social Analysis of Local Politics   190
Conclusion   235

Appendix I   Demands of the Central Committee of Resistance to
     Oppression   249
Appendix II   Occupational Categories of Elected Officials   252
Bibliography   255
Index   265

Maps

1. Departmental Alignment in June, 1793   12
2. Political Alignment of the 1793 Departmental Delegations   13
3. Caen, 1793   33
4. Haute-Vienne Districts and District *Chefs-lieux*   197
5. Parishes and Sections of Caen   218
6. Limoges, 1793   219

Tables

1. Departmental Alignment Following the May 31 Revolution   11
2. Calvados Deputies to the National Convention   76
3. Haute-Vienne Deputies to the National Convention   78
4. Chronology of the Federalist Revolt   103
5. Occupations of Calvados Departmental Administrators,
   1790–1793   194
6. Occupations of Haute-Vienne Departmental Administrators,
   1790–1793   194
7. Occupations of Caen District Administrators, 1790–1793   200
8. Occupations of Limoges District Administrators, 1790–1793   200
9. Occupations of Caen Municipal Officials, 1790–1793   205
10. Occupations of Limoges Municipal Officials, 1790–1793   205
11. *Contribution Mobilière* of Caen Municipal Officials,
    1790–1793   210
12. *Contribution Mobilière* of Limoges Municipal Officials,
    1790–1793   210
13. Sectional Representation in Caen and Limoges, 1790–1793   220

Preface

This study represents an effort to pursue a regional analysis of provincial politics during the early years of the French Revolution. I have chosen for that purpose a comparative approach, focusing on Caen, a federalist center in 1793, and Limoges, a departmental seat that opposed the federalist revolt. There are two reasons for undertaking a comparative study. First, examining two towns that were in many ways similar should make it possible to determine what was unique to each town and to isolate the factors that led to their political differences. Second, the comparative method will better explain regional variation in local responses to national events.

For the comparative method to succeed, of course, the cases being compared must be carefully chosen. Caen is an obvious choice—it is the only one of four centers of the federalist revolt that has not already been extensively researched. Since Series L in the departmental archives has until recently remained virtually unclassified, little serious research has been undertaken concerning the Revolution in Caen.

Limoges meets the criteria for a second town in this comparison. First, it was a Jacobin town. In the weeks following May 31, 1793, the Limoges and Haute-Vienne administrators were initially noncommittal and then openly hostile to suggestions from other departments that they join in a protest directed against Paris and the National Convention. Additionally, Limoges resembled Caen in size and administrative function. Although Caen was somewhat larger than Limoges at the end of the Old Regime (Caen's population stood at just over 35,000 and Limoges' at approximately 22,000), both were among the thirty largest towns in France. Each town was the seat of an intendancy and the site of the important regional courts. Neither town hosted a *parlement*, Caen falling in the jurisdiction of Rouen and Limoges in that of Bordeaux. Limoges was a bishop's seat and Caen was not, that honor falling to the nearby town of Bayeux. The Church must thus be said to have been more important to Limoges, but both towns possessed numerous religious establishments. The role and fate of the clergy during the Revolution was much the same in the two towns. A more interesting contrast is the fact that Caen possessed a sizable Protestant minority, whereas Limoges did not.

Each town was an important regional trade center, Caen dominating Lower Normandy and Limoges doing likewise for the Limousin and the Marche. Limoges lay on the crossroads between Lyon and La Rochelle, between Bordeaux and Paris. Caen bisected one route between London and Paris, though war often disrupted trade between these two capitals. Because of Caen's proximity to the coast, merchants there traded more actively in international markets, though the Orne River and the port of Caen were not capable of handling ocean-going vessels until the very eve of the Revolution. Agriculture presented the greatest economic difference between the two towns. Whereas Caen lay at the heart of a rich grain district, the area around Limoges was hilly and rocky, very poor for cultivation.

This book is first and foremost a study of revolutionary politics, of what molded and determined those politics at the local level. More than simply to compare the local politics of two towns, however, my goal has been to establish the links between local and national political actors, between local and national political issues. Although the nature of local politics tells us a great deal about national political divisions, we need to consider social and economic factors to understand why local politics took the shape they did. Indeed, since I consider those factors to be primary, the manuscript begins and ends with them. Chapter One establishes the economic context in each town and also discusses urban geography and associational patterns among both the social elite and the lower classes of Caen and Limoges at the end of the Old Regime. Chapter Two explores the development of political alignments and confrontations during the first three years of the Revolution. By 1793, the local elite dominated the political arena in Caen, while in Limoges that arena was much more open and contentious. An examination of the events of 1789 through 1792 sheds some light on how that contrasting situation came to be. Chapter Three departs from the local scene to shift our focus to Paris in 1792 and 1793, where an emerging political crisis was increasingly drawing the attention of provincial leaders. My concern in that chapter is to emphasize the ongoing political dialogue between Paris and the provinces and the degree to which national and local issues were intertwined. Chapters Four and Five describe and discuss the federalist revolt and the subsequent repression and reorganization of departmental administrations, stressing the themes established in Chapters Two and Three. Throughout these chapters, the sections devoted to Caen are somewhat lengthier than those devoted to Limoges. This denotes no implicit judgment as to relative importance but rather the simple fact that Caen produced a revolt, with the resultant mountain of documentation, while Limoges did not. Chapter Six analyzes the social and economic factors that, in my view, explain the political differences already established. The Conclusion returns to the broader context of French revolutionary politics in order to appraise the explanatory value of the conceptual interpretations offered by Albert Soboul, Edward Whiting Fox, and Alexis de Tocqueville (discussed first in the Introduction) and to ask whether a regional analysis can help us to understand the federalist revolt and the French Revolution.

Acknowledgments

It is humbling to think that in the length of time it has taken me to complete this modest project, the French challenged and deposed their king, had a revolution, and saw Napoleon come to power. At least in my case, I did not lose my head in the process.

It has been ten years since I began research on the project, and even longer since I first conceived the idea in a graduate seminar at Berkeley. A great many people have helped me along the way, and I should like to thank a few of them here. Lynn Hunt gave me crucial early guidance and advice and throughout the writing and revising of the manuscript has been unfailingly generous with her time and good counsel. Among my graduate school colleagues, David Lansky listened patiently to my ideas and provided a sympathetic sounding board in the early stages of research and writing. During my first lengthy research trip in France, John Merriman introduced me to the pleasures and perils of living in Limoges, and his subsequent reading of the entire manuscript was enormously helpful.

A special note of thanks must go to M. J. Sydenham, who offered much-needed encouragement to a struggling young assistant professor and generously agreed to read this study. I benefited greatly from his extensive comments and criticisms. Jack Censer, Steven Vincent, and Steve Batalden have also read the manuscript at various stages, and I appreciate their advice and encouragement as well.

I should also like to acknowledge the assistance of the archivists and librarians in Caen, Limoges, and Paris, without whom this study would not have been possible. At the other end of the process, it has been a pleasure to work with the entire editorial staff at Louisiana State University Press. At several points in the preparation of the manuscript, Butler University has supported me with faculty fellowships and financial assistance.

Finally, I would like to thank my wife, Betsy Lambie, who endured a winter in Caen with me, and a summer in Limoges. Her careful eye has saved me, or perhaps I should say the reader, from any number of transgressions against the English language. Betsy has read this manuscript almost as many times as I have, and for that she has my unending gratitude.

Abbreviations

A.C. Caen	Archives Communales, Caen
A.C. Limoges	Archives Communales, Limoges
A.D. Calvados	Archives Départementales, Calvados
A.D. Haute-Vienne	Archives Départementales, Haute-Vienne
A.N.	Archives Nationales
B.M. Caen	Bibliothèque Municipale, Caen

Provincial Politics in the French Revolution

Introduction

On June 2, 1793, surrounded by the menacing ranks of the Parisian National Guard, the French National Convention proscribed and placed under watch twenty-nine of its members. The forty-eight sections of Paris, rallied by Robespierre and the Jacobin club, had revolted on May 31, demanding the abolition of the Commission of Twelve (called in May to investigate the Commune of Paris) and the exclusion from the Convention of twenty-four deputies. The proscription of twenty-nine Girondin deputies two days later marked the culmination of the May 31 revolution and was the breaking point in the eight-month political struggle between the Montagnard and Girondin factions. The Montagnards, under the growing leadership of Robespierre, emerged victorious and were to rule France until Thermidor.

But the political victory of the Montagnards came much less easily in the departments of France. Nearly fifty of the eighty-three departments protested the proscription of the deputies. Many formed departmental committees of public safety to coordinate these protests. In some, constituted local authorities convened primary assemblies. A much smaller number engaged in violent resistance to what they considered an incomplete and unrepresentative National Convention. Indeed, not until October did the cities of Bordeaux and Lyon submit to republican troops, bringing the insurrection to an end.

As early as June, the provincial protests were labeled as manifestations of "federalism," and the scattered resistance was described as a "federalist" revolt. Jean Julien of Toulouse opened his report to the Convention in early October, 1793, as follows: "Citizens, the people have conquered, federalism has expired, the misled departments have rallied to the Convention, and to indivisibility."[1] In this two-hundred-page document, Julien detailed a well-developed plot, extending back to at least January, 1793, that he claimed had united internal enemies of the Republic in an effort to undermine the liberty won by the Revolution and deliver France to the tyrants whose armies were then besieging the country.

The use of the label "federalist" to describe either the political intentions of the Girondin deputies or those of the departments that rose in their defense is problematical, but it has been adopted almost unquestioningly by historians of the Revolution. Thus, the uprisings in the provinces from June through August, 1793, have collectively been termed the "federalist revolt" and are generally understood to have been a reaction to the proscription of the Girondin deputies.

Beyond this, however, lies considerable disagreement, both with respect to the nature of the division within the National Convention and with respect to the character and significance of the federalist revolt. Historians have, for the most part, addressed these two questions separately, choosing to focus either on the Girondin/Montagnard conflict in Paris or on one of the provincial federalist centers.

Twenty years ago, Michael Sydenham published the first serious analytical treatment of the group of deputies that has come to be called the Girondins. In *The Girondins,* Sydenham carefully examines the political history of the first nine months of the National Convention, with particular attention to the political and social affiliations of alleged Girondin deputies (for example, which salons in Paris they attended), and concludes that no such political faction existed. He acknowledges the existence of a Montagnard faction but insists that one can go no further than this, that one can establish a division only between the Montagnards and the rest of the Convention. The group traditionally called the Girondins, he argues, was nothing more than a political myth created by a small group of Jacobin deputies to advance their own political fortunes.[2]

---

1. Jean Julien (de Toulouse), *Rapport fait au nom du Comité de Surveillance et de Sûreté Générale sur les administrations rebelles* (Paris, 1793), B. M. Caen, Rés. Fn. B404².
2. M. J. Sydenham, *The Girondins* (London, 1961).

Alison Patrick has directly challenged this view in her book, *The Men of the First French Republic*. Citing voting records and speeches of the deputies, as well as their participation in committees or on political mission, Patrick asserts that one can indeed speak of a Girondin faction within the Convention, identified primarily by its opposition to the growing strength of the Montagnards.[3]

If we accept the reality of a Girondin faction (and Patrick is very persuasive in her argument), the crucial question of what produced the political division between the two factions remains. The traditional Marxist interpretation of the Revolution, expressed by such prominent French historians as Georges Lefebvre and Albert Soboul, has associated the Girondins with the *haute-bourgeoisie*, specifically the commercial bourgeoisie, arguing that their politics reflected their social and economic interests. In Soboul's words, the Girondins "were passionately attached to the idea of economic freedom, freedom to undertake trading enterprises and to make uncontrolled profits, and they showed their hostility to economic regulation, price controls, requisitions, and the forced use of *assignats*, all measures which were, by way of contrast, strongly advocated by the *sans-culottes*."[4] The problem here is that very few members of the National Convention can reasonably be defined as sans-culottes. Lawyers, landowners, and merchants predominated among both Montagnards and Girondins. A 1980 study contends that virtually no difference in social background existed between these two contending factions within the Convention.[5]

The relationship between the Girondin/Montagnard conflict and the federalist revolt is an obvious one. The Girondins are generally associated with federalism, and it was undeniably the proscription of the twenty-nine deputies that sparked the provincial revolts in June, 1793. Lefebvre and Soboul describe the provincial protest as a revolt of the commercial bourgeoisie rising in defense of their economic interests. To quote Soboul again: "This rising was essentially the work of the middle classes who dominated the departmental administrative organs and who were anxious about their property."[6] That the revolt was centered in such commercial towns as Bordeaux,

---

3. Alison Patrick, *The Men of the First French Republic* (Baltimore, 1972).
4. Georges Lefebvre, *La Révolution Française* (Paris, 1951), 273–74; Albert Soboul, *The French Revolution, 1787–1799*, trans. Alan Forrest and Colin Jones (New York, 1975), 276–77.
5. See Jacqueline Chaumié, "Les Girondins et les Cent Jours," *Annales Historiques de la Révolution Française*, XLIII (1971), 329–65; Chaumié, "Les Girondins," in Albert Soboul (ed.), *Actes du Colloque Girondins et Montagnards* (Paris, 1980), 19–60.
6. Soboul, *The French Revolution*, 318.

Marseille, Lyon, and Caen is cited as evidence in support of this argument.

Although this interpretation of the federalist revolt has not gone un-challenged, it has withstood criticism more successfully than the Marxist analysis of the Girondin/Montagnard conflict. That criticism has come from two directions. Sydenham, though he has not looked closely at the provincial protests, has denied the relationship between federalism and the Girondins, arguing instead that the revolts were essentially royalist in nature. This view must be dismissed, as Sydenham himself would now agree. Supporters of the monarchy did indeed participate in the revolts, particularly in Lyon and Toulon, but the principal aims and leaders of the movement were not royalist. Issues other than the fate of the Girondin deputies combined to motivate the provincial rebels, but the restoration of the monarchy was not among them.[7]

At the local level, one can discern two strains of scholarly interpretation of the federalist revolt. The greater number of studies have adopted a sympathetic view of the federalist rebels, describing the proscription of the Girondin deputies as an illegal attack on the National Convention and interpreting the revolt itself as a legitimate effort to defend national sovereignty. In this group, we can include Henri Wallon's two-volume survey of the federalist movement and Georges Guibal's work on Provence.[8] Fewer studies have taken the opposing view, implicitly accepting the proscription of the Girondins as an expression of popular will and describing the provincial protests as an irresponsible action taken by local administrators who failed to heed the desires of their constituencies. Here we can cite Paul Nicolle's study of the Orne and Daniel Stone's work on Rennes.[9]

Few of these works, however, seriously consider the social basis of the fed-

---

7. Sydenham, *The Girondins*, 21. See also M. J. Sydenham, "The Republican Revolt of 1793: A Plea for Less Localized Local Studies," *French Historical Studies*, XI (Spring, 1981), 120–38. Despite Sydenham's legitimate objections to the term "federalist," I have chosen to use it in this book, both because it has been general practice for nearly two centuries and because I see no clear and satisfactory alternative. The label "republican" could apply equally to those who supported the May 31 revolution and those who opposed it and thus would itself be controversial. The label "provincial" is less value-laden but also less discriminating, and to adopt it in this book would be a source more of confusion than of clarity.

8. H. Wallon, *La Révolution du 31 mai et le fédéralisme en 1793* (Paris, 1886); Georges Guibal, *Le Mouvement fédéraliste en Provence en 1793* (Paris, 1908).

9. Paul Nicolle, "Le Mouvement fédéraliste dans l'Orne en 1793," *Annales Historiques de la Révolution Française*, XIII (1936), 481–512, XIV (1937), 215–33, XV (1938), 12–33, 289–313, 385–410; Daniel Stone, "La Révolte fédéraliste à Rennes," *Annales Historiques de la Révolution Française*, XLIII (1971), 367–87.

eralist revolt, a question that has been addressed by three more-recent studies. William Scott and Alan Forrest, writing about the early years of the Revolution in Marseille and Bordeaux, respectively, each lend support to the orthodox Marxist interpretation. Both historians are cautious about attributing too much to social and economic factors, but their conclusions stress the dominant role played in local politics by the commercial elite of these two federalist centers. Challenging the argument of Scott, and the interpretation of Lefebvre, is the unpublished dissertation of John Cameron, Jr. In his study of Marseille, Cameron asserts that "there was little or no economic or social difference" between the Marseille federalists and their opponents and that the revolt of the sections in Marseille was essentially a reaction against local terrorists, which intensified and broadened after the June 2 proscriptions.[10]

The social character of the federalist revolt thus remains as controversial as the goals and motivations of its adherents. This controversy is in part a product of the inherent weaknesses of local studies. The monographs cited here do not give us a full understanding of federalism for two reasons: they do not compare the situation in one area with that in other federalist centers or, perhaps more importantly, with that in Jacobin towns; and they do not establish firmly enough the relationship between local and national politics. These works have advanced our understanding of revolutionary politics in various federalist towns, but the question still remains: What motivated certain towns to join in the federalist movement while others supported the Montagnard Convention?

This question is firmly tied to the Patrick/Sydenham debate regarding the existence of a Girondin faction. Patrick herself suggested that a look to the provinces might help to elucidate the nature of the Girondin/Montagnard conflict.[11] Surely the character of local constituencies and the political situa-

10. William Scott, *Terror and Repression in Revolutionary Marseille* (London, 1973); Alan Forrest, *Society and Politics in Revolutionary Bordeaux* (Oxford, 1975); John Burton Cameron, Jr., "The Revolution of the Sections in Marseille: Federalism in the Department of the Bouches-du-Rhône in 1793" (Ph.D. dissertation, University of North Carolina, Chapel Hill, 1971), 3.
11. Patrick, *Men of the First French Republic,* 192. As if in response to Patrick's call, several articles focusing on the federalist revolt have appeared in recent years. See Bill Edmonds, "'Federalism' and Urban Revolt in France in 1793," *Journal of Modern History,* LV (March, 1983), 22–53; and M. H. Crook, "Federalism and the French Revolution: The Revolt in Toulon in 1793," *History,* LXV (October, 1980), 383–97. For a recent attempt to analyze the differences between Girondins and Montagnards by focusing on national politics, see Patrice Higonnet, "The Social and Cultural Antecedents of Revolutionary Discontinuity: Montagnards and Girondins," *English Historical Review,* C (July, 1985), 513–44.

tion in given departments should tell us something about the deputies who represented them in Paris.

In his very sound article on federalism, Bill Edmonds focuses precisely on local politics in particular cities (Lyon, Marseille, and Toulon) in an effort to understand the character of the revolt. He makes three main points in his analysis: first, that "violent shocks from outside combined with unusual local circumstances" to trigger protest in the provinces; second, that a qualitative difference existed between federalist "protest" and federalist "revolt"; and third, that the revolts were principally "a defensive reaction against Montagnard centralism" and not an aggressive assertion of provincial interests.[12] I am in general agreement with the first two points, although where Edmonds stresses local political conflicts, I would stress the interrelation of local and national political issues as a fundamental aspect of the federalist movement. Edmonds and I further disagree on whether one can discern a "popular" component to the federalist revolt. Edmonds argues that the federalists enjoyed considerable popular support, whereas I maintain just the opposite in this book. This disagreement is partly due, I think, to the fact that Edmonds focuses his attention on Lyon, Marseille, and Toulon. I would argue that Bordeaux and Caen are more representative federalist cities.

Edward Whiting Fox, in a very provocative book, has proposed a framework of analysis that may help resolve this multifaceted debate. He asserts that the French monarchy, developing in the sixteenth and seventeenth centuries, was built on the administrative and agricultural towns of the French hinterland. Fox argues that the commercial towns, principally the ports, were not fully integrated in the new state—that, in fact, there existed a self-contained commercial society with its own distinct social system and values—and that the dichotomy between the agricultural hinterland and the commercial periphery came to a head during the Revolution. The confrontation came, as he sees it, during the drafting of the constitution and reached its crisis point in June, 1793. Fox suggests that "because this Federalist revolt against the Jacobin government was based mainly in port cities, it seems plausible that it represented the last stand of the old commercial society against integration in the administrative state."[13]

Fox is not the first historian, of course, to utilize an interpretative frame-

12. Edmonds, "'Federalism' and Urban Revolt," 53.
13. Edward Whiting Fox, *History in Geographic Perspective: The Other France* (New York, 1971), 105.

work stressing geography and the growth of the state. Alexis de Tocqueville singled out state centralization as the most fundamental development of the Old Regime monarchy, a development consolidated by the Revolution and Napoleon. Tocqueville saw this centralization both as a cause of the Revolution and as a reason for its failure. The aristocracy resented the encroachments of the crown on its traditional prerogatives and consequently forced the convening of the Estates General. But once the Revolution erupted, the people, having for so long been ruled by a despotic state, failed to responsibly exercise their newly gained political liberty. This is the second major theme of Tocqueville's book: the conflict between liberty and equality that the French people could not satisfactorily resolve. The French people, Tocqueville felt, preferred legal equality under a dictator to political freedom under representative government. State centralization under the monarchy had in effect so stifled the Frenchman's capacity for political action that he was unable to accept, after 1789, the responsibility for self-government.[14]

This encroachment of the state, however, had not extended to the limits of the kingdom's boundaries in 1789. Tocqueville distinguished between the *pays d'élection* and *pays d'état,* observing that the latter enjoyed greater autonomy on the eve of the Revolution and presumably a greater propensity for responsible self-government. Tocqueville said little about the respective attitudes and experiences of the *pays d'élection* and *pays d'état* during the turmoils of the Revolution itself. It requires but a moment's reflection, though, to realize that the *pays d'état* roughly equal Fox's commercial periphery, while the *pays d'élection* match, on the map, the administrative hinterland that Fox describes.

The juxtaposition of Fox's and Tocqueville's analyses yields a conceptualization in which state centralization and commercial development are the dynamic elements. Their interaction in late-eighteenth-century France produced a political confrontation between the hinterland, already integrated in the centralizing state, and the commercially oriented periphery. Clearly, economic and social factors remain important in this analysis. Fox posits the existence of distinct social systems and values in the hinterland and the periphery, though he does not describe those social systems. In this conceptualization, the Marxist interpretation is modified, not rejected. The

14. Alexis de Tocqueville, *The Old Regime and the French Revolution,* trans. Stuart Gilbert (New York, 1955). See especially 57–108, 212–22.

state becomes a more active agent than Marxists allow, and the unit of social analysis becomes regions, rather than classes, which have proved so difficult to define in a precapitalist society such as eighteenth-century France.

The federalist revolt provides an excellent context within which to examine the relationship between national and local politics, between Paris and the provinces, between elected officials and their constituencies during the Revolution. All of these were highlighted during the three months following the May 31–June 2 revolution of the Paris sections. More than previous Paris revolutions, this outburst elicited an immediate and widespread response from the departments of France. Although the reaction proved to be short-lived, for several weeks it was an intense expression of grievances against Paris and the Jacobin minority, a reaction itself led by a relatively small number of administrators, whose final victory would not come until 9 Thermidor.

The proscription of the Girondin deputies and the revolt that followed came barely eight months after the National Convention had opened. Dissension and factionalism within the Convention marked this period. The drafting of a new constitution, the primary task of this renewed legislative body, was hopelessly mired in vituperative debate. Letters from the departments poured into Paris decrying this delay and calling for unity within the Convention. The Girondin deputies, who formed a majority, first attempted to break the stalemate not through compromise but rather by trying to silence their political opponents. Their two-pronged effort failed on both counts, first in the unsuccessful trial of Marat and then with the ill-fated Commission of Twelve, formed to investigate the activities of the Paris sections and municipality. In the end, it was the Montagnards, backed by the Paris sections and finally supported by the moderate Plain, who carried the day in early June. With the uprising of June 2, we see the resolution of a political crisis that had simmered for two-thirds of a year.

It is because this conflict existed over such a relatively long period that the revolt that followed its climax offers such an important insight into national and local politics and the interrelation between the two. The federalist revolt was not simply a protest of the proscription of twenty-nine deputies, though this action did trigger the revolt. The provincial protest, which initially included nearly fifty departments, was more broadly directed against the dominance of Paris in national politics. Particularly offensive, and threatening, to departmental administrators was the unprecedented political activity of the Paris crowd. Both deputies and departmental administrators talked in early

1793 of shifting the Convention to Bourges, where the national representatives could deliberate in a calm and untroubled atmosphere, or of accomplishing the same goal by bringing troops to Paris to protect the Convention from outside interference. Underlying these fears was the feeling that a fair and just constitution, the anticipated remedy for all France's ills, could not be delivered under the intimidating surveillance of the Paris sections—certainly not by a legislature that had been stripped of twenty-nine of its members.

The impatience for a new constitution and the apprehension about Parisian domination were not fleeting issues. They had preoccupied people in Paris and the provinces for several months. Widely circulating newspapers and journals reported on events and spread rumors. Many of the deputies maintained regular contact with their constituents by letter. The departments closest to the capital often sent their own delegations to the Convention to carry messages and then report back regarding conditions in Paris. This volatile political atmosphere erupted into violent protest in the months following the proscription of the Girondin deputies.

Historians have tended to exaggerate the scope of the federalist revolt, with most estimating the number of protesting departments at roughly sixty. However, even with reliance placed primarily on the account of Henri Wallon, whose sympathies lay clearly with the Girondins and federalists, it is evident that only forty-seven departments firmly protested by letter the May 31 revolution, while thirty-four either declared open support of the Montagnard Convention or remained indifferent.[15] A majority of the protesting departments took no significant action beyond the letter of protest. Most of these had retracted their protests by late June or early July, after the new

15. Wallon, *La Révolution du 31 mai, passim.* The Vendée and the Deux-Sèvres were, of course, engaged in royalist insurrection. These two complete the total of eighty-three departments that existed at that time. Bill Edmonds and I differ somewhat in our categorization of federalist departments. We both rely on Wallon to a considerable extent, and our differences are thus indicative of the degree to which Wallon's often ambiguous characterization of departmental political postures requires subjective interpretation. Sometimes Wallon is misleading. Based on his work alone, one might well group the Haute-Vienne with the federalist departments, as Edmonds does. I think this is clearly in error. After reading Edmonds' article I went back through Wallon's analysis, department by department, and made one or two adjustments in my own breakdown. Edmonds employs four categories for the federalist departments, compared with my two, and identifies forty-three federalist departments, compared with my forty-seven. Edmonds includes the Aisne, Haute-Saône, and Haute-Vienne, while I do not; I include the Alpes-Maritimes, Cantal, Maine-et-Loire, Marne, Meurthe, Puy-de-Dôme, and Pyrénées-Orientales, while he does not. Edmonds groups the departments I have described as "engaging in prolonged resistance" under two headings: "Contribution to 'federalist' armed forces"; and "Armed revolt." I include the Ain, Jura, and Morbihan, while Edmonds does not. He indicates

constitution had been published. Only thirteen departments engaged in prolonged resistance to the Convention. The departmental alignment is given in Table 1 and Map 1.

The map shows that the departments supporting the Montagnard Convention were located in the north and northeast. The departments protesting the proscription of the Girondin deputies lay in the west, southwest, and south. The four centers of prolonged federalist resistance—Bordeaux, Marseille, Lyon, and Caen—were all commercial towns in these peripheral areas. The thirteen departments that engaged actively in the revolt were clustered around those four centers.

A striking correlation emerges between the distribution of federalist departments and that of departments whose delegations to the Convention were predominantly Girondin. Map 2 represents the political alignments of the 1793 departmental delegations, as constructed by Alison Patrick. It shows that the departments of the southern, western, and coastal areas were generally Girondin, while the Montagnard departments lay in the central, northern, and eastern parts of France.

The geographical distribution of the federalist/Girondin departments and the Jacobin/Montagnard departments lends added weight to Fox's thesis of a political split between the commercial periphery and the administrative hinterland of France. There are exceptions to the pattern, however. Several important commercial towns—Rouen and Nantes notable among them—did not join in the federalist revolt. Several departments of the hinterland—the Côte-d'Or, the Marne, the Meurthe—did not initially support the Montagnard Convention. Some departments that sent Montagnard delegations to the Convention—the Côte-d'Or and the Sarthe, for example—still protested the proscription of the Girondins. The reverse was true as well. The Haute-Vienne and the Aisne, despite sending predominantly Girondin delegations to Paris, supported the Montagnard Convention after June 2. Closer scrutiny, then, is required before it can be determined whether Fox's thesis remains as persuasive at the local level as it appears to be on a national scale.

---

that the Loire-Inférieure, Orne, and Sarthe contributed troops to the federalists, while I am quite certain they did not. Finally, Edmonds includes the Var among his departments engaging in armed revolt, while I am inclined to consider resistance in the Var predominantly royalist. These are mostly, though not entirely, minor differences. We do not disagree substantially on the number of protesting departments or the geographic distribution. I do not believe that our differences can be resolved by reference to Wallon. Local archives and local histories will have to be consulted.

TABLE 1 Departmental Alignment Following the May 31 Revolution

Jacobin departments (departments supporting the Montagnard Convention)

Aisne	Haute-Loire	Nord
Allier	Haute-Marne	Oise
Ardennes	Haute-Saône	Pas-de-Calais
Ariège	Haute-Vienne	Saône-et-Loire
Aube	Haut-Rhin	Seine
Bas-Rhin	Indre	Seine-et-Marne
Basses-Pyrénées	Indre-et-Loire	Seine-et-Oise
Charente-Inférieure	Loiret	Seine-Inférieure
Cher	Loir-et-Cher	Vosges
Corrèze	Meuse	Yonne
Creuse	Moselle	
Eure-et-Loir	Nièvre	

Federalist departments (departments protesting the Girondin proscriptions)

Ain	Finistère	Maine-et-Loire
Alpes-Maritimes	Gard	Manche
Ardèche	Gers	Marne
Aude	Gironde	Mayenne
Aveyron	Haute-Garonne	Meurthe
Basses-Alpes	Hautes-Alpes	Morbihan
Bouches-du-Rhône	Hautes-Pyrénées	Orne
Calvados	Hérault	Puy-de-Dôme
Cantal	Ille-et-Vilaine	Pyrénées-Orientales
Charente	Isère	Rhône-et-Loire
Côte-d'Or	Jura	Sarthe
Côtes-du-Nord	Landes	Somme
Dordogne	Loire-Inférieure	Tarn
Doubs	Lot	Var
Drôme	Lot-et-Garonne	Vienne
Eure	Lozère	

Departments engaging in prolonged resistance

Ain	Finistère	Mayenne
Bouches-du-Rhône	Gard	Morbihan
Calvados	Gironde	Rhône-et-Loire
Côtes-du-Nord	Ille-et-Vilaine	
Eure	Jura	

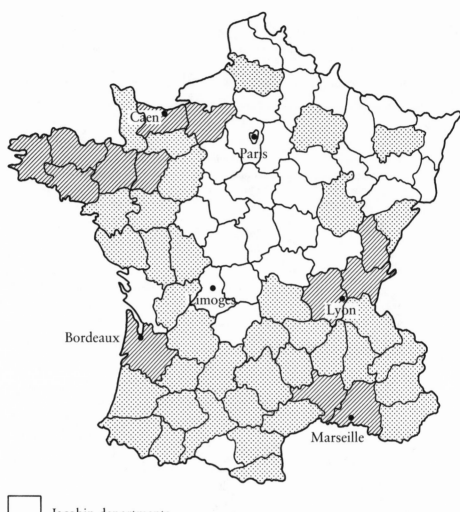

Jacobin departments

Federalist departments

Departments engaging in prolonged resistance

MAP 1. Departmental Alignment in June, 1793

Colleen Baker

MAP 2. Political Alignment of the 1793 Departmental Delegations

Reprinted, by permission, from Alison Patrick, *The Men of the First French Republic* (Baltimore, 1972), 189.

At this point, one encounters difficulties, for Fox does not elaborate on the differing "social systems" that he claims characterized the hinterland and the periphery. A regional model may be a useful heuristic device in describing the political divisions within France during the Revolution, but for a historical explanation of why those regions differed, one must descend to another level. If Fox's thesis is generally accurate, then at the local level one should be able to find a reflection of the administrative/commercial dichotomy in social structures and to see the connections between those structures and local politics.

Several factors merit attention as one searches for those connections. The most obvious is the nature of the local economy in a particular town or area and the social fabric that it produced. Additionally important at a time of revolutionary upheaval are the patterns of sociability both within and between social groups. A number of questions are relevant to this issue. Was the social elite cohesive or divided? Was the elite at odds with the lower classes or linked to them through patron-client relationships? What agents of sociability functioned among the lower classes under the Old Regime, and what impact did this have on their ability to organize and express their views after 1789? These factors varied greatly across France at the end of the Old Regime, and if Fox's thesis is valid, one should see their influence on the political divisions that emerged in the revolutionary era.

The relationship between social structures and political attitudes lies, of course, at the center of controversy in historiography of the French Revolution. Marxist historians, particularly Soboul, have interpreted the events of 1789 as a "bourgeois revolution," a class struggle between the declining aristocracy and the rising bourgeoisie. Critics of this "Marxist orthodoxy" insist that 1789 was not a product of social tensions—that far from being a class struggle, it was instead a political revolution with social consequences.[16]

This debate has principally focused on the causes of the Revolution, but it clearly carries over into conflicting interpretations of the Revolution itself. It is Soboul, again, who has made the most explicit argument with regard to the relationship between political posture and social class. He identifies two competing concepts of representative government in France during the Revolution—one popular and the other bourgeois. The outlines of these two opposing political philosophies emerged clearly in 1792 and 1793. The

16. George V. Taylor, "Noncapitalist Wealth and the Origins of the French Revolution," *American Historical Review*, LXXII (1967), 469–96; see also William Doyle's book, *Origins of the French Revolution* (Oxford, 1980).

Girondin deputies, Soboul argues, championed the concept of a truly representative government, along the lines of the English model, in which elected deputies acted as the autonomous representatives of their constituents. The Parisian sans-culottes, and the Jacobin deputies to some extent, contended that such an arrangement would impinge on the freedom, indeed the sovereignty, of the people and that deputies should serve only as "agents of the people."

These two concepts came into open conflict in 1793 when Marat and the Paris sections demanded the recall of those deputies who had voted for a referendum on the fate of the king. The Girondins responded by defending the inviolability of elected deputies. The sans-culottes in turn insisted on the right—in fact, the responsibility—of all citizens to vigilantly watch and review the conduct of their elected representatives. This confrontation heightened in April and May with the trial of Marat and the formation of the Commission of Twelve. On June 2, 1793, with the proscription of the Girondin deputies, the popular concept of representative government triumphed, at least temporarily. The sans-culottes consolidated their victory in September, 1793, but then saw it institutionalized in the revolutionary government of the year II and finally reversed by the reactionary regime that followed Thermidor.[17]

The political conflict that raged in the capital during the early months of 1793 expressed itself in the provinces of France as well. In neither arena was the debate over what the new regime in France should be a matter confined to 1793. It began in 1790, as the first political clubs came together, and it continued through the Directory. But the lines of debate were most clearly drawn in the spring and summer of 1793, both within the National Convention and among the departments of France. It was this central issue that brought national and local politics together.

Soboul's notion of "agent versus representative democracy" may not be the answer to the political riddle that the French Revolution in a sense represents. But it does offer a possible bridge between the impersonal level of regional analysis proposed by Fox and the personal level of popular politics as acted out in the many cities and towns of revolutionary France. Both ideas merit further study, and the federalist revolt provides an ideal context within which to carry it out.

17. Albert Soboul, *The Sans-culottes*, trans. Rémy Inglis Hall (Princeton, 1980), 106–18.

One

Local Economy and Social Structure

Caen and Limoges under the Old Regime fulfilled similar functions. Administratively and judicially, they were almost identical—each was the seat of an intendancy, each supported important regional courts, and neither played host to a *parlement*. Both towns enjoyed the privilege of nominating mayors and electing municipal councils. Caen countered Limoges' ecclesiastical prestige with an academic reputation—Limoges was a bishop's seat, whereas Caen boasted a university. Both towns served as important regional trade centers—Caen lay at the center of Lower Normandy, and Limoges dominated the Limousin and the Marche.

Looking more closely, however, one discovers fundamental differences in the vitality of the two economies in the late eighteenth century. Rich and productive farmland surrounded Caen. The principal crop, wheat, not only fed the population in all except the leanest years but also produced a surplus that helped finance a thriving textile industry early in the century and a shift into varied commercial activity later, after competition had made local textiles less profitable. The move away from textiles came largely before the 1780s; so the 1786 treaty with England, which created serious unemployment in many northern French textile towns on the eve of the Revolution, did not seriously affect Caen. Even the poor harvests of 1788 and 1789 did not prove disastrous for Caen's economy.

Limoges, on the other hand, lay in a poor agricultural region. The rocky, infertile hills of the Limousin yielded rye, not wheat; and in harsh years, most peasants were forced to supplement their diets with chestnuts. The region did support a modest textile industry, but the local economy in the eighteenth century can best be described as depressed. The Revolution brought little improvement. Five consecutive poor harvests racked the Haute-Vienne, beginning in 1788. Limoges itself suffered a serious fire in September, 1790, a crippling tragedy that was a portent of the economic hardship that plagued the entire department throughout the Revolution.

The contrast in agricultural fertility carried over, though less dramatically, into other economic sectors. Jean-Claude Perrot describes the half-century between 1725 and 1775 as a period of commercial expansion that pushed the population of Caen from 27,000 to 40,000, inspired an impressive wave of road and building projects, and produced a level of urbanization in Caen that "surpassed Paris, four large ports and several celebrated cities of the interior."[1] The Limoges economy expanded, too, during the eighteenth century, but it built upon a weaker base. Georges Verynaud writes that by the beginning of the century, "Limoges had become a poor city."[2] Local industry was in decline, roads were in miserable shape, and the expense of recent wars had overtaxed the population. The reign of Louis XV rejuvenated somewhat the tired Limoges economy. Successive intendants turned their attention to improving the region's roads, and after 1725 a modest textile industry took root, employing one-third of the Limoges work force by mid-century. This growth was limited, however, and could not fully absorb the considerable mendicant population that the cathedral attracted to Limoges.

The growth of the Caen economy, then, proved more dynamic than that of the Limoges economy, but the character of that growth differed as well. One cannot ignore the importance of the rich agricultural basin to the prosperity of Caen. Perrot has demonstrated a strong correlation between Caen's economy and fluctuations in local wheat production and price. Increases in production during the 1730s enriched local farmers and depressed real rural wages, thereby driving the surplus population to the city, where people could find work in the flourishing artisanal trades financed by farm profits.[3] Ironically, the agricultural sector later competed with the artisanal industry

1. Jean-Claude Perrot, *Genèse d'une ville moderne: Caen au XVIII*e *siècle* (Paris, 1975), II, 951.
2. Georges Verynaud, *Histoire de Limoges* (Limoges, 1973), 88.
3. Perrot, *Genèse d'une ville moderne*, II, 801, 948.

that it had encouraged. Salaries for temporary work in agriculture, at peak periods, generally exceeded those for urban labor, and it was difficult for manufacturers to procure raw materials at the same time that labor was available.

A combination of factors—the cost of importing wool and cotton, the high cost of labor, and competition from Upper Normandy—caused a gradual shift within the Caen textile industry from wool production to linen and finally to lace. The wool industry had gone into a steady, and sharp, decline as early as 1740. Manufacturers shifted their efforts to linen production, which maintained its viability until 1760, when the Seven Years War triggered the gradual decline of the linen industry by disrupting the supply of raw materials. Lace production began to grow around 1750, accelerated after 1762, and maintained a peak level from 1772 until the 1790s. A luxury fabric, lace enjoyed a wide market and could be produced by women and children at home without expensive machinery, thus reducing labor costs.[4]

The period of decline in the main textile sectors coincided with the period of Caen's greatest growth, 1725 to 1775. This apparent contradiction is explained by a surge in trade activity after 1750. Throughout the century, textile production tended to be dominated by merchants and speculators rather than manufacturers. Linen production, in particular, became a speculative and capitalistic activity, since much of the flax and all the cotton had to be imported from outside of Normandy. Capital and commercial ties were necessary for the procurement of primary materials and, of course, the sale of final products. This period also witnessed a shift in production from the city to the surrounding countryside, as the putting-out system proved to be more economical than urban production. Linen production in Caen peaked between 1720 and 1740, whereas rural production soared by 800 percent from 1730 to 1760.[5]

On the eve of the Revolution, then, Caen was not predominantly a textile town. The makeup of the labor force reflected the city's diverse economy. To be sure, textile manufacture employed nearly half of the labor engaged in urban production (as opposed to service occupations), and between 1760 and 1792 the number of textile workers had nearly doubled (from 1,343 to 2,572, of whom 1,929 were salaried workers). However, the introduction of

4. *Ibid.*, I, 381–438, II, 725–28.
5. *Ibid.*, I, 417–21.

women and children into the lace industry accounted for much of this increase. The labor force as a whole, moreover, was diverse. Service workers (including transport and commercial employees, servants, and day laborers attached to commercial enterprises) comprised 60 percent of wage earners in 1792. Wage earners represented just over 18 percent of the total population, and the textile industry employed just 30 percent of those wage earners. Compare this situation with that in the textile town of Elbeuf, where 56 percent of the population were wage earners in the 1780s and nearly all of these worked in the textile industry.[6] Caen, by contrast, had a relatively low number of wage earners and a larger number of self-employed artisans, shopkeepers, and merchants.

As textile production became more competitive, manufacturers who could no longer compete in producing wool and linen turned to commerce. Perrot emphasizes, time and again, the commercial mentality of the people of Caen. Norman customary law regarding inheritance and division of property tended to impede capital investment (by failing to distinguish between business capital and family capital) but in no way discouraged commercial speculation. Lace was a commercial commodity par excellence—it required little capital investment, it utilized cheap labor, and its market extended from Paris and the Breton coast to the North Sea. During the 1760s, lace making generated gross product of as much as four million *livres* per year for Caen, an amount that outstripped by far the contributions of the other textile branches and made lace making one of the leading sources of urban wealth. In 1776, Caen boasted forty-six lace entrepreneurs, a 150-percent increase since 1750.[7] Many lace merchants expanded their activities and became true *négociants,* dealing not only in lace but in other luxury commodities as well.

Between 1750 and 1789, production in Caen increased only slightly, while trade in and out of the city, by land and by sea, increased by 50 percent. The importance of commerce to the local economy is evidenced by the size of the two regional fairs in the area. Since the 1740s, the wholesale fair at Guibray (held in August) and the retail fair in Caen (held in the spring) had been the second- and third-largest fairs in France. The two fairs were complementary rather than competitive. Caen merchants controlled the

6. Jeffrey Kaplow, *Elbeuf during the Revolutionary Period: History and Social Structure* (Baltimore, 1964), 67–69; Perrot, *Genèse d'une ville moderne,* I, 265–73.

7. Perrot, *Genèse d'une ville moderne,* I, 318–19, 353, 358, 381, 385, 430–32, 518.

stalls at Guibray, located near Falaise, and that fair in particular attracted a national clientele.[8]

Merchants from throughout northern France and as far south as Lyon attended both fairs. They offered goods ranging from drugs and spices to hardware and textiles of all sorts. Horses and cattle were also sold in most years. At mid-century, the volume and value of goods available at Guibray tended on average to be twice as great as those of goods offered at Caen. As the century progressed, that gap narrowed. In addition, after 1770, the Caen fair proved generally more successful, for approximately 75 percent of the goods brought to market there were sold, compared with 50 percent at Guibray. This attests to the growing commercial dominance of Caen within Lower Normandy.[9]

The two fairs did show some decline in the latter part of the century, brought on in part by improvements in the national road network and the increasing tendency of merchants to buy directly from producers. The last outstanding year for the Caen fair was 1767, when goods valued at 8,853,000 *livres* were brought to market and sales totaled 6,946,000 *livres*. By 1778, following a period of agricultural depression, those figures had dropped to 5,719,000 and 4,191,000 *livres*, respectively. The last years of the Old Regime were more prosperous, however, and the royal inspector reported particularly successful fairs in 1785 and 1787. The role of these fairs in the regional economy would remain important well into the nineteenth century.[10]

Two periods of war contributed to the commercial boom of the late eighteenth century in Caen. Both the War of Austrian Succession (1740–1748) and the Seven Years War (1756–1763) closed the coastal shipping lanes and forced trade within France to travel overland. Forced reliance on inland routes inspired extensive road improvement efforts, particularly following the Seven Years War. This improvement, in turn, facilitated internal trade and further boosted Caen's commerce. By the 1780s, traffic was moving daily between Caen and Rouen, Paris, Alençon, and Cherbourg. Perrot describes what he calls a "Building-Transport cycle." Each period of national road improvement was followed by major street renovation and building

8. *Ibid.,* I, 467–71, II, 729–48.
9. *Ibid.,* I, 490. See also A.N. F¹² 1232 (Foire de Caen), and F¹² 1235 (Foire du Guibray).
10. A.N. F¹² 1232; Henri Sée, "Notes sur les Foires en France et particulièrement sur les Foires de Caen au XVIIIᵉ siècle," *Revue d'Histoire économique et sociale,* XV (1927), 366–85.

projects within Caen. Twenty-five streets were redone between 1750 and 1789, and major construction projects on the docks, the fairgrounds, and the grain market were carried out. Thus, the expansion of Caen's commercial role was primarily responsible for the rapid urbanization of the city.[11]

Caen did not develop as a significant maritime port until late in the century. The larger part of Caen's trade went inland, for two reasons. One was the improving condition of the royal highways. The other was the difficulty of navigation on the Orne, which followed a meandering, silt-obstructed route from Caen to the English Channel. This did not prevent Caen merchants, however, from casting longing glances toward the ports of England and the North Sea. Between 1747 and 1782, the people of Caen sent twelve petitions to Paris requesting that a major project be undertaken to make the Orne fully navigable. The 1747 petition joined the signatures of fifty-six Caen *négociants* with those of fifty nobles and seigneurs, who appreciated that an upgrading of the port of Caen would enhance the possibilities of selling their grain.[12] The petitioners' dreams were partially realized in 1785 with the completion of a canal straightening the course of the Orne and making Caen accessible to small seagoing vessels. The renovations proposed in these petitions, however, would not be fully realized until the Second Empire. Indeed, the persistent aspirations of the people of Caen for major port status have consistently been thwarted, up to the present day, by the continued growth of Le Havre, Cherbourg, and Saint-Malo.

The aspirations of the people of Limoges were not so lofty. Limoges could never become more than a regional center of trade, and its inhabitants seemed to sense that. The surrounding region boasted no thriving agriculture that might generate profits for commercial speculation. The Vienne River would never be navigable except for light boats and the occasional log boom bringing wood to the city for construction and fuel.

The industry that had grown up around mid-century remained modest in scope on the eve of the Revolution. Textiles continued to employ the largest number of workers, approximately 30 percent of the total work force. The Laforest *fabrique* alone, built in 1765, employed nearly 1,800 workers by the late 1780s. The construction trades also provided work for a significant number of laborers, both in Limoges and through seasonal migration to Paris. The porcelain industry, which would make Limoges famous in the

11. Perrot, *Genèse d'une ville moderne*, I, 452–61.
12. *Ibid.*, I, 25, II, 598. For the 1747 petition, see A.N. F[14] 142[B].

nineteenth century, was only in its infancy in the 1780s. Kaolin, the white clay used in the manufacture of porcelain, had been discovered in the area in the late 1760s. The Grellet brothers financed the first porcelain manufactory in Limoges in 1771, employing about two dozen workers. By 1783, with Gabriel Grellet now in sole control, the enterprise was selling kaolin to producers in Copenhagen, Amsterdam, St. Petersburg, Zurich, Paris, Marseille, and several other cities. In 1784, Grellet sold the manufactory to the king, and it became more or less a subsidiary of the porcelain works in Sèvres. Grellet remained as director, but business declined, perhaps because of neglect on Grellet's part. In 1785 and 1786, the accounts showed deficits of more than twenty thousand *livres*. The king dispatched royal inspectors to ascertain the problem, and in April, 1788, François Alluaud replaced Grellet as director. The business showed a brief resurgence, but then the Revolution intervened, and by 1794, the fledgling porcelain manufactory had virtually shut down. All three of these prominent commercial families— Laforest, Grellet, and Alluaud—would be influential in local politics during the Revolution.[13]

The Church, the royal administrative and judicial offices, and regional commerce joined this modest industrial sector in supporting the town's population. The local economy did improve over the course of the century and, as in Caen, the face and shape of the city changed somewhat. But credit for the urban renewal and road improvements that did take place after 1730 must go to a succession of ambitious intendants and not to the lethargic local elite. The intendants Louis Tourny (1730–1743), Anne Robert Jacques Turgot (1761–1774), and Marius Jean Baptiste Nicolas d'Aine (1775–1783) supervised the widening of roads, the demolition of the town walls, and efforts to purify the water supply. They received minimal support from the municipality, whose finances during this period have been described as "less than brilliant."[14] As a result, local main roads still required work in 1789, and Limoges continued to enjoy a reputation as a filthy, unpleasant city well into the nineteenth century. The walls, at least, had entirely disappeared by the 1780s.

13. A.N. F¹² 1493 (Porcelaines: manufactures de Limoges et de Sèvres, 1759–90); A.D. Haute-Vienne, L1240, 1243–44 (papers of the porcelain works, 1790–94); Henri Stein, "Gabriel Grellet et la manufacture de porcelaine de Limoges sous la règne de Louis XVI," *Bulletin de la Société Archéologique et Historique du Limousin*, LXXVIII (1939), 62–79. For information on the Laforest textile factory, see A.N. F¹² 558 and R. Daudet, *L'Urbanisme à Limoges au XVIIIᵉ siècle* (Limoges, 1939), 105.

14. Daudet, *L'Urbanisme à Limoges*, 174.

The Limousin simply was not a wealthy province, and nothing changed that reality when a sizable portion of it became the Haute-Vienne in 1790. Indeed, with the Revolution came one disaster after another. The treaty of 1786 had mild repercussions in the Limoges textile industry, and 1788 brought the first of five successive poor harvests. In September, 1790, a serious fire ravaged a major section of Limoges. Throughout the Revolution, the department turned to its neighbors and to the national government for assistance in feeding its population. The departmental administration concluded a particularly bleak economic report to the Legislative Assembly by describing the Haute-Vienne as "one of the poorest and most unfortunate regions of the Empire."[15]

The Revolution, then, saw the economic contrasts between Caen and Limoges increase. Caen's early shift from textiles into commerce spared it the crisis suffered by other northern French cities after the 1786 trade treaty between England and France. The fertile plains of Calvados rebounded more quickly from the poor harvests of 1788 and 1789 than did the inhospitable fields of the Haute-Vienne. After an abundant harvest in 1792, the infrequent shortages that recurred in Caen were caused only by the refusal of farmers to bring their grain to market. Their reluctance grew after May, 1793, when the Convention enacted the grain *maximum*. But it was not until the federalist revolt, when the central government prevented outside supplies from reaching Caen in the traditionally lean months on the eve of the harvest, that the grain situation became truly threatening for the people of Caen.

In the Haute-Vienne, on the other hand, grain shortages posed a persistent problem. In June, 1791, the city of Limoges owed up to 360,000 *livres* for grain purchases in 1789 and 1790 alone. The noble mayor of Limoges, Jean Baptiste Pétiniaud de Beaupeyrat, who had commercial contacts and credit in all the large ports of Europe, had advanced two-thirds of this sum.[16] Surrounding departments provided a portion of the grain, but purchases were also made in London, Hamburg, and Amsterdam. In No-

---

15. Léon Jouhaud, *La Révolution Française en Limousin, pages d'histoire vécue, 1789–1792* (Limoges, 1947), 266. Jouhaud reprints the entire seven-page report on the economic situation of the department.

16. Louis Guibert, *La Dette Beaupeyrat* (Limoges, 1888). Pétiniaud, son of a bourgeois *négociant* who had acquired noble status for his son by purchasing the office of *secrétaire du roi*, was popular in Limoges when first elected mayor in 1789. He was reelected in 1790, but his popularity waned as he refused to join the Jacobin club. His requests for repayment of his loans were not popular either, and suspicions existed that he might have profited from the grain deals. Not until 1826 was the balance of 142,000 *livres* finally repaid to the Beaupeyrat family.

vember, 1791, a public fund drive raised nearly 22,000 *livres* in loans for the purchase of grain.[17] Each year since 1787 had seen poor harvests, but 1792 promised to be more abundant. In October, however, the commissioners in charge of subsistence reported to the departmental administration that the situation had not improved. Spring frost and summer rain had ravaged what they had hoped would be a good harvest. Fog in August and frost in mid-September had hurt the buckwheat and chestnut crops. The chestnut trees, traditionally the last resource during periods of dearth, had already been severely depleted by a freeze in 1789. The departments of the Vienne, the Charente, and the Indre, suppliers of past years, were short themselves that year. Administrators predicted that the current harvest would feed the department only until February and that 600,000 quintals of grain would be needed to sustain the population through the rest of the year. The outlook for 1793 appeared bleak indeed.[18]

The contrasting economic situations in the two towns were reflected in their patterns of population growth throughout the century. Caen's population grew dynamically during its period of economic expansion, 1725 through 1775. In 1725, the town's estimated population stood at just over 27,000. By 1753, that figure had grown modestly to 32,000; and the census of 1775, an accurate count, showed an impressive increase to 40,858 inhabitants, the high mark of the century. By 1793, after a period of economic stagnation and the disruption caused by the Revolution, the population had dipped to 34,996. Immigration accounted for roughly 75 percent of the population growth in Caen, with emigration responsible for virtually all of the decline. Even during the unstable early years of the Revolution, births exceeded deaths in the town. Between 1790 and 1793, when population declined by 2,799, there was a natural growth (births/deaths) of 1,211; 2,029 people moved into Caen, but 6,039 emigrated to the countryside, other towns, or abroad.[19]

17. A.D. Haute-Vienne, L212 (correspondence, municipality of Limoges), and L215–216 (1791 grain loan, Limoges).

18. A.D. Haute-Vienne, L56 (Délibérations du Conseil Général du Département de la Haute-Vienne, 1792–93). See also Alfred Fray-Fournier, *Le Département de la Haute-Vienne, sa formation territoriale, son administration, sa situation politique pendant la Révolution* (Limoges, 1908), I, 297–99, 322–27.

19. Perrot, *Genèse d'une ville moderne*, I, 103–65. The 1725 and 1753 population figures were based on the *gabelle* rolls; in 1775, a *rôle nominatif* was compiled for half the town (probably the crowded, central districts), while population in the other half was estimated through a hearth count; in 1790, a head count was taken so that the five section boundaries could be drawn up; in 1793, a careful census was taken by municipal officials.

In Limoges, the population remained near 20,000 inhabitants throughout the century. The charity offered by the Church consistently drew the poor to Limoges, especially in hard times, but this immigration never produced a surge in population comparable to that experienced in Caen between 1750 and 1770. The general pattern of population movement in the two towns was in fact reversed. Whereas Limoges attracted the poor during periods of hardship, Caen's population grew during prosperous times and declined in times of misfortune. This pattern prevailed during the early years of the Revolution. While Caen's population dropped between 1790 and 1793, Limoges actually grew from 20,132 to 23,671 inhabitants during those years, despite a natural decline of 2,157.

That Limoges' inhabitants were in general poorer than those of Caen, drawn to the town by desperate need rather than opportunity, is further evidenced by the number of "active" citizens in each town. In accordance with the law of December 22, 1789, 1,431 of the 20,132 people of Limoges paid sufficient taxes to enjoy the right to vote, whereas 3,566 out of 37,795 in Caen enjoyed that privilege. The ratio of "active" citizens to population was thus roughly 30 percent higher in Caen than in Limoges.[20]

The dynamic population growth of Caen produced by 1789 an urban geography very different from that of Limoges. In the last half of the eighteenth century, Caen was beginning to assume the character of a modern city, particularly in the social differentiation of its neighborhoods. According to Jean-Claude Perrot, before 1770 the considerable numbers of immigrants into Caen tended to settle in the artisanal and commercial center, where they blended relatively quickly into the social fabric of the city. Around that time, however, the central parishes reached their saturation point, and a period of economic stagnation set in as well. Immigrants now settled in the faubourgs, joined there by the marginal population from the center, moving to the economically more diverse outskirts of town, where rents were lower and where a garden plot or fishing could easily supplement one's income. By 1789, a circle of newer immigrants surrounded the band of older immigrants closer to the center. The line of the demolished town walls was replaced by an invisible boundary separating the prosperous, commercial central districts from the faubourgs, inhabited largely by the urban poor. The faubourgs resembled small villages, very tightly knit and commu-

20. A.D. Haute-Vienne, L229 (Recensements, mouvement de la population, 1788–96); Verynaud, *Histoire de Limoges*, 122; *Brochures Normandes: Caen sous la Révolution*, B.M. Caen, Rés. Fn. Br. C226–64.

nal, with a real sense of neighborhood solidarity. The inhabitants of those outlying districts were never well integrated in municipal affairs, either before or during the Revolution.[21]

In Limoges, there was no shift of population to the faubourgs during the eighteenth century comparable to that in Caen. The town was physically smaller than Caen, and the demarcation between center and faubourgs was less severe. One reached the countryside more quickly walking from the center of Limoges, and the people of the faubourgs were thus in closer contact with their "downtown" neighbors.

R. Daudet, the principal historian of eighteenth-century Limoges urbanism, writes that while *gens de robe* tended to live away from the artisanal and commercial quarter, the social differentiation of Limoges neighborhoods did not develop until the nineteenth century. Limoges neighborhoods had grown up around corporations—butchers lived on the rue Torte, tanners lived along the Enjoumard stream, and so on—and these patterns persisted at the end of the eighteenth century. The social segregation that had developed in Caen by the eve of the Revolution did not yet exist in Limoges.[22]

The two towns also differed in the patterns of associational life and sociability among their inhabitants. Of particular interest here are the Freemason lodges that attracted the elite of both towns and the penitent confraternities that flourished in Limoges but were absent in Caen.

Freemason lodges first appeared in both Caen and Limoges in the 1760s. The idea that the Revolution grew out of a conspiratorial Freemason movement has long ago been laid to rest. Several studies, however, have suggested more subtle links between the social and cultural milieu of Freemason lodges and the democratic currents of the Revolution.[23] It is not my intent to consider the larger question of the impact of Freemasonry on the Revolution but rather to examine Freemason lodges in Caen and Limoges as a locus of social contact. From membership rolls of the various lodges, we can gauge the extent to which the ties forged by Freemasonry carried over into political rivalries during the Revolution.[24]

21. Perrot, *Genèse d'une ville moderne*, I, 54–55, 267, 525, II, 605, 622, 634–35, 811–16, 926.

22. Daudet, *L'Urbanisme à Limoges*, 56, 104.

23. See Maurice Agulhon, *Pénitents et francs-maçons de l'ancienne Provence* (Paris, 1968); Ran Yedid-Halevi, "La Sociabilité maçonnique et les origines de la pratique démocratique" (Thèse de troisième cycle, Ecole des hautes études en sciences sociales, 1981); Lynn A. Hunt, *Politics, Culture, and Class in the French Revolution* (Berkeley, 1984), Chap. 5; and Michael L. Kennedy, *The Jacobin Clubs in the French Revolution: The First Years* (Princeton, 1982).

24. Membership lists for Masonic lodges are located in the Salle des Manuscrits of the Biblio-

The Freemasons of Limoges have a particularly interesting history in the decade before the Revolution. In 1778, Pétiniaud de Beaupeyrat, a wealthy, noble merchant and future mayor of Limoges, sat as *vénérable* of the only lodge in Limoges, the Frères Unis. Four years later, an internal crisis developed within the Frères Unis, reportedly caused by Pierre Dumas, a young lawyer. The lodge assigned Pétiniaud to investigate the matter, and his report resulted in Dumas' resignation and a splintering in the lodge. Dumas and several others immediately formed a second lodge, La Clairvoyante, which in 1783 became l'Heureuse Réunion. Members of l'Heureuse Réunion included François Alluaud, a future Jacobin and Limoges district director in the 1792–1793 term; Pierre Déroche, a Jacobin and mayor of Limoges from 1792 through 1794; Jean Baptiste Audouin, future adjunct to the minister of war, who regularly corresponded with the Limoges Jacobin club from Paris; and Pardoux Bordas, one of two Montagnards on the Haute-Vienne delegation to the National Convention. All four participated in steering Limoges and the Haute-Vienne away from federalism in 1793. Dumas himself was a Jacobin club member and sat on the departmental administration from 1790 until 1793. By contrast, the lodge of the Frères Unis in 1788 included a number of future members of the Amis de la Paix, a monarchist club responsible for considerable turmoil in Limoges from 1790 through 1792. Thus, the split among Limoges Freemasons foreshadowed, to some extent, the revolutionary conflict between Jacobins and the Amis de la Paix.

In Caen, on the other hand, all but one of the five lodges meeting in the 1780s placed members on one or more of the local administrations, and none was dominant in that respect. Far from quarreling among themselves, the Caen lodges demonstrated the compatibility and cooperativeness that characterized the Caen elite during the Revolution. The apparent social cohesion of the Caen elite was further cultivated by the town's Académie des

---

thèque Nationale. I found the rolls of five Caen lodges in FM² 189–90 and two Limoges lodges in FM² 258–59. I verified that these were the only lodges in Caen and Limoges by consulting Alain Le Bihan, *Loges et Chapitres de la Grande Loge et du Grand Orient de France* (Paris, 1967), 54–55, 104–105. The lodge names and dates of the membership rolls are as follows: for Caen, Coeurs-sans-Fard (1786), Constante Fabert (1789), Thémis (1785), Vraye Union et de l'amitié parfaitte (1781), and l'Union et Fraternité (1788, 1790, 1792); for Limoges, La Clairvoyante, which became l'Heureuse Réunion in 1782 (1782, 1785, 1788), and Frères Unis (1779, 1780, 1782, 1784, 1788). See also René Norbert Sauvage, "La Loge maçonnique la Constante Fabert à Caen, en 1785," *Mémoires de l'Académie Nationale des Sciences, Arts et Belle-lettres de Caen* (1918–20), 397–406; and *La Franc-maçonnerie Limousine, son passé, son présent, ses ambitions* (Limoges, 1949), in the Bibliothèque Nationale, 8°H. Pièce 2255.

Belles-lettres, which especially attracted to its meetings those men who supported Caen's urban development.[25]

Associations in Caen, then, tended to bind the elite together, while in Limoges the Freemasons had split into factions in the years before the Revolution. Among the lower classes of the two towns, however, quite the reverse was true. There is no trace of an organized associational life among the *menu peuple* of Caen, particularly those who had settled in the faubourgs. In Limoges, by contrast, virtually every adult male belonged to a penitent confraternity.

Seven penitent confraternities existed in Limoges at the end of the Old Regime. These lay societies, generally organized around a parish church, drew their members from all levels of society, from among the wealthy and the poor, and offered to their members a rich associational experience. Each confraternity elected officers, maintained a membership roll, recorded minutes of meetings, and made important contributions to charity and public assistance in the community, functions that by the eighteenth century had superseded the confraternities' original purpose as devotional and pietist groups. Each confraternity met in a particular parish church, but the confreres were intensely insistent on their independence from both clerical and civil authorities. After a period of decline in the late seventeenth century, the confraternities rebounded strongly in the mid-eighteenth century, and on the eve of the Revolution virtually every male head of a household in Limoges belonged to a confraternity. The importance of these organizations to Limoges' sociability is attested to by the fact that although they were suppressed by law in 1792, they revived after the Revolution and by 1809 again counted nearly four thousand members.[26]

Maurice Agulhon has argued that these confraternities left a substantial legacy to the popular societies that formed during the Revolution.[27] The case of Limoges is among the most striking. The Limoges Jacobin club held its meetings in the former assembly hall of the *pénitents gris*, used a method of voting similar to that of the confraternity, and adopted a form of membership roll identical to that which the old confraternity had used. Jacobin club

25. Perrot, *Genèse d'une ville moderne*, II, 693–94.
26. Louis Guibert, "Les Confréries de Pénitents en France et notamment dans le diocèse de Limoges," *Bulletin de la Société Archéologique et Historique du Limousin*, XXVII (1879), 5–193.
27. Agulhon, *Pénitents et Franc-maçons*.

members urged their confreres to join the club and to donate chapel funds to the patriotic contribution.[28]

More importantly, the penitent groups created men who were accustomed to associational life and inculcated values that would later be associated with the Revolution. Louis Guibert writes that a commitment to equality and fraternity was among the most salient features of Limoges confraternities. Agulhon suggests that many of these men became Jacobin militants after 1789, although he does not go so far as to argue that a direct correlation exists between Jacobinism and confraternities. In Limoges, where nearly all men belonged to a penitent confraternity, obviously not all penitents became Jacobins. No clear pattern emerges from the few membership rolls that still exist, but the names of many men who were leaders in Limoges during the Revolution—François Alluaud, Jean Baptiste Audouin, de Chaise Martin (leader of the Amis de la Paix), J. Pétiniaud, and a number of other Jacobin club leaders and municipal officials—also appear as officers of Limoges confraternities in the decade before 1789.[29]

One exception to the social heterogeneity of these groups was the confraternity organized around the parish of Saint-Pierre-du-Queyroix. This group distinguished itself from other Limoges confraternities in that its membership seems to have been restricted to rich *négociants* and petty noble families.[30] No membership list survives for the Saint-Pierre penitents in the 1780s, but there may have been some continuity between this group and the Amis de la Paix.

Confraternities did not flourish in northern France, and there appears to have been no comparable social association among the lower classes of Caen. This may explain, in part, the weakness of the popular movement in Caen during the Revolution. By contrast, the existence of confraternities certainly contributed to the vitality of popular politics in Limoges in 1792 and 1793. There seems to have been a relationship linking the confraternities, the formation of the Jacobin club, and the later political divisions in Limoges, even if the evidence is suggestive rather than conclusive. Clearly, the penitent confraternities and the larger question of the link between pat-

28. *Ibid.*, 279–80; Guibert, "Les Confréries," 156–57.
29. Guibert, "Les Confréries," 19, 111; A.D. Haute-Vienne, G731, 13G1, 16G14 (papers relating to penitent confraternities).
30. Michel Tintou, "Réorganisation de la confrérie du Saint-Sacrement de Saint-Pierre-du-Queyroix, en 1763," *Bulletin de la Société Archéologique et Historique du Limousin*, XCVI (1969), 141–50.

terns of sociability under the Old Regime and revolutionary politics represent fruitful areas for future research.

The social fabric of the two towns had little effect on local politics under the monarchy, because political activity itself was extremely limited. During the Revolution, this would change. But the contrasting economic situations of the two towns did have an impact on the character of their local governments at the end of the Old Regime, as it would in later years.

In Caen, the mayor, *échevins,* and town notables defended local prerogatives vis-à-vis the intendants and consistently protested royal encroachments. The substantial public works undertaken between 1750 and 1789 were funded principally by local taxes (both from the city and the rich, surrounding farmlands), and not by the royal treasury. The situation in Limoges was nearly the reverse. The local elite took little initiative in public improvement projects, largely because of the paltry state of municipal finances. They looked instead to the intendants for planning and to the royal coffers for support.[31]

The comparison here is strikingly similar to that which Tocqueville makes between the self-reliant *pays d'état* and the politically lethargic *pays d'élection.*[32] Tocqueville argues that provincial self-government had been eroded in the *pays d'élection* by the expanding monarchical bureaucracy, leaving those regions politically inert and dependent on the central government. The economic disparity between Calvados and the Haute-Vienne had produced very different attitudes toward the central government. The burgeoning commercial community of Caen looked abroad, to foreign ports, for the source of its vitality and resented the restrictions and impositions that emanated from the capital. Limoges, on the other hand, looked to Paris and Versailles for much-needed assistance during periods of hardship. These attitudes toward the state, developing under the Old Regime as well as under the Revolution, would receive full expression during the chaotic months of the federalist revolt.

31. Perrot, *Genèse d'une ville moderne,* II, 578–85; Jean Yver, "Une Administration municipale 'orageuse' à Caen à la fin de l'Ancien Régime: La Mairie de M. de Vendoeuvre," *Mémoires de l'Académie Nationale des Sciences, Arts et Belles-lettres de Caen* (1931), 241–68; Verynaud, *Histoire de Limoges,* 95–100; Daudet, *L'Urbanisme à Limoges,* 35, 88, 109.
32. Tocqueville, *The Old Regime and the French Revolution,* 212–21.

Two

Revolutionary Politics Take Shape

1789–1792

The Revolution began in Caen much as it did in Paris, with a storming of the most obvious and imposing symbol of the Old Regime. Built in the eleventh century by William the Conqueror, the Château dominated the landscape from its perch on a hillside above the city, as indicated in Map 3. On July 21, 1789, probably inspired by news from Paris, a crowd invaded the Château and armed themselves. They encountered no serious resistance.

The significance of this episode lies less in the actual event than in the contemporary response to it. Two published diaries offer a unique insight into public opinion in Caen during the Revolution. The diaries, printed side by side in one volume, are made especially interesting by the contrasting social backgrounds of their authors. One, Pierre François Laurent Esnault, was a bourgeois *avocat* whose father and grandfather had been *procureurs* at the *bailliage* court of Caen. Jean Jacques Victor Dufour, the other diarist, was a gardener, an *homme du peuple*, as the editor describes him. Esnault wrote his journal near the end of the Revolution (after 1795), and his accuracy suffers for it. Dufour wrote his diary more or less day by day, which gives it a more spontaneous, but less reflective, flavor. The objectivity of both is dubious, but they offer important and distinctly different contemporary viewpoints.[1]

1. Georges Lesage (ed.), *Episodes de la Révolution à Caen racontés par un bourgeois et un homme du peuple* (Caen, 1926). For this chapter in particular, I have relied extensively on these

Esnault noted in his journal that the attack on the Château had reportedly been inspired by Protestants, "men who sought to abolish the Catholic religion in order to establish their own exclusively, and to avenge the Bartholomew's Day massacre."[2] The interpretation here is definitely suspect—there is no evidence that Caen Protestants persecuted the majority Catholic population at any time during the Revolution. But his comments do indicate that Protestants were active in local affairs in Caen and that Catholics viewed their political participation with some alarm. Indeed, the question of whether Protestants could be elected as delegates to the Estates General had been a matter of local discussion. Local electors appealed to Versailles for a ruling before the issue was decided. In the end, the third estate *bailliage* assembly chose as deputies two Caen Protestants, both of whom had ties to the commercial elite. The first was Michel Louis Lamy, a wealthy merchant; the second, Gabriel de Cussy, was a former *directeur de la monnaie* in Caen. The relations between Catholics and Protestants were not volatile in Caen, as they were in Nîmes and Montauban, for example. The Protestant minority did play a very important role in local affairs, however, and the disproportionate presence of Protestants among elected officials continued throughout the Revolution.[3]

Victor Dufour had surprisingly little to say about the taking of the Château. He did note that only four days previously the duke of Harcourt, the provincial governor, had positioned six cannons, four on the bridge of Vaucelles and two in the Cours la Reine, and trained them across the river on the faubourg Vaucelles (one of the poorest quarters in Caen) in case of revolt. This observation is embellished by Esnault's comment that after July 21, "honest and peaceful townspeople were alarmed to see arms in the hands of immoral and unprincipled people."[4] As further instances will show, the elite of Caen wished that politics remain an orderly business, the

---

two sources for anecdotal and "public mood" material. To identify which diarist I am citing, footnotes will henceforth refer to either Lesage (Esnault) or Lesage (Dufour).

2. Lesage (Esnault), 10. The translation is mine, as it will be in all instances, unless otherwise noted.

3. Félix Mourlot, *La Fin de l'Ancien Régime et les débuts de la Révolution dans la généralité de Caen, 1787–1790* (Paris, 1913), 235. See James Hood, "Protestant-Catholic Relations and the Roots of the First Popular Counterrevolutionary Movement in France," *Journal of Modern History*, XLIII (June, 1971), 245–75; and Daniel Ligou, *Montauban à la fin de l'Ancien Régime et aux débuts de la Révolution, 1787–1794* (Paris, 1959).

4. Lesage (Esnault), 10, and (Dufour), 21. Esnault is clearly referring to the *menu peuple* and those who would rouse them.

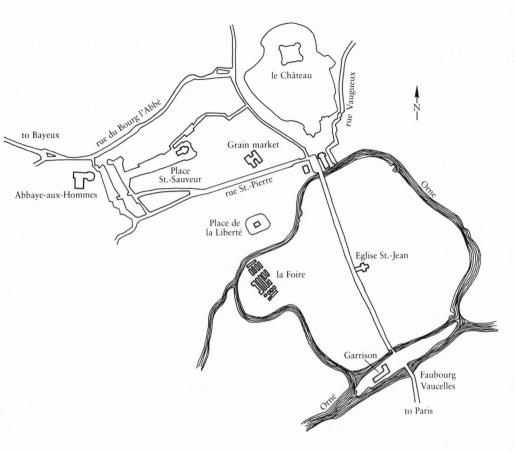

le Château

rue Vaugueux

rue du Bourg l'Abbé

to Bayeux

Grain market

N

Place
St.-Sauveur

Orne

Abbaye-aux-Hommes

rue St.-Pierre

Place de
la Liberté

Eglise St.-Jean

la Foire

Garrison

Faubourg
Vaucelles

Orne

to Paris

MAP 3. Caen, 1793

Colleen Baker

affair of men of substance, and particularly that it not descend to the level of public, popular contention.

The days following the storming of the Château continued to be unsettled, as the scarcity of grain provoked several disruptions at the market. A more serious outburst of violence jolted Caen less than four weeks later. On August 12, an angry crowd murdered the viscount Henri de Belzunce. A young major in the second Bourbon infantry regiment, garrisoned in Caen, Belzunce was described as handsome and spirited but arrogant and avowedly royalist. He maintained a visible presence around town and, with an aide, frequently provoked trouble at patriotic fetes. His actions, particularly his open display of arms, became so offensive that the General Committee of Caen (a temporary municipal council created in July, 1789) requested his transfer. Belzunce refused to go. On August 11, he publicly promised to reward any of his soldiers who could strip the medals of Necker and the Breton Union from the uniforms of a rival regiment. Belzunce himself led a group of his men to perform the feat, brutally striking a soldier in the process and raising the ire of the townspeople against the young noble and his regiment. Later that evening, one of his second lieutenants walked with four or five other soldiers toward the bridge of Vaucelles. The lieutenant allegedly fired on a sentinel of the bourgeois militia, who returned fire and killed him. Scattered shots rang out through the night, and by morning the mood of the populace had been raised to a fever pitch. An anonymous citizen sounded the tocsin, and a crowd invaded the garrison, towing a cannon in its wake. Members of the General Committee quickly intervened in an attempt to prevent violence, as Belzunce—who was blamed for having provoked the incident—protested his innocence and offered to appear at the town hall. With that course of action agreed upon, the National Guard led him to the Château, there to be confined for his own protection.

Meanwhile, the provincial commander, perhaps unwittingly, sent orders for the Bourbon regiment to leave Caen. Its departure alarmed and enraged the crowd, which again went to find Belzunce. They marched him to the Place Saint-Pierre, where a national guardsman struck him down as he made an effort to flee. In the bloody scene that followed, his body was chopped into bits and his head paraded about town.[5] According to the memoirs of Frédéric Vaultier, it was this sickening slaughter that stuck in the memories

5. Frédéric Vaultier, *Souvenirs de l'insurrection Normande, dite du Fédéralisme, en 1793,* avec notes et pièces justificatives par M. Georges Mancel (Caen, 1858), 299–303. Frédéric Vaultier, just seventeen years old in 1789, completed his rhetoric studies at the University of

of the people of Caen, and not the irresponsible antics of a young fool who had antagonized the "patriots" in town. No one ever came to trial for the murder of Belzunce.

Three individuals stand out from the crowd for the noteworthy roles they played during these few days. One was Jean Michel Barbot, who owned a small tobacco shop in the parish Saint-Pierre.[6] Although not directly implicated in the murder, he enjoyed a reputation as a popular leader, and some accused him of instigating the attack on Belzunce. Barbot ran for the vice-presidency of his section in 1790 and was later president of the Carabot club. A bully of sorts, he obtained for himself, by questionable means, the position of clerk at the Tribunal of Commerce. Despite his poor reputation in some quarters, his sway over the crowd was clear. Each day before his shop he read aloud, often to large crowds, *Le Courrier dans les Départements,* a newspaper written by the future Girondin Antoine Joseph Gorsas. Barbot frequented town hall, it appears, and often acted as a messenger or town crier for municipal officials. He turned up at almost every important event or crisis, though he never held elected office.[7]

The two other figures exerted a more calming influence on the populace, or at least tried to do so. One of them, Pierre Mesnil, was a wealthy Protestant merchant and a captain in the National Guard in 1789. Victor Dufour remarked upon his efforts to protect Belzunce from attack, describing Mesnil as "a very prudent and wise man." Elected to the district council in 1790, he became a departmental administrator in 1792.[8] François Le Carpentier, a teacher of philosophy at the *collège* Dumont, also did what he

---

Caen in 1793 and probably wrote his "souvenirs" of the federalist revolt around 1840, after a career at the University of Caen. Georges Mancel, who edited and annotated Vaultier's memoirs, gives no precise date for the completion of the manuscript, saying only that Vaultier wrote the account "over thirty years after the revolt." Thus, it could have been completed as early as 1825. Vaultier died in 1843. The considerable volume of notes and documents that Mancel has appended to Vaultier's memoirs includes an account of the massacre. See also *Extrait du procès-verbal du Comité Général et National de la ville de Caen, relatif à la mort du Belzunce,* B.M. Caen.

6. Saint-Pierre lay at the heart of the main artisan quarter, in the most densely populated part of Caen.

7. A.D. Calvados, L10125 (interrogations following the federalist revolt); A. C. Caen, D1, D2 (Délibérations du Corps municipal et du Conseil Général de la Commune, 18 février 1790–3 janvier 1792 and 4 janvier 1792–11 Germinal an II); Lesage, (Esnault), 18. Esnault describes Barbot as an "homme aussi laid au physique que dépravé au moral," his standard criticism of those he disliked or of whom he disapproved.

8. A. D. Calvados, L189 (Registre des arrêtés du Conseil Général du département du Calvados, 11 août 1792–26 juillet 1793), I40 (Eglise de Caen, état civil-Protestant declarations, 1788); Lesage (Dufour), 22.

could to prevent trouble. He did in fact avert serious bloodshed on the eve of Belzunce's death when he defused a confrontation between the Bourbon regiment and a National Guard battalion. Respected for his fairness and moderation, Le Carpentier served as an early secretary of the Jacobin club and in 1791 was elected one of the town *notables*.[9] All three of these men later actively participated in the federalist revolt.

Suspicion of and animosity toward the nobility, at their most violent in the Belzunce affair, were ever present in Caen. They received their next open expression in October, 1789. Like most other towns, Caen had assembled a bourgeois National Guard in late July, primarily for defense against the dangerous bands rumored to be roaming the countryside. By August 7, the guard had been formally organized into twenty-seven companies of one hundred men each. But alongside this new force there continued to function a company of "volunteers," whose existence the guardsmen vocally protested. Patriots considered the volunteers superfluous at best and a threat at worst, for they were reputed to be armed and paid by the nobility. The General Committee made an effort to disband them on August 16 by prohibiting the bearing of arms except by those on National Guard duty. This measure proved largely ineffective; so on October 6, sectional assemblies voted formally to suppress the volunteers. The National Guard disarmed them without delay.[10]

If tension between the second and third estates dominated the revolutionary period in Caen, the religious question must be said to have been second in importance, though the two were clearly related. Félix Mourlot remarks upon the division, perhaps even hostility, between the low and high clergy on the eve of the Revolution. The latter felt that the king was tipping the balance toward the lower clergy with regard to election procedures. Either because of those procedures or by choice, the five bishops of Lower Normandy exerted little influence on the election of delegates to the Estates General. The first estate's electoral assemblies were the most tumultuous of any of the three orders, and the clergy's elections in the *bailliage* of Caen were the only ones "marked by a truly democratic character." The clergy sent

9. A. C. Caen, D1; René Norbert Sauvage, "Les Souvenirs de J.-B. Renée sur la Révolution à Caen, 1789–93," *Normannia*, VI, (1933), 577.

10. Mourlot, *La Fin de l'Ancien Régime*, 363; Lesage (Dufour), 23–24. One can appreciate the nobles' fear that the bourgeois guard might not adequately protect their families and property against an angry crowd. They cannot have been encouraged by the frequent admonitions to guardsmen, often publicly posted, that drinking was not allowed while on duty.

mostly parish priests to Versailles, and Mourlot remarks upon the considerable sympathy between the lower clergy of Caen and the third estate.[11]

With the legislation of the constitutional oath, however, the clergy closed ranks to some extent. Passed by the Constituent Assembly in July, 1790, and signed into law by Louis XVI on August 24, the civil constitution of the clergy reorganized the Church in France. The new constitution mandated the election of clergy by electoral assemblies, limited the powers of bishops, and required all clergy to swear an oath of loyalty to the nation, the king, and the law, the same oath sworn by all elected officials. The Assembly hoped to receive the approval of the pope, but when Pius VI remained silent, a decree requiring immediate compliance with the law was passed and was signed by Louis on December 26, 1790. The high clergy almost universally opposed this new measure, but the low clergy was divided, with many following their bishops. By early 1791, only seven bishops had sworn the oath, and slightly more than 50 percent of the lower clergy had done so.[12]

In Calvados, Bishop Cheylus refused to accept the oath and exhorted his priests to do likewise. Many did, but the department was not among the most refractory—50 to 70 percent of the priests eventually swore the constitutional oath.[13] In Caen itself, however, only two of the thirteen parish priests conformed to the new law, and a spirited public polemic ensued regarding the legitimacy of the civil constitution. Interestingly, the two priests who swore the oath served the principal artisan and working-class parishes in Caen, Saint-Pierre and Vaucelles.[14] Only with difficulty were the eleven *refractaires* replaced by constitutional priests, as several of those initially elected refused to serve. In February, 1791, the conflict spilled over into municipal politics when the mayor, Le Forestier de Vendoeuvre, resigned over the issue of the oath. On January 13, he had delivered a lengthy discourse to the municipal council attacking the civil constitution of the clergy and defending those who refused to take the oath. When it became clear that his convictions were not shared by the council or the majority of the public, he resigned.[15] The resignation of Vendoeuvre brought a special election, and

11. Mourlot, *La Fin de l'Ancien Régime*, 186–91.

12. Jacques Godechot, *Les Institutions de la France sous la Révolution et l'Empire* (Paris, 1951), 224–28.

13. Michel Vovelle, *La Chute de la Monarchie, 1787–1792* (Paris, 1972), 230.

14. *Brochures Normandes: Caen sous la Révolution*, B. M. Caen, Rés. Fn. Br. C182–225.

15. A. C. Caen, D1. A copy of Vendoeuvre's discourse can be found in *Pièces sur la normandie*, B. M. Caen, Fn. A562/1–14.

the choice of a new mayor signaled a shift in Caen politics, as the people of Caen once again demonstrated their aversion to the nobility.

Le Forestier de Vendoeuvre, seigneur of an estate not far from Caen, had first been named mayor by Louis XVI in 1781 and had served for nearly seven years. His term had been a stormy one, though. The king had showed displeasure at the strained relations between Vendoeuvre and the intendant, and the people had protested the mayor's excessive spending and autocratic manner. His election in February, 1790, may have been due to his willingness to stand up to the king and the intendants in defense of municipal independence. But Vendoeuvre's inability to work with the elected *notables* seems to have carried over into the revolutionary period.[16]

His successor, Pierre Louis Bonnet de Meautry, was, to be sure, a noble and a chevalier de Saint-Louis. But if under the Old Regime there were a fair number of bourgeois living nobly, then Bonnet de Meautry, by contrast, must certainly be called a noble living poorly. His sentiments lay more with the sans-culottes than with his fellow aristocrats. Very early, he dropped de Meautry from his name; and in 1793, he would be the only Calvados deputy to the National Convention to sit with the Montagnards. Bonnet was a captain in the National Guard and in July, 1790, headed Caen's delegation to the Festival of the Federation in Paris.[17] Our bourgeois commentator, Esnault, offers a clear indication of Bonnet's reputation among the high ranks of Caen society: "One saw with profound sadness a gentleman of exemplary conduct, of unequalled generosity and charity, replaced by a man who was reproached as being, for several years, at the head of *biribi* and other games forbidden by the police, the only source of support which remained to him."[18] The political shift that began with the election of Bonnet was confirmed in the November, 1791, municipal elections, which marked a final repudiation of the Old Regime elite and nobility of Caen. Municipal councils thereafter would be dominated by the commercial elite.

The election of Bonnet as mayor was soon followed by a change in the local church hierarchy. The refusal of Bishop Cheylus to swear the constitutional oath made necessary the election of a new bishop. Gervais de la Prise, curé of Saint-Pierre in Caen, was chosen by an electoral assembly and installed as bishop on March 16, 1791. Less than three weeks later, he re-

---

16. Yver, "Une Administration municipale 'orageuse,'" 241–268.
17. Mourlot, *La Fin de l'Ancien Régime*, cxii.
18. Lesage (Esnault), 47.

signed, citing the refusal of Cheylus to formally step aside as the reason he could not, in good conscience, assume the episcopal duties. The electoral assembly met again, more sparsely attended this time, and on April 18 elected Claude Fauchet on the third ballot. The choice was at first an unpopular one. Fauchet was not from Calvados, he had a reputation as a radical, and the former bishop published a denunciation of his election. Cheylus' refusal to resign posed no crisis of conscience for Fauchet, though, and he arrived on May 11 for installation. His compassion and eloquent oratory rapidly won him support.[19]

The new bishop quickly assumed an active role in departmental affairs. As early as June, his public criticism of two administrators made him again a center of controversy. Fauchet apologized for his error in judgment, became an active participant at Jacobin club meetings in Caen, and was soon elected president of that body. In November, 1791, though still a controversial figure, Fauchet won election on the first ballot to represent Calvados in the Legislative Assembly. He continued as bishop of the department and frequently communicated with the Caen Jacobin club.

Fauchet remained an influential figure in local affairs. One of his vicars, Chaix-d'Estanges, became curé of the parish Saint-Etienne in Caen and was later a leader of the federalist revolt. Gohier de Jumilly, elected curé of the parish Saint-Jean shortly after the bishop's arrival, also supported Fauchet and was active in the revolt. Fauchet himself was among the twenty-two deputies initially denounced by the Paris sections in April, 1793. Arrested after the assassination of Marat, he came to trial with the proscribed Girondins and was executed in October, 1793.[20]

On November 5, 1791, the issues of religion and the aristocracy combined to produce the most dramatic incident in Caen's revolutionary history, "l'Affaire des 84." On the preceding day, Bunel, former curé of Saint-Jean and a refractory priest, had held a mass in the church Saint-Jean, in accordance with the law and with the permission of the constitutional curé. A large number of nobles, resident in that parish, had attended the mass with their

19. Vaultier, *Souvenirs*, 78–87; Lesage (Esnault), 55–57. See also Olwen Hufton, *Bayeux in the Late Eighteenth Century* (London, 1967), 173. Hufton writes that the failure of the Constituent Assembly to call a national church council to affirm the civil constitution and confirm the jurisdiction of new bishops led to the resignation of Gervais de la Prise.

20. A. C. Caen, K16 (Elections à l'assemblée législative, 1791); Vaultier, *Souvenirs*, 83–87, 288–89; Lesage (Dufour), 76; Jean Chrétien Ferdinand Hoefer, *Nouvelle Biographie Générale*, XVII (Paris, 1858–78), 163–65.

servants. The latter had been rumored to be armed with pistols, and the noblemen, of course, had worn their swords. The insolent tone of the servants had offended some "patriots" (as they were referred to in the municipal council report), but the mass had ended without incident, and Bunel had announced another service for the following day.

It should be noted that the elected constitutional curés were at this point not very popular with the people of Caen. Their masses were not generally well attended, and many people remained loyal to their old parish priests. On October 8, 1791, the departmental administration published an order from the minister of the interior that declared refractory priests free to celebrate mass as long as they did not disrupt public order. Those attending the November 4 mass clearly saw this order as a moral victory over the radical elements in Caen, in particular the members of the Jacobin club. This attitude led to the taunts and insults that so offended the "patriots."

The municipality, fearing trouble, asked Bunel to postpone his mass. The curé readily agreed, but his decision was not adequately publicized, and a number of aristocrats assembled at Saint-Jean anyway. A group of concerned "patriots" appeared at the church as well. The two groups exchanged words, minor scuffles ensued, and several shots were fired. Two municipal officers arrived with two companies of National Guard grenadiers and dispersed the crowd.[21] The municipal council immediately convened with the district and departmental administrations to consider security measures. As they deliberated, word came that a group of armed nobles and servants had gathered at the Place Saint-Sauveur, located in a well-to-do neighborhood near the Abbaye-aux-Hommes (where the municipal council met). The combined administrations sent a municipal officer to order the nobles back to their regular companies. (The municipality had called all citizens to arms when trouble first broke out at Saint-Jean, but they should have reported to their assigned National Guard stations.) For reasons that remain unknown, the officer instead led them to the square in front of the town hall, where they were questioned and disarmed. The search and interrogation produced a letter that referred to a coalition of nobles, allegedly formed to protect "persons and property." Presented with this evidence, the municipality ordered the arrest of those disarmed, as well as several others, mostly aristocrats and wealthy bourgeois. A total of eighty-four men and women

21. *Brochures Normandes: Caen sous la Révolution*, B. M. Caen, Rés. Fn. Br. D156–209.

were jailed in the Château and their crimes reported to the Legislative Assembly.[22] The three administrations, meeting jointly, ordered all strangers in Caen to report to the town hall to turn in their arms, forbade unnecessary public assemblies, and authorized National Guard captains to search suspect houses for strangers bearing arms.[23]

Several accounts of the affair, both contemporary and secondary, illuminate the situation in the weeks preceding November 5. One local antiquarian notes that since the beginning of the Revolution, the unsettled situation in the countryside had forced a considerable number of nobles to seek safety in Caen, where they stayed with friends or in their own town houses. Lacking any occupation, they closely followed public affairs and grew alarmed at what they perceived to be an increasing disrespect for property (particularly their own) and public order. This led to the formation of committees and proposals for reestablishment of respect for the law. The meetings of these committees were not unknown to the Jacobin club and the municipal council, but they could not be legally prohibited. It is significant that the Régiment d'Aunis, the only remaining military alternative to the bourgeois National Guard, was transferred from Caen on November 3, despite the protests of the departmental administration. This may well have increased the aristocrats' apprehensions.[24]

Our two contemporary chroniclers, Esnault and Dufour, offer distinctly different impressions of the episode. Esnault writes that the aristocrats and wealthy bourgeois (*les honnêtes gens,* as he calls them) feared the increasing influence of the Caen Jacobin club and held secret meetings to plan strategy and propose suitable candidates for the upcoming municipal elections. He acknowledges the lack of circumspection of "les royalistes" and the brash words of young nobles from out of town but insists that the gathering at the

22. The confiscated letter began, "Le désir de protéger les personnes et les propriétés, et la nécessité de réclamer l'exécution des loix à chaque instant violées, ont provoqué la réunion des honnêtes gens." It went on, in sixteen articles, to describe the formation of committees to coordinate efforts to preserve order. The letter identified by name two prominent nobles and spoke of secret meetings in private homes. The municipality also claimed to have found other letters. My account of these two days relies primarily on *Consultation délibérée à Paris pour les 84 citoyens détenus dans la Tour de Caen, depuis le 5 novembre 1791,* a thirty-nine-page report prepared for the Legislative Assembly by three of its members, Deseze, Vulpian, and De la Malle. B. M. Caen, Rés. Fn. Br. D156−209.

23. A. C. Caen, D1.

24. A.N., F⁷ 3661¹ Calvados (mostly correspondence to the minister of the interior); Bonnel, "Communication au sujet des troubles de 4−5 novembre, 1791," *Bulletin de la Société des Antiquaires de Normandie,* XLIX (1942−45), 487−94.

Place Saint-Sauveur was due to confusion and an honest desire to restore order.[25] Dufour describes this same group of upright citizens as a "compagnie noire" that wished to make a counterrevolution. He says that 150 to 200 men assembled on the Place Saint-Sauveur and that several people had earlier been wounded near Saint-Jean. Another observer wrote two days later that "the scene yesterday of which Mlle ⎯⎯⎯ spoke to you was crushing for the aristocratic party, which has grown insolent over the past month."[26]

Whatever the truth may have been, and it remains elusive, the Legislative Assembly agreed with Esnault. After three of its members had made a report citing the municipality's call to arms and the lack of sufficient evidence of conspiracy, the Assembly ordered the release of all but two of those arrested.[27] The decision was not a popular one in Caen. The Jacobin club and the National Guard opposed it, and Louis Caille, a lawyer and president of the club, proposed that the municipal and district administrations petition the Legislative Assembly to retract the decree. The municipality and district rejected Caille's suggestion, and on February 3 at 2:00 A.M., the municipal officers, with the aid of a small guard, released the prisoners from the Château. No trouble marred the release, though a small group of "enragés" were rumored to have waited all night in ambush, fortunately at the wrong entrance![28]

Three significant observations can be made about this episode. First, it was perceived by the people of Caen at the time as a "noble conspiracy." Not all of those arrested were nobles—some were bourgeois *rentiers*—but the most prominent among them were of the nobility. The confrontation thus heightened the tension between the second and third estates of Caen. Second, no elected officials, either former or present, were implicated in the affair. The controversy did not create any lasting political divisions, nor did it embroil the local political arena. If anything—and this is the third point— it strengthened the bonds of the local political elite in the face of a challenge

25. Lesage (Esnault), 69–71.
26. Lesage (Dufour), 78; a letter signed Loiseau, reprinted by Bonnel, "Communication au sujet des troubles," 490–92.
27. *Consultation délibérée à Paris*. The prisoners were ordered released on the basis of what today would be termed a technicality. The three deputies found that the arrests had been motivated by the discovery of the anonymous letter. Since the National Assembly had declared letters and personal correspondence inviolable, the letter should never have been seized; and there existed no other strong evidence against the accused.
28. A. C. Caen, D2; Lesage (Esnault), 81.

from the old aristocracy and interference from the Legislative Assembly in Paris. The municipal council had seen a threat to public order and had acted resolutely to eliminate that threat. The evidence against the accused seemed clear, yet the Legislative Assembly overturned the accusation and ordered the release of the suspects. Here we see an early, albeit minor, confrontation between local and national authority. This issue would assume greater importance by 1793.

Another crisis developed even before the resolution of the Affair of 84, and it eventually led to a second brutal murder. As before, bourgeois animosity toward the nobility triggered the chain of events. At issue in this instance was the composition of the departmental Criminal Tribunal. The tribunals were created by the law of February 7, 1791, but because the law required interpretation and clarification, final enactment did not come until nearly one year later.[29]

The new court encountered opposition in many parts of the country. In Caen, its installation was scheduled for January 23, 1792, but the National Guard's refusal to participate forced the municipality to postpone the ceremony. The guard acted in support of the Caen Jacobin club, which had vehemently protested the jury list proposed by Georges Bayeux, the Calvados *procureur-général-syndic.*

In a January 26 report to the minister of the interior, the departmental directory described the disruptive events of the previous few days. On January 24, the day after the aborted installation, a delegation from the Jacobin club, led by Chaix-d'Estanges and Louis Caille, invaded the directory's chambers.[30] The unruly group claimed that aristocrats outnumbered patriots on the jury list and particularly denounced the inclusion of two university professors who had signed a letter protesting the constitutional oath. In the words of the directory report:

> A voice was then raised and stated, "we will not permit on the Criminal Tribunal a Boucher Deslongpars and a Deshameaux, who in the electoral assembly declared

29. Godechot, *Les Institutions de la France,* 119–21.
30. A.N., F⁷ 3661¹ Calvados; A. C. Caen, I275 (Société des Amis de la Constitution, 1790–93); B. M. Caen, Rés. Fn. A1900/1. Unfortunately, the registers of the Jacobin club for the period before September, 1793, no longer exist. One assumes that they were destoyed by frightened club members as the failure of the federalist revolt became apparent. The information available regarding the club comes from contemporary accounts, some printed declarations of the Jacobin club (which often listed the current president and secretaries), and administrative reports and letters.

themselves enemies of the bishop of Calvados"; and on the observation of the president that M. le Boucher Deslongpars had been named commissioner to the Tribunal by the executive power, M. Destanges stated that neither the King, nor decrees, nor administrative bodies would oblige them to recognize persons who did not have their confidence, and that the members of the Directory themselves, who currently enjoyed their confidence, would be frankly informed and not tolerated if they came to lose that confidence.[31]

A series of letters from the department president, Doulcet de Pontécoulant, to the minister of the interior, Cahier de Gerville, elaborates on the evolution of the affair and its final resolution. Doulcet acknowledged that the jury list, the root of the problem, was "véritablement fort mauvais" and merited change, but he noted the directory's reluctance to cede to popular demand by changing it. He commented that Bayeux, by his support of the monarchy and his aristocratic sympathies, had lost the confidence of citizens throughout the department and stood little chance of regaining it. In a second letter, dated February 2, Doulcet sounded much more optimistic:

> We are constantly gaining ground on the factious elements. We have pursued them into a corner. Yesterday *at the club*, we won a complete advantage over them. The success was almost entirely due to Bougon-Longrais, our secretary-general, who on several occasions has had the honor to meet you in Paris. *Caille* was defeated, and to such a degree that his brother in arms D'estanges felt compelled to abandon him and even mount his carcass to complete his defeat.
>
> At the end of the meeting I was elected President of the Club. I learned of it this morning from a large number of good citizens of this town who had long since ceased going there. They pressed me, they demanded that I accept; myself, I demanded that they attend meetings regularly, and I volunteered. There is the battle decidedly engaged and suffering a necessary fight to the death. Either we restore the authority of the law in Caen, and respect for it in the Club, or we abandon all, business and the country.[32]

Here we see a prime example of the legalism and the insistence on orderly debate in the political arena that were the most prominent characteristics of the Calvados administration throughout this period. Despite the merits of the Jacobin club protest, it had been lodged in an unruly and unsanctioned manner, and to accede to the protestors' demands would, in the minds of the administrators, have clearly established a disastrous precedent.

---

31. A.N., F[1b]II Calvados 1 (personnel and tribunals).
32. A.N., F[7] 3661[1] Calvados. Chaix-d'Estanges' name is spelled in at least three different ways in the documents. He was reportedly born Chaix-de-St.-Ange, and changed his name to Destange or d'Estanges at the time of the Revolution (Vaultier, *Souvenirs*, 288).

Doulcet wrote again to the minister one day later and reported that he had just presided over a peaceful Jacobin club meeting attended by more than two thousand people. In subsequent letters, he suggested to the minister that an example be made of Chaix and Caille, but soon he moderated his opinion, noting that the two men continued to exercise "a prodigious influence over the people of the faubourgs" and that the authorities should proceed with a prosecution only if they could be assured of success. To accuse the two leaders of *lèse-nation* before the Legislative Assembly, and then see them acquitted (as Doulcet thought probable), would only make them popular heroes. He observed that Fauchet, then a deputy to the Assembly, had himself written to the Jacobin club urging it to join with the municipal council in demanding an annulment of the entire jury list. With respect to any prosecution, Doulcet thought the municipal council to be hesitant because of the powerful influence of the club and considered the departmental directory unwilling to risk its current good standing with the populace. Several municipal officials did resign in the wake of the controversy, citing violation of the law and the inability of the council to deliberate free of the club's overriding influence, but their colleagues exhorted them to retract their resignations. In the end, only one followed through on his action.[33]

No prosecution resulted from this affair, and Doulcet's victory over his "factious" opponents appears to have been short-lived. Less than two months later, Caille again sat as president of the Jacobin club, and in November, 1792, he was elected *procureur-syndic* of the district (an ironic position for one who had been accused of flouting the law and public authority!). Chaix-d'Estanges continued to hold forth from the pulpit of Saint-Etienne. The departmental directory did dismiss the two professors from the jury list but made no further concessions, and on February 11, the Criminal Tribunal was finally installed.[34]

Despite the apparent victory of Louis Caille and the Jacobin club, this episode marked an important shift in Caen political life. Since late 1790, the Jacobin club had acted as an independent agent in Calvados politics—attempting to influence local elections, supporting Claude Fauchet, urging prosecution in the Affair of 84. What Doulcet and other administrators objected to in February, 1792, was the extralegal manner in which the club

33. A.N., F^7 3661^1 Calvados, and F^{1b} II Calvados 1; A. D. Calvados, L10052 (documents pertaining to the installation of the Criminal Tribunal).

34. A. D. Calvados, L386 (Transcriptions des procès-verbaux des délibérations du conseil général du district de Caen, 15 juillet 1790–15 janvier 1793); A. C. Caen, D1.

acted, riling the populace in support of its demand. Doulcet sympathized with the club's objection to the jury list but would not tolerate the popular tumult that accompanied it. In the following weeks, Doulcet appears to have succeeded in bringing the Jacobin club under control. Although Caille returned as president, the club did not henceforth exercise the independent influence that it had had to that point. The local administrations now dominated political affairs. By 1793, the Jacobin club would be playing only a secondary role in Caen politics.

For Georges Bayeux, however, the trouble had just begun. Intimidated by the public outcry directed against him, Bayeux excused himself from departmental meetings and retreated with his family to their country home. On February 13, the departmental directory informed Bayeux that calm had been restored and that nothing should prevent his return to duty. Several weeks passed before he heeded that call, and his relationship with his colleagues clearly deteriorated. He soon accused several members of the directory of misallocation of funds, and they in turn redirected the accusation against Bayeux. On May 1, 1792, five Calvados deputies to the Legislative Assembly wrote to the minister of the interior requesting that at the first opportunity he rid their department "of one of the most perfidious enemies of the republic," namely Bayeux. They charged that he had led the departmental administration to take illegal actions and was contributing to a disruption of public order.[35] The Legislative Assembly opened an investigation, but with no immediate result. Bayeux's sympathy with the monarchy was well known, and it is probably no coincidence that only two days after the monarchy fell, he was arrested and charged with communicating with émigrés, as well as complicity with the ministers Armand Marc Montmorin and Claude Antoine Valdec de Lessart, themselves suspect after August 10.

Bayeux was imprisoned in the Château, and his wife traveled to Paris to plead his case to members of the Assembly. Their investigation of his papers produced no conclusive evidence, and on the night of September 5, she returned to Caen with an order from the Comité de surveillance et de sûreté général for his release. The procureur of Caen refused to act alone, though, and an old friend and municipal official, Jean Lasseret, offered no help. The mayor, Auvray de Coursanne, insisted on consulting the municipal council. The council took no action that night, while the news of Bayeux's ordered

35. A.N., F⁷ 3661¹ Calvados.

release spread throughout town. The following day, Auvray went to the Château to release the prisoner, accompanied by several officials. Instead, the citizens on guard arrested and imprisoned them. Not until late in the afternoon did the National Guard secure the freedom of Bayeux and the others. Realizing his still-precarious situation, Bayeux headed toward the Abbaye-aux-Hommes, meeting place of the departmental and municipal councils, accompanied by a National Guard escort. Just short of their goal, on the Place Saint-Sauveur (the same spot that had spawned the Affair of 84), they encountered an unruly crowd. Members of the administration, clearly concerned for Bayeux's safety, soon arrived on the scene but could not prevent the shot and blows that killed Bayeux. The National Guard stood helplessly by as his head was cut off and paraded around town, the same fate that had befallen the unfortunate Belzunce.[36]

Madame Bayeux demanded the arrest and prosecution of her husband's murderers, but to no avail. A number of rumors circulated during the weeks following the tragedy. One of these suggested premeditation on the part of the National Guard, charging that the guardsmen had intentionally led Bayeux through the Place Saint-Sauveur with the knowledge that a crowd awaited him there and that he would be attacked. The area could have been avoided by means of an equally direct route from the Château to the Abbaye. The guard was also criticized for its failure to protect Bayeux after the situation had clearly become dangerous.[37]

A second rumor accused Jean Charles Hippolyte Bougon-Longrais, the young secretary-general of the department, of conspiring in the murder of Bayeux. Bougon was an active and respected figure in public affairs from the very start of the Revolution. He sat on the first *comité révolutionnaire* in Caen; and in late 1789, when he was only twenty-four years old, he was one of two emissaries sent by the municipality to the Constituent Assembly to solicit the establishment of a *cour supérieure* in Caen.[38] An *avocat* by profession, Bougon was elected *procureur* of the commune in February, 1790, but could not accept the post because of his youth. One year later, he became secretary-general of the departmental administration. Named *accusateur public* by an electoral assembly in April, 1791, he was again disqualified

36. A. C. Caen, D2. See also Vaultier, *Souvenirs*, 290–93; and Lesage (Esnault), 90–92.
37. Lesage (Esnault), 92.
38. A. C. Caen, I1 (Députation à Versailles de Signard d'Ouffières et de Bougon-Longrais, 1789–90).

because of his age.[39] Respect for Bougon's abilities was often grudging, as more than a few people resented his ambition and egotism. One contemporary observer, noting the popular suspicion of Bougon after the murder of Bayeux, commented on the young man's character: "M. Bougon-Longrais, a young lawyer, born in Caen, was a self-conceited, proud, vain, and presumptuous fellow, all based on very superficial talents, but which he believed to be at least equal to those, infinitely more substantial, of his benefactor [he suggests that Bayeux had obtained the post of secretary-general for Bougon], against whom he was animated by the basest jealousy and the blackest ingratitude."[40] A more charitable biographer dismisses the suspicions as unfounded, claiming they were probably inspired by Bougon's known friendship with Fauchet, who had long been a detractor of Bayeux.[41] Whatever Bougon's motives or involvement, no serious investigation was mounted against him. Indeed, he succeeded Bayeux as *procureur-général-syndic* and went on to play an influential role in departmental politics.

In the controversy surrounding the Criminal Tribunal, as well as during the Affair of 84 in November, 1791, the Caen Jacobin club played an important role. Officially called Les Amis de la Constitution, the society was formed in late 1790 and immediately contributed several pamphlets to the debate over the constitutional oath of the clergy. Early presidents of the club included Jean Baptiste Lomont, deputy to the Legislative Assembly and Convention; Bonnet de Meautry, also a deputy to those assemblies; and Pierre Jean Lévêque, president of the departmental council in 1793. But undoubtedly the most influential leader of the Caen Jacobins was Bishop Claude Fauchet, despite the fact that he did not arrive in the department until May, 1791. Under his leadership, the activism of the club increased. The coalition of nobles that surfaced in November had allegedly been formed to prevent the manipulation of municipal elections by the increasingly active Jacobin club. Barely two months earlier, six members of the departmental directory had appealed to the Constituent Assembly and the minister of the interior for permission to shift their meetings to the nearby town of Bayeux, citing the intimidating presence of the club in Caen and warning that "ar-

39. A. D. Calvados, L10058 (correspondence to departmental administration); A. C. Caen, K35 (Procureur de la Commune, 1790–an III).

40. Sauvage, "Les Souvenirs de J.-B. Renée," 598.

41. Jeanne Grall, "La très courte carrière d'un procureur général syndic, Bougon-Longrais (1765–1794), procureur général syndic du Calvados," in *Droit privé et institutions régionales: Etudes historiques offertes à Jean Yver* (Paris, 1976), 335.

bitrariness, insubordination, and despotism, as much popular as military, threaten to subvert everything." The minister responded by letter on August 26, acknowledging their "alarming position" but stating that he could not authorize the transfer of their meetings to another town.[42]

It was during this period that the split between the Jacobins and the Feuillants occurred in Paris. The regional paper printed in Caen, *Affiches, Annonces et Avis Divers de la Basse-Normandie,* announced the split in its issue of July 24, 1791. As a sidelight, the editor included the following tidbit: "It is rumored in Paris, that M. Robertspierre is crazy: this opinion appears to be generally held; people are only divided as to the date of this unfortunate event: several persons place it rather early." One month later, the paper reported that the Jacobins were prevailing in their struggle with the Feuillants, with more departmental societies affiliating with the former than with the latter.[43] The Caen club broke communication with the Paris Jacobins, favoring the Feuillants, but shortly reestablished ties with the Jacobins. Esnault suggests, probably exaggerating, that Fauchet changed his mind on the matter and that this was the deciding factor.[44]

The club's decision to continue its affiliation with the Jacobins undoubtedly contributed to the increasing opposition to the club among "les honnêtes gens" of Caen. The *Affiches,* clearly catering to the aristocracy and wealthy bourgeois in its editorial policy, joined in the attack on the Caen Jacobins. A series of articles in October asked the rhetorical question, What is a club? Responding that it was a group of men assembling to discuss and deliberate on affairs of state in order to influence public opinion, the editor concluded that all clubs were therefore useless and dangerous. "Do we not already have a National Assembly? Do we require several?" The clubs may have begun with good intentions, but vanity now reigned among them. They misled rather than enlightened.[45]

The problem came to a head in February, 1792, when the club opposed the newly constituted Criminal Tribunal. We have seen in the correspondence of Doulcet his concern for the threat to public order and lawful government and the temporary departure of Louis Caille from the club. Doulcet's elec-

---

42. A.N., F[7] 3661[1] Calvados (Letters of August 21 and August 26, 1791).

43. *Affiches, Annonces et Avis Divers de la Basse-Normandie,* July 24 and August 21, 1791, A. D. Calvados.

44. Lesage (Esnault), 65.

45. *Affiches, Annonces et Avis Divers de la Basse-Normandie,* October 9, 13, and 16, 1791, A. D. Calvados.

tion as president raised hopes of a moderating trend, but no significant shift in club attitudes occurred at this time. If anything, the club's ties to the Paris Jacobins grew stronger. Robespierre apparently made some public defense of the Caen Jacobins, and the club sent the following appreciative address to him on March 7, 1792:

GREETINGS TO THE INCORRUPTIBLE ROBESPIERRE

The Society of Caen knows that the father of patriotism was at his post when it was necessary to defend his children of Calvados, hounded by stylets of calumny; she knows it . . . and comes silently to add a palm to his civic crown.

Robespierre, this name that makes glory, this name that brings fear into the hearts of tyrants, will be the watchword that will rally us to fight them.

We do not pretend to render that name more celebrated in making this address: the undertaking was beyond our powers; it is only the precious token of our gratitude and the particular tribute of public esteem.[46]

By the end of the year, however, the Caen Jacobins had reversed their position and broken with the parent club. In the wake of Bayeux's murder and the September massacres in Paris, the Caen club repudiated the excesses of the Paris Jacobins. Louis Caille was very likely instrumental in this switch. Sent by the club to Paris in January, 1792, Caille had argued with Robespierre and developed a dislike for the Paris leader. He is known to have been friendly with the Girondin deputies, particularly the Marseille delegation, led by Charles Jean Marie Barbaroux.[47]

Even more important, however, was the influence of the Calvados deputies to the Convention. We have here a clear example of the channels of communication between Caen and the capital regarding issues of local, as well as national, importance. Late in 1792, the Caen Jacobin club wrote to the Calvados delegation soliciting advice as to whether it should end its affiliation. In a letter written by Lomont and signed by the other deputies (with the exception of Bonnet), the delegation firmly recommended that the club break with the Paris Jacobins. By January, 1793, it had done precisely that. In doing so, the Caen Jacobins not only severed their ties with the parent

46. Vaultier, *Souvenirs*, 122.

47. "Le Fédéralisme dans le Calvados," *Annales du Centre Régional de Recherche et du Documentation Pédagogiques de Caen*, Service Educatif Nouvelle Série, Dossier 3 (Caen, 1977), A. D. Calvados. This is an edited collection of twenty documents, including biographical information on several federalist leaders, compiled by M. O. and J. Macé, J. Grall, A. Parmentier, and E. Gautier-Desvaux.

club but demonstrated their esteem for the Calvados *conventionnels,* most of whom supported the Girondins.[48]

Even as it broke with the Paris Jacobins, however, the Caen Jacobin club was clearly in decline. Few members attended meetings. Those who did reportedly spent the time singing patriotic songs, for lack of more serious business.[49] The decline of the Caen Jacobin club can be attributed in part to the growth of another club, the Carabots. The precise origin of this group is not certain, but it apparently had its roots in the people's militia that formed in the summer of 1789. Primarily artisans and small shopkeepers who had armed themselves in the raid on the Château, the members of this militia were exuberant in their newfound role but found themselves relegated to the lower ranks after the official organization of the National Guard. In order to preserve something of their élan and rapport, they formed a group and called themselves the Carabots, a derogatory derivation of *caporaux* (corporals). The Carabots made the jump from obscure fraternity to documented club on February 10, 1793, when fifty of them assembled on the Place de la Liberté, formerly the Place Royale. It is interesting that they chose this square, fronted by the homes of wealthy *négociants,* rather than the Place Saint-Sauveur or the Place Saint-Pierre. Two days later, they assembled again, with a banner, arm bands, and a *procès-verbal* of their previous meeting. They vowed to accept only recognized republicans in their society and swore "to maintain the Republic—one, indivisible, and popular—liberty, and equality; to observe the laws that had these principles as their foundation; and to exterminate all those who wanted another government." They proclaimed their motto to be, "Execution of the law, or death."[50]

48. I found neither the letter from the club nor the deputies' reply in any of the archives I consulted. They are mentioned, however, in a February 12, 1793, letter from Bonnet de Meautry to an unidentified friend in Caen. He noted his refusal to sign the letter authored by Lomont and said that he had written his own letter to the Jacobin club on January 1, 1793, in which he recommended that they not break relations with the Paris club. He received no reply. He remarked, in closing, that he had heard that the Caen club was languishing and from this presumed that his friend no longer attended. Bonnet's letter can be found in A. C. Caen, I275, and is reprinted in Vaultier, *Souvenirs,* 122–23.

49. Lesage (Esnault), 102.

50. See Vaultier, *Souvenirs,* 9–11, 126–37; Charles Renard, *Notice sur les Carabots de Caen* (Caen, 1858), located in B. M. Caen, Rés. Fn. Br. C315–368; and Georges Mancel, *La Société des Carabots* (Caen, 1857). Georges Lefebvre noted that since the fifteenth century, rural brigands had been known as *carabots* in Picardy and Normandy. Neither Vaultier nor Renard mentions this possible derivation of the club name, but Mancel dismisses it entirely. See Georges Lefebvre, *The Great Fear of 1789,* trans. Joan White (New York, 1973), 23.

It is difficult to say much about the Carabot club, because it left little trace of its existence. Aside from the proclamation issued on the date of its foundation and a proposal that it presented to the departmental administration during the federalist revolt, no documents relating to the club have survived in the archives. No membership list exists. But the date of the club's official foundation (in early 1793, when "anarchism" and "factionalism" in Paris and the Convention were being widely denounced by departmental administrations and popular societies) and the stress on respect for the law in both the motto and the oath suggest that the Carabots were moderates who did not support Jacobin radicalism. They maintained an active and public presence, though, and apparently made respectable citizens somewhat uneasy by bearing arms. Both Esnault and Vaultier report that the Carabots soon eclipsed the Jacobins in popularity and influence.[51]

Nowhere in the documents, however, do the Carabots ever appear in an adversarial relationship with the local administrations. Indeed, several departmental administrators were reportedly members of the club, which often acted as an unofficial arm of the administration. On March 3, 1793, when a group of young men disrupted army recruitment, the Carabots sounded the alarm and assisted officials in restoring order. Occasionally, club members were overzealous in their actions—on April 20, the municipal council sent several men to head off a group of 150 armed Carabots on their way to Argences in search of grain. But officials often turned to them for manpower to assist with recruitment, grain requisitions, and transport. On March 12, a Carabot accompanied Louis Caille to Evrecy on official business, and on May 19, the departmental administration assigned the Carabots to inspect foreign mail. Departmental and municipal officials even called on Carabots to carry out occasional domiciliary searches in the spring of 1793. In April, Bougon-Longrais, on mission to Paris, closed a letter to two colleagues by embracing in spirit "you and all the faithful carabots."[52]

This limited evidence suggests that the Carabot club acted as a client group of the departmental administration and probably of the Caen merchant elite. Certainly, many of the artisans and shopkeepers who made up the club's membership depended on the wholesale merchants for their live-

51. Lesage (Esnault), 102; Vaultier, *Souvenirs*, 136.

52. Lesage (Esnault), 103; A. D. Calvados, L10024 (loose minutes of departmental administration meetings, 1793), L10151 (papers pertaining to Bougon), and L10529 (Bougon's letter to departmental administration, April 12, 1793).

lihood and did business with them on a regular basis. Their choice of the Place de la Liberté as a meeting place suggests a clientage relationship, as does the fact that one of the Carabot leaders, Jean Michel Barbot, was chief clerk at the Tribunal of Commerce. The Carabot club definitely enjoyed a more collaborative relationship with the departmental administration than did the Jacobin club, which the Carabots now replaced as the most active Caen popular society. It is also significant, particularly given the evidence suggesting a clientage relationship between the club and the Caen commercial elite, that the ascension of the Carabots came just months after the merchant community had achieved its greatest representation on the Caen municipal council.

In Limoges, there was no Château to be stormed, and the Revolution there began much more quietly than it did in Caen. On July 26, 1789, the tricolored *cocarde* made its first appearance in a demonstration directed against the nobility, and several days later the Great Fear brushed Limoges, but nothing of truly dramatic proportions occurred. Shortage of grain had forced municipal control of bread prices since 1788, and in August, 1789, a patriotic committee formed to aid in the provision of the city. For the next year, the search for grain remained the predominant issue facing local authorities.[53]

No significant disruption upset the customary pattern of Limoges life until the night of September 7, 1790, when a fire blazed through the *quartier* Manigne in the heart of the city. The fire raged out of control until early morning, destroying 160 houses and leaving 800 families homeless. The National Guard and the Royal-Navarre regiment valiantly fought the fire and prevented loss of life, but the town hall lacked the financial resources to help those whose property had been destroyed. The entire department lay exhausted after two years of dearth, forcing the administration to ignore legal restrictions and tap the *caisse des domaines* for emergency funds. Departmental and municipal officials appealed to the king and the Constituent As-

---

53. Two books provide good general accounts of the early years of the Revolution in Limoges. They are Jouhaud, *La Révolution Française en Limousin*, and Verynaud, *Histoire de Limoges*. See Lynn A. Hunt, *Revolution and Urban Politics in Provincial France* (Stanford, 1978), 136, for a map detailing the formation of municipal committees in the major towns in France in 1789. In Caen, the committee replaced the old council and remained in power until new elections in February, 1790. In Limoges, the committee functioned alongside the Old Regime municipality until that date.

sembly, but aid from those sources covered only one-twentieth of the need. The Limoges Jacobin club wrote to the Paris Jacobins and other provincial clubs about the terrible misfortune. The clubs responded generously; assisted by a benefit performance of the Théatre Français, they raised over eight thousand *livres* to assist the fire victims, still only a pittance in the face of enormous destruction. With other private donations and the help of neighbors and relatives, the people of Limoges managed to overcome this tragedy, but economic hardship would burden them for several years to come.[54]

Only three months after the fire, political controversy erupted in Limoges. It centered around the founding of a new club, Les Amis de la Paix, organized to balance the influence of the previously established Société des Amis de la Constitution, the Limoges Jacobins. It appears that the results of the municipal elections in November, 1790, inspired the formation of the Amis de la Paix. Eight out of twelve of the municipal officers elected were members of the Jacobin club, and moderates alleged that the Jacobins had achieved these results by limiting the number of electors. The number of voters was indeed much lower than in the previous election, though the impact of that decline is unclear.[55]

The founders of the new club proclaimed in a pamphlet their intention to arouse civic responsibility in order to increase voter turnout. The social attitudes, and perhaps an indication of the social status, of the Amis are revealed in the pamphlet's reference to "the crowd scarcely capable of examining the truth," which had allegedly been swayed by the Jacobin club propaganda. In a similar observation, this time with respect to the nearby rural inhabitants, the pamphlet described "those people of the country-

---

54. Alfred Fray-Fournier, *Le Département de la Haute-Vienne*, I, 320–22, and *Le Club des Jacobins de Limoges, 1790–95* (Limoges, 1903), 27; Jouhaud, *La Révolution Française en Limousin*, 36. See also Kennedy, *The Jacobin Clubs in the French Revolution*, 128.

55. Léon Jouhaud, in *La Révolution Française en Limousin*, claims that all but one of the municipal officers were Jacobins, but four names do not appear on either of the membership lists I have found, so I am reluctant to accept his statement. It is difficult to assess the importance of the low voter turnout. A comparable drop in numbers occurred in Caen between the February and November, 1790, elections, so perhaps the trend was general. Roland Marx has noted a similar decline in voter participation for Alsace. In Strasbourg (Bas-Rhin), the turnout declined from 61 percent in January, 1790, to 21 percent in November, 1791 (he has no figures for November, 1790). In Colmar (Haut-Rhin), 81 percent of the electorate voted in January, 1790; 37 percent in November, 1790; and only 14 percent in November, 1791. See Roland Marx, *Recherches sur la vie politique de l'Alsace prérévolutionnaire et révolutionnaire* (Strasbourg, 1966), 56–62. In Limoges, voter turnout remained low in 1791, when the moderates made a recovery; so low turnout in 1790 can hardly explain the election results for that year.

side . . . simple and credulous, who know not how to distinguish the truth from the coarsest seduction."[56]

The Amis de la Paix first met on December 11, 1790. There was initial widespread skepticism regarding the intent of the new club, but publication of its prospectus quieted those doubts somewhat. In this document, the Amis professed their desire for open discussion, obedience to the law, and respect for the new constitution. In an obvious challenge to the exclusivity of the Jacobin club and the Société Patriotique et Littéraire, a club composed of individuals too young to join the Jacobins, the Amis made membership fees low and declared their meetings open to the public. The other two clubs soon followed suit, and all seemed resigned to a period of intense, but peaceful, competition for members.

The Société Patriotique was the first to abandon the status quo of uneasy coexistence. In a December 29, 1790, meeting, the Société Patriotique charged the Amis with the instigation of public quarrels, in cafes and on street corners, between its own members and members of the other two clubs. Those present voted to avoid public confrontation but to bring all grievances to the attention of the society.[57] The Jacobin club, too, intensified its campaign against the Amis de la Paix. As early as December 13, the Jacobins had granted the right to all national guardsmen to attend meetings in full uniform, a clear attempt to recruit new members. Pierre Dumas, club member and captain in the guard, soon led his company to join the Jacobin club en masse.

Both the municipal and departmental administrations at first refused to consider the squabbles between the Amis and the other two clubs. As Jacobin club membership grew, however, the issue came again before the departmental administration, introduced by the *procureur-général-syndic,* Pierre Dumas, who was also, of course, a Jacobin club leader. In an undated December letter addressed to the municipal council, the Jacobins expressed their concern over reports of a nationwide conspiracy and rumored Amis de la Paix involvement. They noted that clubs with similar names had caused trouble in Nîmes, Nancy, Brest, and Lyon.[58] On December 28, Dumas remarked on the coincidence of recent public disruptions in Limoges with the

---

56. *Exposition de la conduite et des principes de la Société des Amis de la Paix* (January, 1791), A. D. Haute-Vienne, L812; hereafter referred to as *Exposition.*

57. A. D. Haute-Vienne, L811 (Société Patriotique et Littéraire, procès-verbaux).

58. Fray-Fournier, *Le Club des Jacobins,* 20.

formation of the Amis. He moved that the club be instructed to dissolve and its members to join the Jacobin club in order to avert serious trouble, and the motion was easily passed by the departmental directory, the district directory, and the municipal council.

The Amis protested this decision. They charged first that the local councils were biased, claiming that of the thirty-nine members of the departmental directory, the district directory, and the municipal council, at least twenty-three belonged to the Jacobin club.[59] They also defended their club's attention to legal requirements and noted that the Jacobin club had been founded six months before the Constituent Assembly legalized political associations. They vowed to continue their respect for authority by complying with the dissolution order. However, instead of dissolving their club, the Amis proposed an affiliation with the Limoges Jacobins in order to retain an element of autonomy. The Jacobin club rejected the proposal, refusing to affiliate with any group not already recognized by the Paris Jacobins. The Amis stood fast and defended their right to assemble by noting the continued existence of the Société Patriotique et Littéraire. Faced with an apparently unresolvable conflict, the municipal council ordered the suspension of the Amis de la Paix on December 30, 1790. Not wishing to serve as a pretext for the continued resistance of the Amis, on January 1 the Société Patriotique sent delegates to the Jacobin club to request a union of the two popular societies. Unification took place two days later. The Amis de la Paix was dissolved, and its suspension soon became official.[60]

There are obvious parallels between this episode and the Affair of 84 in Caen. The members of the Amis de la Paix, like the Caen coalition, were seen as "enemies of the constitution and troublemakers seeking to return France to the Old Regime."[61] Unlike the Caen coalition, however, the Amis were not predominantly nobles. There were nobles among the members, to be sure, but the officers of the club included Ardant-Dupicq, a *négociant* and municipal officer; Lambertie, a lawyer; Pétiniaud de Juriol, a noble *négociant;* and Fournier *le jeune,* a lawyer. Many of the Amis were wealthy

59. I do not know how they arrived at these numbers. Counting ten departmental directors, including the president and *procureur-général-syndic,* six district directors, including the president and *procureur-syndic,* and thirteen municipal officials, including the mayor and *procureur,* I total twenty-nine, fifteen of whom were members of the Jacobin club. This is still a majority, but not quite as overwhelming as twenty-three of thirty-nine.

60. A. D. Haute-Vienne, L811 and L812 (documents pertaining to the Amis de la Paix).

61. A. D. Haute-Vienne, L812 (Jacobin club address).

bourgeois, including Louis Naurissart, *directeur de la monnaie* and future mayor, four *négociants,* two *marchands,* and two clerks. At least eight of the Amis were municipal *notables* in the 1790–1791 term.[62]

The lack of full membership rolls for the Amis de la Paix makes a detailed social comparison with the Jacobin club impossible. But in general, it is fair to contrast the *haut-bourgeois* character of the Amis with the *moyen-bourgeois* character of the Jacobins, who also admitted a considerable number of *petit-bourgeois* artisans and workers into their ranks. It seems probable that the *moyenne-bourgeoisie* dominated the Jacobin club until at least the year II, though there is some disagreement on this question. Alfred Fray-Fournier has argued that the intellectual superiority of the bourgeoisie allowed it to maintain control of the club throughout its existence. Another local historian, however, insists that in 1792, "the bourgeois element was overwhelmed by an influx of workers and artisans."[63]

It may well be that the better-educated bourgeois were able to dominate the Jacobin club with eloquent oratory, but a membership list prepared in the year III shows that artisans and workers constituted the single largest occupational group in the club almost from the date of its foundation. Adopting Léon Jouhaud's dividing line and comparing members who joined the club in 1790 and 1791 with those who joined from 1792 through 1794 yields several interesting observations. First, of the 419 members listed, 72 percent joined in 1790 and 1791. In that group of 303 individuals, artisans and workers accounted for 37 percent, professionals for 21 percent, and merchants for 18 percent. The remaining 24 percent was distributed roughly among lawyers, landowners, military men, and others (students and bourgeois *sans état*). In the period 1792 through 1794, the percentage of artisans and workers did increase to 44 percent, while the percentage of professionals and commercial men declined to 17 percent and 11 percent respectively; but none of these changes are drastic. Moreover, only 116 men joined the club during this later period. Thus, if workers and artisans can be said to have overwhelmed their bourgeois colleagues in the club, they had done so as early as 1791. It seems more likely that Fray-Fournier's assessment is cor-

---

62. *Exposition; Délibérations de la Municipalité de Limoges* (November, 1790), B. M. Limoges. No membership list for the Amis de la Paix exists. However, a petition to the king prepared in April, 1791, bears the names of 208 citizens of Limoges, most of whom were likely members of the club, which reportedly numbered 300 members before its dissolution.

63. Fray-Fournier, *Le Club des Jacobins,* x; Jouhaud, *La Révolution Française en Limousin,* 55.

rect, but clearly the Limoges Jacobins could not ignore the viewpoint of the town's petty bourgeoisie and workers, or at least did not choose to do so.[64]

The abolition of the Amis de la Paix did not bring an end to the opposition between its adherents and the Limoges Jacobins. A number of events combined to maintain a tense situation in Limoges through May, 1791. The new legislation regarding the organization of the Church provided one source of friction. The antipathy between the supporters of the new and old regimes was exacerbated by the controversy surrounding the civil oath of the clergy. As in the case of Caen and Calvados, Limoges registered a lower rate of acceptance of the oath than did the Haute-Vienne as a whole. Sixty-five percent of the parish priests in the department swore the oath, while in Limoges only five of twenty-three priests, or 22 percent, did so.[65]

The most ardent defender of the oath was a professor of theology and former Dominican priest named Jean Foucaud. One of the founders of the Jacobin club and very active in its affairs, Foucaud delivered an address on January 13, 1791, in which he established a theological foundation for the civil constitution.[66] He later published a tract based on this speech, which four professors of the Limoges *collège,* all of them ecclesiastics, publicly attacked. They charged Foucaud with a fraudulent interpretation of Church doctrine. This produced something of a public scandal, which was aggravated on February 25 when the four professors, who had refused to swear the oath, disrupted the installation of their replacements. The municipal council responded with an order forbidding any unauthorized public assembly of more than three people, temporarily restoring quiet to the town.[67]

That peace remained a fragile one, though, made tenuous by the emergence early in the year of a new armed force, a company of dragoons. Technically an adjunct to the National Guard, the company was formed by the most active members of the Amis de la Paix. The requirement that each man in this mounted cavalry unit provide his own equipment effectively re-

64. A. D. Haute-Vienne, L813 (Société Populaire, an III membership list). The list does not include the unknown number of individuals who were expelled before the year III and may therefore exaggerate slightly the artisan/worker predominance. Each entry on this roll includes the member's name, age, place of birth, occupation (before and during the Revolution), residence, and date of admission to the club.

65. I am indebted to Professor Timothy Tackett for these figures. They are based on the research of Paul d'Hollander, working in France on a *thèse de troisième cycle.*

66. Fray-Fournier, *Le Club des Jacobins,* 24.

67. A. D. Haute-Vienne, L812 (response of the municipal officers to the petition to the king of the former Amis de la Paix).

stricted membership to the wealthier segment of the population. Two of the wealthiest men in town, the future mayor Louis Naurissart and the aristocratic president of the departmental administration, Jean Baptiste Pétiniaud de Beaupeyrat, donated some of the equipment. The officers of the Royal-Navarre regiment generously offered to train the dragoons, whose frequent banquets were often flavored by royalist songs. Enrollment in the elite company reached nearly four hundred.[68]

Barely ten days after the municipal council had banned public assembly, an incident occurred that would lead to the abolition of this new armed corps. On March 8, a small group gathered on a Limoges street corner and burned a copy of the Amis de la Paix prospectus. An outraged *notable* (in all likelihood, a former Amis) reported this to the municipal council as a violation of the February 25 decree against public crowds and demanded that action be taken against those responsible, including the president and secretaries of the Jacobin club, who he claimed had incited the incident. The council, sparsely attended, did issue a decree of accusation, but without the necessary formal indictment from the municipal *procureur*. This forced a reconvening of the full council, which was evenly divided between adherents of the Jacobins and of the former Amis. The vote on the issue deadlocked eleven to eleven, with Jean Baptiste Nieaud, the mayor, inclined to cast the deciding vote in favor of the Jacobin club, which he had helped to found. Before he could do so, however, the eleven moderates (three officers and eight *notables*) walked out of the meeting and refused to attend future sessions. All eleven were former members of the Amis de la Paix.

As this crisis developed within the municipal council, agitation began once again on the streets of Limoges, melding political and religious issues. Supporters of the traditional clergy circulated a petition calling for the reinstallation of the refractory curé of the parish Saint-Michel, as well as the four *collège* professors. Their efforts produced a number of public disputes, and four petition gatherers were finally charged with undermining respect for the law. The municipal council deplored this divisive situation, which it attributed to the continued provocations of the former Amis, the efforts of refractory priests and the *collège* professors, and the formation of the controversial dragoons. An assembly of National Guards, meeting on March 29, supported the position of the municipal council but laid responsibility for

68. Jouhaud, *La Révolution Française en Limousin*, 79–81; Léon Jouhaud, *Les Gardes nationaux à Limoges, avant la Convention* (Limoges, 1940), 43–47.

the current troubles explicitly on the existence of the company of dragoons. The guardsmen blamed the dragoons for a number of recent duels, legally prohibited, and two public brawls during the previous weeks. The municipal council, itself under public attack, appealed for help to the district administration, which in turn appealed to the departmental directory. The directory responded by ordering the convocation of sectional assemblies so that active citizens might calmly discuss their differences, an action that municipal officials feared would exacerbate, not resolve, the current difficulties. Nonetheless, sectional assemblies were scheduled for April 4.

On the eve of those assemblies, armed groups gathered on Limoges street corners. Small bands of uniformed dragoons moved about town taunting their Jacobin opponents as tensions once again reached a dangerous level. The mayor responded to the immediate threat by ordering the National Guard to disband the armed groups, and in this manner, calm was restored. But with regard to the larger problem of political polarization, the municipal council, still meeting without its moderate members, remained tentative and unsure. Once again, it appealed to a higher authority, this time directly to the departmental administration, requesting postponement of the sectional assemblies and suspension of the dragoons. The departmental council approved the former request and ruled that the municipality itself had the authority to order the latter action. On April 6, the municipality issued that order, instructing the dragoons to rejoin their regular National Guard units. Few of them returned to the National Guard, but the company of dragoons was effectively dismantled.[69]

In a later report, the municipal council charged that the former members of the Amis de la Paix, deprived of their armed company, now turned to the Royal-Navarre regiment for support. Most of the soldiers in this regiment were German, barely conversant in French and not well loved by the populace, despite their valiant efforts at the time of the Limoges fire. With the demise of the dragoons, the Royal-Navarre increased its nightly patrols. It was not long before an incident occurred; but only insults, and no blows, were exchanged. Still, the Royal-Navarre commander, Montigny, ordered his men henceforth to patrol with charged guns, prepared to meet force with force. The municipal council considered this an entirely unwarranted response and warned Montigny that he would be held responsible for any

69. A. D. Haute-Vienne, L812.

trouble. Montigny refused to retract his order and doubled the patrols. On April 19, six municipal officers, plus the mayor, signed an order referring the entire affair to the National Assembly and requesting the transfer of the Royal-Navarre regiment. Seven *notables* objected that the full council had not been consulted, but the officers ruled that this was not required for a simple police matter. Several former Amis appealed to a rump session of the departmental directory, meeting without three of its members and the *procureur-général-syndic,* and secured a request to the minister of war for postponement of any transfer. However, the full directory, with its Jacobin members in attendance, soon reversed this decision. Both factions now decided to take their case to the highest authority. The former Amis and their supporters drafted yet another petition to the Constituent Assembly, which was countered by a petition written by Jacobin club members.

The petition of the former Amis claimed that the National Guard was to blame for the recent troubles, that the April 19 municipal order had been illegally drafted, and that the municipal council had lost the confidence of the populace. More than two hundred people signed this petition. The Jacobin club countered that the Amis de la Paix supporters were a collection of former nobles and wealthy individuals who sought to protect their own interests by undermining the Revolution, that the dragoons and the Royal-Navarre regiment had served those interests, and that the municipal council had acted responsibly and constitutionally throughout the affair. More than four hundred residents of Limoges signed the Jacobins' petition. The name of Léonard Gay-Vernon, recently elected bishop, headed the list of signatures, which also included the names of a number of municipal and district officials. The minister of war did order the transfer of the Royal-Navarre regiment, but not before a May 16 brawl had left several national guardsmen seriously injured.[70]

The departure of the Royal-Navarre regiment brought an end to the armed confrontations on the streets of Limoges, but it did not resolve the opposition between moderates and radicals in local politics. Indeed, Amis de la Paix supporters regained control of the municipal council in the elections of late 1791. This contrasts sharply with the situation in Caen, where there was no prolonged struggle for control of municipal politics. The challenge

70. A. D. Haute-Vienne, L812 and I/K103 (Pamphlet relatif au conflit opposant la municipalité de Limoges au régiment de dragons, 1791). See also Jouhaud, *Les Gardes nationaux,* 45–47.

to the "patriot party" came largely from the nobility, and as nobles emigrated or withdrew from public life (as most did), the issue became moot. Local elections in Caen were relatively uncontentious, and the local political elite was remarkably unified. In Limoges, on the other hand, the conflict between the Amis de la Paix and the Jacobins had fractured local unity and created an intensely politicized atmosphere by the end of 1791. The transfer of the Royal-Navarre may have defused the potential for violence, but in essence it removed from the scene only pawns in the political conflict. The former Amis continued to be active in local affairs, and the erstwhile dragoons remained available, though unorganized. The confrontation between radicals and moderates never produced the sort of violent and deadly clash that Nîmes had witnessed in 1790, but the tension lay always just below the surface. Most importantly, as in Nîmes, Marseille, and Lyon, this political rivalry brought artisans and workers firmly into the political arena, as the bourgeois leaders of the Jacobins and of the Amis sought support among the sans-culottes. In Caen, by contrast, the popular classes remained on the fringes of local politics.

The election of a constitutional bishop in February, 1791, contributed to the tense situation in Limoges. The bishop's palace was located there, and we have already seen evidence of the public controversy in the city over the civil oath of the clergy. The choice of Léonard Gay-Vernon as the new bishop introduced to public prominence a fervent Jacobin who would exercise a strong influence on local affairs throughout the Revolution. Gay-Vernon, born into a Saint-Léonard family "de petite noblesse," had most recently served as curé in Compreignac, a town of about two thousand people roughly fifteen miles north of Limoges, where he had been elected mayor in 1790. His election as bishop came on the third ballot, and then only by a slim margin over the Abbé Gouttes, a delegate to the Constituent Assembly. The former bishop, Duplessis d'Argentré, denounced the election of Gay-Vernon and called on all priests to reject his leadership.[71]

Gay-Vernon was affiliated with the Limoges Jacobin club almost from its creation and became president not long after his election as bishop. His brother, Jean Baptiste, was also a priest and a member of the club. The new bishop named his brother an episcopal vicar, and in 1792, the latter was elected to the departmental administration. When Gay-Vernon left for Paris in late 1791 as a delegate to the Legislative Assembly, he remained in con-

71. Fray-Fournier, *Le Département de la Haute-Vienne*, II, 166; Jouhaud, *La Révolution Française en Limousin*, 124–126.

stant contact with his brother and the Jacobin club. One departmental administrator attributed to the bishop "the greater number of the troubles that afflicted the Limousin. . . . He became the motive force behind all the intrigues and follies of the club."[72] The influence of Gay-Vernon on attitudes in Limoges cannot be denied. In April, 1794, he estimated at 380 the number of letters he had already sent to the Limoges Jacobins. We will see that his letters were not ignored.[73]

The civil constitution of the clergy remained a divisive issue in Limoges through the summer of 1791. On August 6, the departmental directory, with Pétiniaud de Beaupeyrat as president, provisionally suspended a law of June 1 that called for the creation of four parishes in Limoges. The directory complained that the proposed parish lines, drawn up by the district (allegedly under pressure from Bishop Gay-Vernon), were haphazard and irrational. A crowd gathered in front of the departmental meeting hall to protest the decision. Pétiniaud felt morally compelled to resign rather than revoke the suspension, leaving that action to the remainder of the departmental directory. In the minds of Limoges moderates, Pétiniaud's resignation represented the hounding from office of a man of substance and integrity, a leading figure of the traditional elite who linked, by virtue of his title and commercial activities, the second and third estates. For Pétiniaud's detractors, his resignation marked another victory for Limoges Jacobins.[74]

Despite the apparent victory of the Jacobin club over the Amis de la Paix and the radicalization of the municipality, the Limoges moderates rallied their forces to make a comeback in the fall of 1791. In early November, Louis Naurissart, *directeur de la monnaie,* was elected mayor; and the newly elected municipal council was dominated by wealthy *négociants,* including Pétiniaud de Beaupeyrat as a *notable.* It is difficult to pinpoint the reason for this turnaround, but the Limoges sans-culottes had a simple explanation. A letter written by members of the 2nd Battalion of Haute-Vienne volunteers, sent from their camp in Villers-Cotterets to the Jacobin club in Limoges, clearly expresses their suspicion of vote buying:

Permit us to offer you our felicitations on the good fortune that our town will enjoy under the paternal government of Naurissart, Marc Dubois and other excellent citizens, whom an infernal cabal has kept from official position up to this

72. P. Granet, "Extraits du journal de Génébrias de Goutte-pagnon, 1774–1794," *Archives Historiques du Limousin,* IV (1892), 382.
73. Fray-Fournier, *Le Club des Jacobins,* xx.
74. A.N., F⁷ 3697 (report of the departmental directory to the minister of the interior, August, 1791).

time. . . . We are sure that aristocrats, swindlers, refractory priests, speculators, nuns, and prostitutes have sung a *Te Deum,* as thanksgiving, for so happy an event. . . . As for those indignant patriots, perhaps they made a long face, but what does it matter?! They have dominated too long! Moreover, most of them have no money and cannot buy the votes of active citizens. All irony aside, brothers and friends . . . we view the counter-revolution as accomplished in our town. But please caution our rich municipal officials and their promoters that they respect our families, or else we will come and give them a lesson that will long be spoken of; and we will not take twenty days to make the trip to Limoges, as we did to come to this place.[75]

One sees that the Limoges patriots at least had a sense of humor, but the situation for them was a serious one. In a response to the 2nd Battalion, the Jacobin club admitted that its meetings were now sparsely attended and that émigrés were boldly returning to their homes. Revolutionary fervor seemed to have waned.

Louis Naurissart had been mayor of Limoges before, from December, 1780, until August, 1784. He had been a third-estate delegate to the Estates General, where his efforts on the finance committee had eventually procured 300,000 *livres* in aid for the Limoges fire victims. In March, 1791, he had resigned as deputy after a public furor in Limoges over his allegedly poor attitude and his conservatism. His *hôtel* in Limoges was one of the most stylish in town, and in 1788, he completed construction of a luxurious rural château. "He loved to play the grand seigneur, protecting the arts, the artists, and the comedians. He truly had the temperament of an aristocrat, enjoying, moreover, the fortune necessary to maintain a role conforming to the tastes of the *haute-bourgeoisie."*[76] His rudeness and inability to manage crowds proved serious liabilities during his second tenure as mayor.

A challenge to the Naurissart mayoralty came in February, 1792, barely three months after the elections. The trouble was occasioned by the return to Limoges of two commissioners, Ganny and Bégougne, sent by the municipality to take delivery of grain purchased the previous fall in Vatan and Châteauroux. The two, members of the Jacobin club, had nearly been killed in Châteauroux during a riot aimed at preventing the removal of the grain. They returned empty-handed, despite the fact that the grain had allegedly

75. The letter is reprinted in Jouhaud, *La Révolution Française en Limousin,* 100–101.
76. Ernest Vincent, "Souvenirs de la Révolution: Les tribulations d'un ancien maire de Limoges," *Le Populaire du Centre* (October, 1958). Vincent wrote a series of historical articles for this newspaper, which have been clipped and filed in the library of the departmental archives.

been paid for by the previous commissioners, Mallet and Garraud. Denunciations of the municipal council abounded. Citizens of Limoges demanded a public accounting of the mission, which Ganny and Bégougne were willing to give but which the municipal council apparently opposed. The departmental administration initially ordered that the report be given behind closed doors, fearing for the safety of those who might be implicated. Jacobin supporters decried this precaution as an effort to protect Mallet and Garraud.

Two days later, on February 26, the mayor and several municipal officials reported to the departmental directory that a crowd planned to escort Ganny and Bégougne to town hall the next day on "a chariot of triumph." They feared a riot. The directory issued orders to National Guard commanders to select twelve men from each company for the protection of the departmental and district directories and the municipal council. They also ordered two gendarmerie brigades to form mounted patrols for crowd control. It soon became clear, however, that the National Guard was divided over the issue and itself posed a threat to public order. The departmental and district directories met the next afternoon in emergency session and read a petition from Ganny and Bégougne describing their dilemma: if they reported in public, they would violate an order; and if they did not, they would be accused of duplicity, and their lives would be in danger. As the administrators discussed the situation, a group of armed national guardsmen invaded the meeting hall, and a spirited crowd gathered in the courtyard. The administrators refused to continue in the presence of armed men but finally agreed to a semipublic hearing the following day.

Naurissart did not attend that hearing, announcing by letter that the current threat to his safety prevented him from attending. Bégougne reported on the two commissioners' recent mission, recounting the dangers they had encountered. He mentioned three letters that he and Ganny had sent to the Limoges municipality. All three had gone unanswered, greatly discrediting them in the eyes of the Châteauroux officials. A report from Garraud and Mallet was read as well, increasing the tumult in the hall. Bégougne responded bitterly to that report, denouncing its authors and the mayor. At this point the National Guard brought laurel crowns to Ganny and Bégougne, which they graciously accepted. They called on the crowd to respect property and the law and suggested that Mallet and Garraud be given until April 1 to either deliver the grain or return the money. The crowd seemed satisfied at this and moved off to pay visits to the homes of Mallet, Garraud, and Naurissart, where they contented themselves with obtaining drink and a small amount of grain.[77]

On February 29, a letter arrived from the Indre administration, stating that the situation had been resolved, that calm had returned to Châteauroux, and that the grain would eventually be delivered. It is difficult to assign responsibility for this colossal mix-up, but Naurissart must be criticized for his failure to respond to the commissioners' three letters, barring the unlikely possibility that he received none of them. The mayor apparently failed to respond to another letter as well, this one from a farmer in a nearby village, who claimed he had written to Naurissart offering to supply Limoges with all the grain it needed. He was very surprised at receiving no response, since he had previously supplied the town and had shown he could be trusted.[78] The best that can be said of the mayor is that he failed to diligently carry out his responsibilities in this instance. Perhaps he was hoping to favor friends in the merchant community with contracts for the procurement of grain. Clearly, there were those in Limoges who suspected such manipulation at the time, but there is no hard evidence to demonstrate collusion.

Naurissart informed the town council on February 29 that the threat to his personal safety would prevent him from attending meetings in the foreseeable future. He promised to remain in regular communication, so as not to abandon completely his duties, and to keep the council informed of his address in Paris.[79] His letters soon ceased, however, and by August, the departmental administration had dismissed Naurissart for failure to perform the functions of his office.

This episode marks the return of the Jacobin club to a preeminent position in Limoges politics. Its demands for a public accounting had prevailed in February. In August, following the toppling of the monarchy in Paris, the Limoges sections refused to adjourn after electing a new mayor until a complete renewal of the municipal council had been carried out. Voters chose a new council, with eleven of the thirteen officers Jacobin club members, and

77. A. D. Haute-Vienne, L197. This dossier contains a departmental *procès-verbal* recounting the events of February 24–29, 1792.

78. A. D. Haute-Vienne, L850 (March 12, 1792, statement of M. Lafleur, farmer in Marcheval).

79. A. D. Haute-Vienne, L850 (Naurissart letter of February 29, 1792).

regular elections in December installed a municipality that even more clearly expressed Jacobin views.[80]

An understanding of the events and personalities of the early years of the Revolution is essential to a full appreciation of the developments of 1793. During those two or three years, revolutionary politics took shape in the towns and cities of provincial France. This period marked a transition from the politics of the Old Regime, restricted in terms of both access and authority, to the more open and responsible politics of the new regime. It was a period of flux, because the new regime remained in a process of definition. Traditional elites either faded from the scene or were thrust from it, to be replaced by new elites. In both Caen and Limoges, those new elites took it upon themselves to define and control the local political arena. As we have seen, members of the elite in Caen proved much more successful in that effort than their counterparts in Limoges.

In neither city, however, was the struggle for political power a particularly bloody one. From 1789 to 1792, both Caen and Limoges experienced a controlled popular fervor and tumult that only rarely erupted into violence. In Caen, the murder of Belzunce and the later killing of Bayeux were looked upon with shock and dismay by the generally law-abiding populace. Even among the sans-culottes, as far as we can tell, neither act was trumpeted as a noble blow for patriotism, though the bulk of the populace clearly perceived both men as enemies of the Revolution. The Affair of 84, rife with the potential for bloodshed, was controlled by the municipal authorities. Even later, during the Terror, those accused would suffer no more than imprisonment.

In Limoges, the 1790 fire and the more serious grain shortage may have subdued the crowd and helped prevent popular violence. Or perhaps his own prudence allowed Naurissart to escape the fate of Bayeux and Belzunce. Certainly the situation during that episode was as delicate as any that Caen experienced.

Religious divisions produced by the civil constitution of the clergy increased the political tension in both departments. Difficulties were greatest in the two *chefs-lieux*, where the controversy brought the resignations of Le Forestier de Vendoeuvre and Pétiniaud de Beaupeyrat. The election of con-

---

80. A. D. Haute-Vienne, L182 (August 8, 1792, letter from Limoges citizens to departmental administration), and L441 (documents pertaining to municipal elections and personnel).

stitutional bishops in each case delivered to office dynamic individuals who went on to play important roles in local politics. Both Gay-Vernon and Fauchet maintained an active interest in, and influence on, local affairs after their departure to Paris; and it is significant that in 1793, one supported the Montagnards while the other allied himself with the Girondins.

These two men provide examples of the ties that developed between Paris and the two towns in the years before 1793. Other deputies, as well, actively corresponded with their friends and former colleagues back home. These personal links were very important, and official and institutional ties were also influential. The departmental administrations were, of course, in frequent contact with the various ministers in Paris. The Jacobin clubs exchanged letters with the mother club in Paris and with affiliated clubs in other towns, thereby creating a national network capable of mobilizing political action. The break between the Caen and Paris Jacobins was thus a crucial development, eliminating an important outside input into local political attitudes. Newspapers provided a final important source of information from Paris. Neither the regional paper in Caen nor that in Limoges offered more than brief reports from the capital and other major cities. But we have seen that in Caen, *Le Courrier dans les Départements* was regularly read to public gatherings. Bougon-Longrais had first ordered the Gorsas paper for the municipal council on his mission to Paris in early 1790. The Jacobin club in Limoges also received the Gorsas journal but canceled its subscription in December, 1792, dissatisfied with the moderate tone that Gorsas had adopted.[81]

Other differences between Caen and Limoges were of a more fundamental importance. In Calvados, a strong nobility remained active in local politics in 1789 and 1790, and when in 1791 the nobles saw their position seriously threatened, they mounted an effort to restore it, unsuccessful though it was. In nearly every serious confrontation in Caen between 1789 and 1792, it was an aristocratic action, or a perceived threat from the aristocracy, that was the instigating factor. For the people of Caen, the Revolution very clearly pitted the third estate against the vested interests of the aristocracy.

In the Limousin, on the other hand, the aristocracy was not a dominant force in 1789. Although some nobles occupied positions of power, most disappeared from local administration in the 1790–1791 term. Anti-

81. A. C. Caen, I1; Fray-Fournier, *Le Club des Jacobins*, 95.

aristocratic sentiments were sometimes displayed, but these were secondary to the conflict between *haut-bourgeois* and *moyen-bourgeois* elements. According to Fray-Fournier, the dynamic aspect of the Revolution in Limoges was "l'idée bourgeoise contre l'idée démocratique."[82] This analysis seems appropriate. In a forecast of nineteenth-century politics, we see in Limoges the *haute-bourgeoisie* seeking a restricted electorate and limited popular participation, while the *moyenne-bourgeoisie* sought a broad-based, broadly participative democracy. By 1793, the latter would triumph. The Caen bourgeoisie, more cohesive than the Limoges elite, proved more successful in limiting the political activity of the popular classes, first by bringing to heel the Caen Jacobins and then by supporting the Carabots, a much more moderate and quiescent group.

In Limoges, the central social conflict occurred within the political arena, disrupting and dividing the municipal administration of 1791–1792. The bitter struggle between the Amis de la Paix and the Jacobin club embroiled the municipal council. The Jacobins not only prevailed as the dominant club in Limoges but gained control of the municipal council in 1792. In Caen, the fundamental conflict pitted wealthy bourgeois merchants against the nobility, a group in the process of being excluded from political participation. This conflict erupted most often on the edges of organized politics, with little real impact on them, and allowed the *haute-bourgeoisie* to remain virtually unchallenged in political office until after the federalist revolt.

The nature of the political arena was thus radically different in these two towns when the federalist revolt erupted in 1793. In Caen, the commercial elite dominated the municipal council and, along with the departmental administration, controlled local politics. In Limoges, the commercial elite had been forced from office by an active and powerful Jacobin club, which at least to some extent represented the interests of workers and artisans. The club and its supporters would assert themselves again in 1793 to steer Limoges away from the federalist camp; but in Caen, Jacobin forces had long since been neutralized.

82. Fray-Fournier, *Le Club des Jacobins*, xi.

Three

Crisis in National Politics

1792–1793

On August 10, 1792, in a successful version of the aborted June 20 uprising, the drama of the Revolution shifted from the chambers of the Legislative Assembly to the streets of Paris. Headed by the Marseille *fédérés* and contingents from several other towns, some twenty thousand men assaulted the Tuileries palace, forcing the king to flee to the Assembly, where ultimately he would be suspended from office. The attack climaxed several months of antiroyalist agitation in the forty-eight sections of Paris and heralded the fall of the monarchy in France.[1]

Albert Soboul has written that the six weeks following August 10 profoundly affected the course of the Revolution.[2] The collapse of the monarchy alone would justify such a claim, but three further developments confirm the verity of this statement. First among these was the creation on August 10 of the Insurrectionary Commune in Paris. This semilegal body grew out of the correspondence committee of the forty-eight sections, which had played a prominent role in organizing the assault on the Tuileries and constituted *en permanence* a central organ of the Paris sections. Moderate deputies in the Legislative Assembly accused the Commune of "dictatorship and the usurpation of power," but radical deputies came to its defense, lauding the patriotism of the common people. The opposition between the revolutionary

1. George Rudé, *The Crowd in the French Revolution* (London, 1959), 101–105.
2. Soboul, *The French Revolution*, 259.

Commune and the Legislative Assembly evolved into Parisian antipathy toward the Girondin deputies in the National Convention and remained a crucial component of national politics over the next nine months.[3]

The second important development was the August 11 decree of the Legislative Assembly calling for the election of a National Convention. Although the Convention's principal mandate was to draft a new constitution, it came to exercise powers more extensive than those of the Legislative Assembly. Within four days of its convocation, the Convention had abolished the monarchy and proclaimed a republic. Thereafter, it assumed a legislative, executive, and judicial role and ruled France for three full years, longer than either of its predecessors.

Finally, the September massacres in the prisons of Paris confirmed in the minds of most Frenchmen an unsavory image of the Parisian crowd. The provinces, too, despaired over the failing war effort and experienced the hysterical fear of counterrevolution that inspired the September massacres. In Limoges in mid-July, an angry crowd had beaten to death the Abbé Chabrol just after the declaration of *la patrie en danger*. Chabrol had refused to relinquish weapons in his possession to army volunteers. Georges Bayeux was murdered in Caen even as the prisons were being attacked in the capital. But the atrocities in Paris defied comprehension, and the September 3 circular sent by the Commune to the departments, allegedly written by Marat in justification of the executions, earned for Parisians the label of *anarchistes* and for its author a reputation as the leading *buveur de sang*.[4]

The nature of the August 10 revolution made the calling of new elections a delicate task for the Legislative Assembly. In the days immediately following August 10, the deputies issued a number of circulars explaining the tumultuous events of that day and outlining recommended procedures for departmental electoral assemblies. These circulars addressed two principal concerns. The first was to maintain the authority of the Assembly during the interim period until the Convention could be opened. The suspension of the king, and the very calling of elections, implicitly called into question the Assembly's legitimacy. Sovereignty now lay, some said, with the people; and to avoid dissension and potential chaos, the deputies adopted a cautious tone

3. *Ibid.*, 259–60.
4. Rudé, *The Crowd in the French Revolution*, 110. Rudé includes the following excerpt from that letter: "et sans doute la nation entière . . . s'empressera d'adopter ce moyen nécessaire de salut public."

in their language. Instructions to electoral assemblies took the form of recommendations rather than decrees.

The second concern, more important in the context of this study, was the question of how to describe the events of August 10. Acknowledgment of the predominant role of the Paris Commune would further undermine the authority and leadership of the Legislative Assembly. In addition, such an account might fuel counterrevolutionary sentiments in the country. The first attack on the Tuileries, on June 20, had elicited a wave of protests from departmental administrators, many of whom remained monarchist in their sympathies. Even within the Assembly, there were those who feared and resented the growing militancy of the Paris sections. To credit the Paris Commune with the fall of the monarchy might have deepened the divisions in both the Legislative Assembly and the nation at large. In its *Exposition des Motifs*, the Assembly therefore focused on the actions of the king, its own determined opposition to his intransigence, and the final provocations that had brought about the spontaneous uprising of the people, including the *fédérés*. The report never mentioned the Insurrectionary Commune.[5]

Late in August, the Jacobin club of Paris issued a circular of its own. The *Tableau comparatif des sept appels nominaux fév.–10 août 1792*, a summary of the voting on the most important issues debated in the Legislative Assembly, was intended to inform electoral assemblies of the voting records of those deputies who might be considered for reelection. The suspension of the king, the continuing problem of émigrés and refractory priests, and the lagging war effort all had combined to produce a mood of antiroyalism in much of the country. The *Tableau comparatif* identified those deputies who had voted in support of the monarchy in the Legislative Assembly and recommended that they not be reelected. The circular reached barely half of the electoral assemblies, and as most of these convened on September 2, it arrived in many cases too late to be considered. Its effect is difficult to measure, but in all of France, only one deputy who had consistently supported the monarchy on the listed votes won reelection. This deputy, interestingly enough, was Pierre François Henry-Larivière, a lawyer from the district of Falaise in Calvados and a future supporter of the Girondins. Alison Patrick attributes his reelection to the fact that officials in Bayeux, the site of the Calvados electoral assembly, deliberately delayed printing and circulating the *Tableau*.[6]

5. Patrick, *The Men of the First French Republic*, 150–151.
6. *Ibid.*, 145–48, 170. It is Patrick's contention that Henry-Larivière supported the right

The election of deputies to the Convention proceeded in two stages. Primary assemblies met in late August to choose departmental electors, who in turn elected the deputies. Despite the recent declaration of universal male suffrage by the Legislative Assembly (eliminating the category of "passive" citizen), few voters turned out. Nationwide, as few as 20 percent of eligible voters participated in primary assemblies. Given the existing political climate, it is possible that monarchists chose to stay away from the assemblies; certainly, the exigencies of the harvest reduced participation; and resentment over the constitutional oath may have had an adverse effect. Despite the small turnout, there is little evidence that a republican minority or the popular societies unduly influenced either the primary or the electoral assemblies. Most of the latter met in small towns, not in the departmental *chefs-lieux* where popular societies exerted their greatest influence.[7]

Electoral assemblies were held during the first two weeks of September, and the majority were carried out in orderly and expeditious fashion. Some took as little as four days to complete their task. Others turned their attention to local affairs as well and met for two weeks or more. Of the 750 deputies elected, 201 had been members of the Legislative Assembly; only 83 had been representatives to the Constituent Assembly. Outnumbering both these groups combined were the approximately 300 deputies whose only political experience was in local administration. Thus, while electors preferred candidates with some political experience (fewer than 10 percent had none whatsoever), previous national office was not always the best recommendation.[8]

The men chosen in those elections would guide France for the next eight months, and many would remain in office for three years. The most active among them would function as interpreters of the political climate in the capital for their constituents. Their correspondence constituted an important link between national and local politics during the turbulent period leading up to the revolution of May 31. Indeed, local perceptions of events in Paris strongly influenced provincial responses to the proscription of the Girondin deputies. It is therefore essential to understand the composition and character of the delegations sent to the Convention from Calvados and

---

in these votes, but the record shows that he was absent for all but two of the votes and voted yes on the impeachment of Lafayette. Still, his record in the Convention puts him clearly in the royalist camp.

7. *Ibid.*, 152–55.

8. *Ibid.*, 170–72, 229–30. Patrick and Godechot, in *Les Institutions de la France*, disagree slightly in their estimates of deputies who had experience in local politics. I have therefore adopted the approximate figure of 300.

the Haute-Vienne, as well as the lines of communication that developed between them and their constituencies. Such understanding brings into clearer focus the process by which the crisis in national politics of winter and spring, 1793, had become a nationwide crisis by the summer of that year.

In Calvados, the electoral assembly convened on September 2 in the town of Bayeux. Although this episcopal seat was located less than twenty miles from Caen, the political attitudes of its citizens were more conservative than those in the departmental *chef-lieu*. Throughout the Revolution, Bayeux remained a royalist and aristocratic stronghold of the department. Claude Fauchet, upon his arrival in Calvados as the newly elected constitutional bishop, found the town to be decidedly inhospitable. In July, 1791, Fauchet, along with his vicar-general, Chaix-d'Estanges, stood as defendants before the Bayeux district tribunal for having allegedly changed two Bayeux street signs from "Louis XVI" and "Place Royale" to "Fauchet" and "Parjure." It is scarcely credible that Fauchet would have committed such a frivolous indiscretion, but the charges do illustrate the chilly reception the new bishop received in Bayeux. In any case, a general amnesty granted by the king on September 15, 1791, reprieved both men.[9]

It is impossible to assess the effect of the location of the assembly on the election results. Certainly, it did remove the assembly from the direct influence of the Caen Jacobin club; and the reluctance of the Bayeux authorities to publish the Jacobin *Tableau comparatif* has already been noted. But one can say little more.

Doulcet de Pontécoulant, whom we have already encountered in the affair of the Criminal Tribunal, presided over the assembly. Doulcet, who held the title of count, was born in 1766 into an old noble family, originally of Savoy, which had held the *seigneurie* of Pontécoulant since the eleventh century. He had risen to the rank of lieutenant in the army and had founded the Jacobin club in the district seat of Vire, near the family estate in Condé-sur-Noireau, south of Caen. In 1792, he served as president of the departmental administration.[10]

The electoral assembly chose another familiar figure, Bougon-Longrais, then secretary to the departmental council, as its secretary, but illness forced Bougon to cede his place to Louis Jean Taveau, a departmental admin-

9. Lesage (Esnault), 65–68; Hufton, *Bayeux in the Late Eighteenth Century*, 185–86.
10. A. D. Calvados, F2080 (Nouvelles Acquisitions).

istrator from Honfleur. Bougon's absence from the Bayeux assembly, and his presence in Caen, may have fueled the public suspicion regarding his role in the murder of Georges Bayeux, the *procurer-général-syndic* whose aristocratic jury list had attracted such vehement criticism.

The assembly session itself proceeded uneventfully, with no serious disruptions or disputes. But news of trouble in Caen interrupted the proceedings on September 6. Several Caen municipal officials had been imprisoned temporarily in the Château after ordering the release of Georges Bayeux. The assembly sent a delegation (including Jean Michel Barbot, the future president of the Carabot club) to assist in calming the angry crowd in Caen. They succeeded in securing the release of the municipal officials but could not prevent the death of the unfortunate Bayeux.[11]

The assembly had already completed the election of deputies to the Convention when this disruption occurred. Table 2 lists the delegates from Calvados, with their occupations, districts, and previous political experience. Several important characteristics of the delegation merit comment. First, none of the Calvados delegates were political novices. All but two, Fauchet and Dubois Dubais, had previous political experience in local administration—eight had served as municipal officials, one as a district administrator, and five on the departmental council. Several had served at more than one level. A second notable feature is the experience of these deputies in national assemblies. Only one of the thirteen Calvados deputies, de Cussy, had been a member of the Constituent Assembly, a proportion corresponding very closely to that in the Convention as a whole. But whereas 27 percent of all deputies to the Convention had been delegates to the Legislative Assembly, six of the Calvados deputies (46 percent of the delegation) had been members of that body. We have seen that one of them, Henry-Larivière, had compiled a voting record that should have assured his rejection by the voters. Finally, the delegation, in its geographic distribution, represented the entire department. All six of the districts were represented, and no district sent more than three deputies. Three of the deputies, Lomont, Bonnet, and de Cussy, had personal experience in Caen municipal affairs. Five others had spent substantial time in the *chef-lieu* as departmental administrators or, in the case of Fauchet, as bishop and president of the Jacobin club.

11. A. D. Calvados, L10074 (Elections et actifs 1790–92), and L10124 (documents pertaining to repression of the federalist revolt). Barbot's role in the incident was detailed in a 1793 letter from his wife to Robert Lindet, then on mission to Caen, pleading for the release of her husband.

TABLE 2 Calvados Deputies to the National Convention

Name (in Order of Election)	Occupation	District	Previous Political Experience
Fauchet (Claude)	bishop	Bayeux	Legislative Assembly member (1791–1792)
Dubois Dubais[a] (Louis Thibaut)	cavalry captain	Lisieux	Legislative Assembly member (1791–1792)
Lomont (Claude Jean Baptiste)	procureur du roi à la monnaie de Caen	Caen	departmental administrator (1790–1791) Legislative Assembly member (1791–1792)
Henry-Larivière (Pierre François)	lawyer	Falaise	municipal procureur (1790–1791) Legislative Assembly member (1791–1792)
Bonnet de Meautry[a] (Pierre Louis)	military officer	Caen	mayor (1791) Legislative Assembly member (1791–1792)
Vardon (Louis Alexandre Jacques)	lawyer	Falaise	municipal official (1790) departmental administrator (1790–1791) Legislative Assembly member (1791–1792)
Doulcet de Pontécoulant[a] (Gustave)	army lieutenant	Vire	departmental administrator (1791–1792)
Taveau (Louis Jean)	négociant	Pont l'Evêque	municipal official (1790–1791) departmental administrator (1791–1792)
Jouenne du Longchamp (Thomas François Ambroise)	doctor	Lisieux	municipal official (1791–1792)
Dumont (Louis Philippe)	lawyer	Vire	district administrator (1790–1791) departmental administrator (1791–1792)
de Cussy[a] (Gabriel)	directeur de la monnaie de Caen	Caen	Constituent Assembly member (1789–1791) municipal official (1791–1792)

TABLE 2 (*continued*)

Name (in Order of Election)	Occupation	District	Previous Political Experience
Legot (Alexandre)	lawyer	Falaise	municipal official (1791–1792)
Philippe-Delleville (Jean François)	lawyer	Bayeux	municipal official (1791–1792)

ᵃ Member of the nobility.
Sources: A variety of biographical and administrative records from the Revolution located in the Calvados Departmental Archives.

In addition to the thirteen deputies, the assembly elected five *suppléants* to replace any deputies unable to fulfill their duties. The first of these was Pierre Jacques Samuel Chatry *l'aîné*, a Protestant *négociant* from Caen. Chatry had been active in municipal politics since 1789, first as a member of the Caen General Committee and then as municipal officer and *notable*. In November, 1791, he declined election as mayor of Caen, arguing that it would undermine public welfare for a Protestant to serve as mayor at a time of considerable public ferment over religious opinions. One year later, his younger brother, Jean Louis Isaac, declined the same post because of his conflicting position as a departmental administrator. Both held local public office in 1793 and played leading roles in the federalist revolt. Chatry never took a seat in the Convention; but he was elected to the Council of Elders in year VII, moved on to the Legislative Corps the following year, and was eventually named to the Legion of Honor.[12]

Little is known about the circumstances in which the Haute-Vienne electoral assembly met. The department was one of only four that did not send a full account of the proceedings to Paris.[13] Nor does a *procès-verbal* from the assembly exist in the departmental archives. The absence of a detailed report suggests that the proceedings were uneventful. The assembly, which met in Dorat, was presided over by Pierre Dumas, an *avocat* from Limoges and then president of the Haute-Vienne Criminal Tribunal, as well as a departmental administrator. Michel Lacroix, a district official from Bellac, acted

12. A. D. Calvados, L10074; A. C. Caen, D1 (Délibérations du Corps municipal et du Conseil Général de la Commune, 18 février 1790–3 janvier 1792), D2 (4 janvier 1792–11 Germinal an II), K34 (Mairie 1790–an II).
13. Patrick, *The Men of the First French Republic,* 141.

TABLE 3 Haute-Vienne Deputies to the National Convention

Name (in Order of Election)	Occupation	District	Previous Political Experience
Lacroix (Michel)	notary	Bellac	district procureur-syndic (1790–1792)
Lesterpt-Beauvais (Benoist)	lawyer	Dorat	Constituent Assembly member (1789–1791)
Bordas (Pardoux)	lawyer	Saint-Yrieix	departmental administrator (1790–1791) Legislative Assembly member (1791–1792)
Gay-Vernon[a] (Léonard)	bishop	Limoges	municipal official (1791) Legislative Assembly member (1791–1792)
Faye (Gabriel)	doctor	Saint-Yrieix	departmental administrator (1790–1791) Legislative Assembly member (1791–1792)
Rivaud du Vignaud (François)	military officer	Dorat	municipal official (1791–1792)
Soulignac (Jean Baptiste)	avocat au parlement	Limoges	district procureur-syndic (1790–1792)

[a] Member of the nobility.
Sources: Alfred Fray-Fournier, Le Département de la Haute-Vienne, sa formation territoriale, son administration, sa situation politique pendant la Révolution (Limoges, 1908), I, 132–38; and a variety of biographical and administrative records from the Revolution located in the Haute-Vienne Departmental Archives.

as secretary. The Haute-Vienne elected seven deputies to the Convention, as listed in Table 3.

Some interesting contrasts between the Haute-Vienne delegation and that from Calvados are discernible. The most obvious is in the size of the two delegations—the Haute-Vienne sent seven deputies, while Calvados sent thirteen. Three factors determined this: the size, population, and taxes of each department. Nearly all departments were the same in area, but the "active" population of Calvados nearly doubled that of the Haute-Vienne, and Calvados inhabitants paid nearly three times as much in taxes.[14]

14. Jacques Peuchet, Statistique Elémentaire de la France (Paris, 1805), 148–49, 153–54. Each department measured 288 lieues carrées. Calvados numbered just over 60,000 actifs, compared with approximately 34,000 in the Haute-Vienne. Calvados was the fifth most highly

Like the deputies from Calvados, the Haute-Vienne representatives all had experience in local administration. The difference here lay in the level of administration—the Calvados deputies more often had served as municipal officials, while those from the Haute-Vienne had more experience in district administration. Experience in departmental administration was approximately the same—five deputies (38 percent) from Calvados and two deputies (29 percent) from the Haute-Vienne had been departmental administrators. Experience in national politics was also similar. One Haute-Vienne deputy had sat in the Constituent Assembly, and three (43 percent) of the deputies had been members of the Legislative Assembly, a proportion almost identical to that in Calvados, and significantly above the national average.

The most striking contrast between the two delegations concerns geographic representation. We have seen that the Calvados deputation fairly represented the entire department and that a majority of the deputies had had some contact with Caen affairs as municipal or departmental officials. In the Haute-Vienne delegation, however, two districts—Saint-Léonard and Saint-Junien—sent no deputies to the National Convention. If one considers the three *suppléants* as well, two of the districts were overrepresented— Dorat, where the electoral assembly met, and Bellac. Five of those elected, fully half, came from this less agitated part of the department. Whereas the district of Limoges was well represented—two deputies and one *suppléant*—the town of Limoges was not. Two of the deputies had been departmental administrators and had therefore spent some time in Limoges. Jean Baptiste Soulignac had been a district administrator, but only Gay-Vernon had been a municipal official in Limoges. Moreover, Gay-Vernon served on the council of la Cité, the smaller, ecclesiastical section of town that had been absorbed into Limoges only in November, 1791, just as he left for the Legislative Assembly.

Overall, two salient characteristics of these delegations to the Convention should be emphasized. First, the electors in both departments appeared satisfied with the performance of their representatives to the Legislative Assembly. Each department reelected nearly 50 percent of those deputies, and the two delegations reflected no significant change in political attitudes. The majority of each would support the Girondins in 1793. Second, whereas

---

taxed department in France (combining the *contribution mobilière* and the *contribution foncière*). Comparing population with tax load, one sees that inhabitants of Calvados also paid proportionally higher taxes than inhabitants of the Haute-Vienne.

Caen was well represented among the Calvados deputies to the Convention, the Haute-Vienne delegation included only one deputy who can truly be said to have represented Limoges, the most important constituency in the department.

The deputies who gathered in the National Convention on September 20, 1792, faced an extremely important issue—one that remained largely unresolved over the next eight months. The question of what form the French state would assume loomed in the trial of Louis XVI and even more explicitly in the debate over a new constitution.

From the day of their arrival in Paris until the end of January, the deputies devoted most of their energy to the gathering and evaluation of evidence, the debate over the legitimacy of a trial before the Convention, the actual trial of Louis XVI, and the final vote on his sentence. This period was a painful and difficult one for the deputies, who were only too conscious of the gravity of the judgment that they were called upon to make. They voted not only on the fate of a king but on the fate of the French republic.[15]

Even after the execution of the king, however, the Convention was unable to make progress on its primary task. The drafting of a new constitution, necessitated by the fall of the monarchy, had been the explicit reason for the calling of the Convention. Exhaustion from the ordeal of the trial may partially explain the deputies' inactivity on this project, but another factor must also be considered. The growing divisions within the Convention made agreement on any important issue virtually impossible. Marie Jean Antoine Condorcet presented his proposal for a constitution to the Convention on February 15, but no consensus formed in its support. Sitting with Condorcet on the Constitutional Committee had been Armand Gensonné, Pierre Victurnien Vergniaud, Jacques Pierre Brissot, and Jérome Pétion, all associated with the Girondin faction, and the constitution proposed by Condorcet reflected their views. It would have increased the power of government ministers, at that time predominantly Girondin, and strengthened the role of departmental administrations. The Mountain attacked the document for its failure to guarantee political equality and for its excessive federalist tendencies. A stalemate developed that lasted until after the proscription of the Girondin deputies.[16]

15. See Daniel P. Jordan, *The King's Trial: Louis XVI vs. the French Revolution* (Berkeley, 1979).
16. Sydenham, *The Girondins,* 149–51; Godechot, *Les Institutions de la France,* 275–81.

The trial and execution of the king did not produce much reaction in either Calvados or the Haute-Vienne. For an explanation of this, we must look back to the weeks following the unsuccessful June 20 attack on the Tuileries palace. That violent demonstration by the Paris crowd had elicited nearly universal protest from departmental administrations.

The directory of the Calvados administration drafted a letter to the Legislative Assembly on July 2, 1792. In it, the directors lauded the courage of Louis and the dignified character of the legislators but denounced the factious elements in Paris and stressed that "the French Nation is not in one faubourg of the capital, in one town, in one department; she is in the union of all citizens; she is essentially in that honest and good people that loves liberty, searches for peace, and requires order." The administrators closed their letter with an emotional appeal: "We are taking this opportunity to express to you our feelings. It is finally time that the reign of anarchy cease, that the Revolution end! The Nation has said: I want to be free, and she was; she says today: I want calm and order, and she will obtain them; her will is pronounced."[17]

This address reveals sentiments that had already appeared in Caen political life and that would continue to characterize the political attitudes of the town and the department throughout the following year: the conviction that the nation was embodied not in the capital but in all French citizens; a denunciation of factious elements; a demand for respect for the law; and finally, a desire for an end to anarchy. The praise of the king, however, and the call for an end to the Revolution were expressions that would become unacceptable after the *journée* of August 10 and even more so by January, 1793. That so many such addresses reached Paris in July very likely contributed to the Convention's decision of October 19 calling for the complete renewal of all departmental administrations to purge the royalist element from these councils.[18] Voters in Calvados reelected none of the seven departmental directors who had signed the July letter. The eighth director, Philippe Dumont, was elected to the Convention but felt obliged to defend his reputation in an April 28, 1793, letter to the president of the Calvados administration, in which he denied having supported the July address. Dumont observed that although he and Gustave Doulcet, former president of the department and now also a *conventionnel*, had been present at the July 2

17. A. D. Calvados, L10025 (documents pertaining to departmental *procès-verbaux*, 1790–an II).

18. Godechot, *Les Institutions de la France*, 282–83.

meeting, they had not signed the letter and had in fact argued against it. The taint of that ill-considered expression of support for the king clearly was not quickly forgotten.

The Haute-Vienne directory also protested the outrage of June 20 in a letter to the king. There, however, the backlash was more immediate. The Limoges Jacobin club denounced the directory's letter at a July 16 meeting, and on July 27 the club drafted its own letter to the Legislative Assembly demanding the dismissal of the four directors who had signed the letter to the king. Joseph Durand de Richemont, president of the department and one of the signatories, was one of the founders of the Jacobin club and was generally popular in Limoges, but he only regained favor after a public apology. The departmental administration provisionally replaced the other three, granting them leaves of absence. None of the three won reelection in November.[19]

The purge of royalist sympathizers from departmental administrations, plus the general shift in political attitudes, guaranteed that there would be few official protests of the king's trial or fate. In both Caen and Limoges, a solemn mood greeted news of Louis' execution, though in later years patriotic fetes celebrated the anniversary of the king's death.

A greater concern in the early months of 1793 was the continuing dissension within the Convention and the growing war crisis, which additionally hampered efforts to draft a constitution. France had been at war with Austria since April, 1792; and on February 1, 1793, only one week after the execution of the king, the Convention declared war on Great Britain. By March 7, France had declared war on Spain as well, thereby sowing the seeds of the First Coalition. Now faced by a more formidable array of enemies, the French armies were also plagued by insufficient provisions and dwindling numbers. Many volunteers returned home after a single campaign, and by February the army had dropped from 400,000 to 228,000 men. A new requisition of 300,000 soldiers, ordered on February 24, did not go smoothly. The crippled French army suffered repeated setbacks in a March campaign into Holland. In Paris, news of the defeats aroused the people's patriotism and brought the creation of the Revolutionary Tribunal. But at the front, fortunes did not improve. Troops under General Charles François Dumouriez, the architect of the Belgian campaign, suffered decisive

19. Fray-Fournier, *Le Club des Jacobins*, 61–67; A. D. Haute-Vienne, L176 (documents pertaining to various reorganizations of the departmental administration).

defeats at Neerwinden and Louvain on March 18 and 21. Dumouriez struck a bargain with Frédéric Cobourg, the Austrian commander, agreeing to lead his troops in an attack on Paris and the Convention to restore the monarchy under the constitution of 1791. General Dumouriez arrested four deputies sent by the Convention to dismiss him and turned them over to the Austrians. His troops refused to follow him in his treason, though, and in early April, Dumouriez fled to the safety of the Austrian lines.[20]

Compounding the problems of a failing foreign war was the real threat of civil war. The British and Austrians were, of course, eager to aid and promote internal attacks on the new regime. But the conscription of 300,000 men, ordered on February 24, was equally responsible for the troubles that grew in March and April. In the Lozère, the requisition of men revived royalist insurgency behind the leadership of Charrier, a former member of the Constituent Assembly. Panicky officials in a neighboring department wrote to the Convention of "a terrible insurrection" and the "massacre of all public officials."[21] The most serious revolt, however, occurred in the Vendée. Bands of peasants, led by nobles and refractory priests, coalesced into a force large enough to threaten Nantes. At one point, the counterrevolutionaries crossed the Loire to the north, briefly taking Saumur. The Convention, in response, raised a large army, principally composed of volunteers, to put down this challenge to the Republic. The revolt could not be contained until October, 1793, and then only temporarily. During the intervening months, the Vendéan counterrevolution had a profound effect on other departments in western France.

The conscription of 300,000 men provoked resistance in both Caen and Limoges. On March 3 in Caen, a volatile situation developed on the *prairie*, located at the western edge of town. The previous evening, the municipality had received a hint of the impending trouble in an unsettling letter from one Louis Bellissent, who claimed he would rather die than join the army. Early on March 3, a group of women marched to the town hall and demanded the aid that had been promised to the wives and children of volunteers who had already been away at the front for months. The news of an additional military requisition did not raise the spirits of these disgruntled women. As they protested before the town hall, another group of people, some reportedly armed, gathered at the *prairie* to resist the recruitment. Esnault described

20. Soboul, *The French Revolution,* 296–99.
21. Wallon, *La Révolution du 31 mai,* II, 195–97.

the group as "young bachelors" anxious to avoid military service.[22] Another contemporary observer, himself arrested in the confusion later that day, described those resisting recruitment as coming from "classes that did not share the principles of the Revolution."[23] The Carabots reported this unruly, unpatriotic gathering to the municipal council, which sent several of its members to disperse the crowd. They failed in their efforts and, at 6:00 P.M., gave way to the National Guard, which surrounded the *prairie* and arrested some 230 people. Most were released after questioning, but some thirty resisters remained in detention until April 10. Bonnet (of Calvados) and Jean Michel DuRoy (of the Eure), representatives on mission, ordered their release, citing their youth, the fact that no arms had been found, and the subsequent fulfillment of the recruitment quota. Similar incidents occurred in other parts of Calvados throughout March, but all were minor. The final recorded episode came late in the month, when the district directory ordered the Caen municipal council to arrest a soldier who had been seen in town wearing a uniform sporting epaulettes made of spinach.[24]

Trouble arose in Limoges as well. In contrast to the innocuous character of the March 3 troubles in Caen, though, resistance to recruitment in Limoges developed along lines reminiscent of the conflict between the Jacobin club and the Amis de la Paix. Unofficial word of the military requisition arrived on March 5, and a group of 150 young men gathered in the former church of the Augustins. They asked the municipal council to send a commissioner to preside over the meeting but were refused on the grounds that the meeting was unlawful, as it lacked prior authorization. Temporarily befuddled, the delegation to the council left. In the hours that followed, messengers shuttled back and forth between the Augustins and town hall. Those assembled insisted that authorization was not required, while the council cited the disruption of public order in demanding their dispersal. Finally, a report that "aristocrats" were present at the Augustins, trying to prevent young men from volunteering for the army, spurred mayor Déroche and two municipal officials to successfully break up the meeting.

Around three o'clock the next day, however, four members of the Jacobin club reported that a new gathering of young men had formed, composed of "former dragoons, amis de la paix, or individuals who had continually

22. Lesage (Esnault), 103.
23. Sauvage, "Les Souvenirs de J.-B. Renée," 600.
24. A. C. Caen, D2 and I29 (Affaire du 3 mars 1793).

manifested uncivic opinions." The sizable group had already disrupted public order. The council ordered two companies of grenadiers and chasseurs to disperse the crowd and arrest the leaders ("les présumés coupables"). Those arrested included Pierre Balezy, a former *notable*, and Laforest *cadet*, both associated with the Amis de la Paix, along with a number of servants from some of the prominent Limoges households.[25] There is no evidence that those arrested were ever brought to trial. Balezy, for example, was continually under suspicion during the following summer but suffered only provisional house arrest because he worked as a *teinturier* dyeing uniforms for the army.[26]

Of greater consequence to the Haute-Vienne than the general military requisition, however, was the call for volunteers and supplies to combat the Vendéan rebels. Revolt had erupted early in March, and on the seventeenth of that month a special courier from the Charente arrived in Limoges to inform the departmental administration of insurrection in the Deux-Sèvres, the Vendée, and neighboring departments. Pardoux Bordas (of the Haute-Vienne) and J. Borie (of the Corrèze), representatives on mission, arrived the same day, sent by the Convention to supervise recruitment. Their work in the department proceeded uneventfully, unusual in that elsewhere these early recruitment missions often inspired resentment. Recruitment for the army of the Moselle, the general destination of Haute-Vienne volunteers, went reasonably well, slowed only by the short supply of arms in the department. By March 18, Limoges had already filled its contingent, although some scattered resistance to recruitment persisted in rural cantons.

In addition to its quota of 3,539 men for the regular army, the Haute-Vienne also sent, between March and June, more than 2,000 volunteers to the rebel departments in the west. On March 22, the departmental administration informed the Charente officials that 300 volunteers had left Limoges for Niort on March 18 and that 800 others had probably by then left from other parts of the department. Two hundred twenty-five soldiers from the Corrèze had also passed through Limoges on their way to Niort. Three days later, in a letter to the minister of the interior, the departmental council revised upward to 2,000 its estimate of Haute-Vienne volunteers on their way to the Vendée.

25. A. D. Haute-Vienne, L197 (report of the municipality to the departmental administration).
26. A. D. Haute-Vienne, L849 (list of suspects in Limoges, prepared by the *comité de surveillance*).

The departmental administration pursued its efforts to assist in the battle against the Vendée rebels with considerable zeal. In mid-March, it ordered, at the urging of Limoges Jacobins, a special tax on rich aristocrats and *hommes suspects,* to be levied according to known or presumed wealth. The tax became a donation after Bordas and Borie ruled that no existing law would justify a compulsory tax.

Over the next two months, four additional pleas for help reached the Haute-Vienne from the Vendée and Deux-Sèvres. On each occasion, the department responded by raising additional forces. Departmental administrators spoke stirringly in public session of the responsibility of all citizens to defend the Republic. On May 13, the administration ordered that all National Guard officers down to the grade of *sous-lieutenant* prepare to depart for Poitiers, an action that earned an honorable mention for the Haute-Vienne on the floor of the National Convention.[27]

By the last week of May, reports were so alarming that the administration called a general alert in the department and issued orders for the raising of yet another force to march to Poitiers. When a courier arrived from the Cantal on May 31, reporting news of a serious revolt in the Lozère, the Haute-Vienne could send nothing but gunpowder. The next day, however, good news from Niort allowed the departmental council to countermand the order for additional troops to go to Poitiers. Instead, it instructed volunteers to remain in their district *chefs-lieux* until further notice.[28]

The impact of the Vendée revolt on political opinion in the Haute-Vienne must certainly have been considerable. The department had sent both men and supplies to combat the rebels, and reports of this counterrevolutionary challenge to the Republic roused the patriotism of administrators and citizens alike. In the midst of its fourth consecutive year of dearth, the department saw its traditional sources of grain to the west and northwest, the Charente and the Vienne, threatened by the rebel forces. But it would be an exaggeration to say that the Vendée revolt was the decisive factor in turning the Haute-Vienne away from the federalist movement. The department's manpower had been strained but not exhausted; five hundred to eight hundred troops remained at the ready in district *chefs-lieux* on June 1. In July, the department could muster additional troops to send to the Vendée, and

27. *Réimpression de l'Ancien Moniteur,* XVI, 352 (session of May 9, 1793).
28. A. D. Haute-Vienne, L57 and L146 (departmental correspondence regarding military volunteers).

Limoges could raise a force to repel the advancing Bordeaux federalists. Those troops could have been used in a march on Paris, and we will see that the departmental administration considered that option in early June.

In Paris, the deputies were preoccupied by more than the demands of war at home and abroad. In April, 1793, the Convention easily passed a Girondin-supported proposal for the impeachment of Jean Paul Marat. A Jacobin circular, signed by Marat, "urging the departments to recall their unworthy representatives," inspired the impeachment motion, but the real reasons for Marat's indictment lay in his defense of the September massacres, his inflammatory rhetoric, and his continued championing of the Paris crowd.[29] Marat's April 24 acquittal before the Revolutionary Tribunal represented a victory for the increasingly militant Paris sections and a further blow to the weakening Girondin majority in the Convention.

A more direct attack on the independence and influence of the Paris Commune followed on the heels of Marat's acquittal. In the session of May 18, Marguerite Elie Guadet alleged that an insurrection against the Convention was being planned within Paris and proposed the dissolution of the Commune and the transfer of the Convention to Bourges. Taking a more moderate course, the deputies ordered the creation of a Commission of Twelve to investigate the situation in the capital. Girondin deputies and their supporters dominated this committee, which included not a single Montagnard. On May 24, Louis François Sébastien Viger reported to the Convention that the Commission of Twelve had found evidence of a planned insurrection. On that same day, Jacques René Hébert, the *procureur* of Paris, was arrested for publishing a denunciation of the Girondins in the *Père Duchesne*.

Over the next two days, a parade of delegates from the sections appeared before the Convention to protest Hébert's arrest. Far from modifying its action, however, the Commission ordered additional arrests, and debate in the Convention reached a fever pitch. Late on the night of May 27, after many of the moderate deputies had retired, the Montagnards secured the dissolution of the Commission of Twelve and the release of the prisoners. But the Girondins refused to accept defeat by political maneuver and contested this decision on the following day. In a very close count, with over one hundred abstentions and many Montagnards on mission in the departments, the Convention voted to reinstate the Commission. Three days later, the Paris

29. Patrick, *The Men of the First French Republic*, 109–10.

sections revolted, shifting the arena of contention from the Convention itself to the streets and thereby assuring the final defeat of the Girondin leaders.[30]

The trial of Marat and the controversy surrounding the Commission of Twelve highlighted the two fundamental tensions that underlay national politics throughout this period: dissension within the National Convention and apprehension over the excessive political influence of the Paris crowd. These tensions were acutely felt in the capital; but the provinces, too, appreciated the threat that they posed for the young republic. These two issues, more than any other, generated an active correspondence between deputies in Paris and their constituents in the departments.

A division between moderate and radical deputies had already become apparent during the last months of the Legislative Assembly, but the revolution of August 10 produced a renewed commitment among the legislators to work together and overcome their differences for the sake of national unity. This uneasy truce lasted into September but crumbled almost as soon as the Convention met. As early as September 25, Jacques Brissot and Pierre Vergniaud accused Robespierre and other Montagnards of complicity in the September massacres.[31] In late October, Jean Baptiste Louvet denounced Robespierre in his celebrated speech before the Convention, often described as the opening salvo in the Girondin/Montagnard conflict.[32] Throughout the next two months, the diatribe continued against Robespierre, Marat, and Danton, who allegedly formed a triumvirate intent on establishing themselves as dictators. These personal attacks solidified the opposition between Montagnards and Girondins. Many provincial Frenchmen associated the Montagnards, and in particular "the triumvirate," with the excessive political influence of the Paris crowd and the threat of anarchy that it represented.

News of developments in Paris reached the provinces through both official channels and letters from individual deputies to friends and administrators back home. As already noted, Bishop Gay-Vernon of Limoges corresponded regularly with the Jacobin club after his election to the Legislative Assembly and then to the Convention. Claude Jean Baptiste Lomont, one of Calvados' deputies to the Convention, remained in close contact with his constituency in Caen. Lomont (born Dobiche de Lomont) had been *procureur du roi à la monnaie de Caen* before the Revolution, a position that

---

30. *Ibid.*, 116–18; Soboul, *The French Revolution*, 309–10; Sydenham, *The Girondins*, 173–77.
31. Sydenham, *The Girondins*, 126.
32. Jordan, *The King's Trial*, 51–53.

would have acquainted him with Gabriel de Cussy, former *directeur de la monnaie* and another of Caen's deputies to the Convention. Lomont had been elected to the departmental administration in 1790, had joined the directory, and had presided over the Caen Jacobin club in April, 1791. In the fall of that year, he had been elected to the Legislative Assembly. He appears to have been the deputy to whom the municipal council of Caen most frequently turned for assistance in its dealings with the national government.

Lomont's earliest letters of record date from the last months of the Legislative Assembly. He addressed many of them to Pierre Jean Lévêque, a doctor in Caen, a prominent municipal official, and a personal friend. The two corresponded frequently over the next ten months, both on personal and official business. This liaison is particularly important because Lévêque would be elected a departmental administrator in September, would eventually become president of the administration, and in June, 1793, would be one of the leaders of the federalist movement in Caen.

Much of the correspondence between Lomont and officials in Caen dealt with routine administrative affairs—requests for public works funds, official appointments, and taxation questions. As the situation in Paris grew more unstable, however, letters focused more often on political matters. On August 7, the municipal council forwarded to Lomont a petition addressed to the Legislative Assembly from the Caen sections demanding the suspension of Louis XVI. The deed had been accomplished, of course, before Lomont could deliver the petition.[33]

On September 11, in the wake of troubles in both Paris and Caen, Lomont wrote directly to Lévêque. He graciously acknowledged his election to the Convention and requested clarification of the circumstances of the murder of Georges Bayeux. He made reference to the massacres in Paris and commented that "the people of Paris and Versailles have bestowed an air of justice to the vengeance that they exercised upon the prisoners: there is a sort of Court Martial which pronounces a preliminary verdict, but in Caen nothing at all like that, people say."[34] This was clearly a mild appraisal of the September massacres; but only one month later, Lomont showed more emotion in describing the dissension that had quickly developed in the Convention. In another letter to Lévêque, he wrote: "The enemies of order have long been uniting to sow and support suspicions of the best patriots. Buzot, Brissot, Fauchet, Guadet, Vergniaud, etc., whose patriotism equals their talents, are

33. A. C. Caen, D1.
34. A. D. Calvados, L10276 (Lévêque correspondence).

each day slandered by a handful of men who are as spiteful as they are despicable. And their efforts will be futile: Marat, their writer, is currently loathed, even though the Jacobins of Paris (I speak only of thirty or so leaders) never cease praising him."[35]

Gabriel de Cussy seconded Lomont's opinion in a letter to the municipal council on October 31. He requested that the council read in a public meeting Jean Baptiste Louvet's recent discourse to the Convention denouncing Robespierre. De Cussy assured the people of Caen that the majority of Parisians were good citizens but noted the presence in the Convention of a handful of scoundrels. He suggested that a departmental guard, sent to Paris, might be necessary to expel them.[36]

De Cussy's letter is an interesting one, raising both the idea of expelling a small group of troublemakers from the Convention (a fate that he himself would suffer ten months later) and the possibility that a departmental guard might assist in that task. The Calvados administration had already supported the latter proposal in a letter addressed to the Convention two weeks earlier, perhaps the first call from the departments for the creation of such a guard. On October 21, Philippe Dumont informed the departmental administrators that their letter had been well received by many deputies but that debate had resulted in a tabling of the question.[37] In the following two months, factionalism persisted in Paris, and talk of raising a departmental guard to protect the Convention continued. Finally, on January 2, 1793, the departmental administration wrote to the Convention offering to send a force from Calvados. The most important passage declared:

> You are described as exposed under the axe of the executioner; Paris, the cradle of Liberty, is full of conceited and bloodthirsty agitators: they want to interfere with your opinions: cruel and cowardly men are preaching carnage. Well! the citizens of Calvados are roused. Impatient, they are eager to sign their names in the civic registers; they want to depart, to avenge your threatened Liberty, the debased Sovereignty of the People, and to render Paris worthy of her glory; they will support the work of their Representatives, OR THEY WILL DIE! The fire that inflames them will spread to all Departments, and the French Senate will soon enjoy, despite those who defile its meeting place, the calm necessary for the formation of good laws.[38]

35. *Ibid.*, letter of October 5, 1792.
36. A. C. Caen, I33 (Affaire de la garde départementale de la Convention, lettre de Cussy).
37. B. M. Caen, Fn. Br. 981; Paul Delasalle, *Documents inédits sur le fédéralisme en Normandie* (Le Mans, 1844).
38. A. D. Calvados, L10021 (documents pertaining to deliberations of constituted authorities).

The council attached to this letter a previous order regulating the formation of the proposed departmental force and calling on volunteers with valid *certificats de civisme* to enroll at the secretariats of their district directories.

A January 4 letter from the Calvados delegation to the departmental council confirmed the administrators' fears. Signed by all thirteen Calvados deputies to the Convention, the letter spoke of a "parti désorganisateur" in Paris and of threats of anarchy and claimed that "Pache himself, the Minister of War, is very suspect to the true friends of the Republic." Despite these misgivings, the deputies expressed confidence that the patriotic majority of the Convention would continue to predominate.[39]

Sentiments similar to those in Calvados prevailed in the Limousin. On January 17, following the example of the nearby Corrèze, the Haute-Vienne administration voted to announce to the Convention that the entire departmental force was prepared to march to Paris to ensure the integrity and security of the Convention. The administration ordered all national guardsmen to make ready, with each soldier to receive thirty *sols* per day while on duty. The decree invited individual citizens to go to Paris as well. Two days later, the departmental council wrote to the Convention denouncing the factions and anarchy that threatened the deputies and informing them of the Haute-Vienne's actions:

> At the cry of danger that surrounds you, all of the Citizens of the departments are roused and, from all points of the Empire, their innumerable legions await but the signal of the law to throng to your meeting place; because you must finally be free, and such is the formidable crisis into which events have drawn you that you cannot be so without surrounding yourselves with a departmental force powerful enough to assure the success of your labors, to annihilate the factions and dispel the anxiety of your constituents. Hasten therefore to organize that tutelary force that should save Liberty; all of the Citizens of our department, anxious to cooperate in its formation, fervently appeal for the order to come to your defense.[40]

At subsequent meetings, the departmental council received numerous addresses from other departments asserting the need for departmental guards in Paris to protect the Convention. On February 11, the administration ordered all public officials to swear an oath, recently sworn and circulated by the council of the Haute-Loire, declaring anathema all "Kings . . . Tyrants . . . Dictators . . . triumvirs" and promising to defend the liberty,

39. B. M. Caen, Rés. Fn. Br. C289.
40. A. D. Haute-Vienne, L57 (Délibérations du Conseil Général); letter reprinted in Fray-Fournier, *Le Département de la Haute-Vienne*, II, 204–206.

equality, and sovereignty of the people, as well as the unity and indivisibility of the Republic.[41]

Although neither Calvados nor the Haute-Vienne sent a departmental guard to Paris, other departments did. Both Finistère and the Bouches-du-Rhône, at the unauthorized bidding of their deputies A. B. F. Kervélégan and Charles Jean Marie Barbaroux, sent forces that had arrived in the capital by December, 1792.[42] By February, as many as twelve thousand soldiers had gathered in Paris. The Convention hotly debated the question of calling troops to the capital and on January 13, 1793, adopted a plan for a formal provincial force to protect its meeting place. But Jean Baptiste Boyer-Fonfrède raised questions about the efficacy of such a plan, and the deputies ultimately rejected it. On March 5, the Convention went one step further and ordered the troops already in Paris to return to the defense of their departments.[43] Departmental forces did not therefore remain in Paris. The debate of the question in the Convention and the de facto presence of troops in the capital for at least three months, however, established an important precedent for the following summer.

Correspondence between the capital and the provinces increased during April and May as the trial of Marat and the formation of the Commission of Twelve raised tensions in Paris to a critical level. As early as April 1, Gabriel de Cussy complained to the Caen municipal council of the insults and threats that he and his colleagues endured and expressed his hope that "abominable traitors" masquerading as patriots would soon be expelled from the Convention.

De Cussy wrote again the next day, describing the treason of Dumouriez, the agitation of the Paris sections, and his own fearlessness before death. He denounced Danton and Marat by name. Less than two weeks later, he exultantly reported the decree of accusation against Marat and reviled those who defended that "cruel and cowardly instigator of pillage and assassinations." Once again, he castigated the insolent and insulting Parisian crowd, which had taunted him and three others as they left the assembly hall that day.[44]

41. A. D. Haute-Vienne, L57.
42. Sydenham, *The Girondins*, 194.
43. *Ibid.*, 133, 153. See also Wallon, *La Révolution du 31 mai*, I, 73–81.
44. A. C. Caen, I34 (Lettres des députés du Calvados). The crucial paragraph in de Cussy's first letter reads, "Les gens de bien depuis longtemps abreuvés d'amertume, exposés sans cesse aux injures du peuple, exposés même à la mort vont être vengés. La république va reconnaître des traîtres abominables qui n'avaient que le masque du patriotisme. J'espère que la séance ne sera pas levée sans que des membres de la Convention soient décrétés d'accusation et arrêtés."

Alarmed by these reports of factionalism and anarchy in Paris, the Calvados departmental and Caen district administrations met together on April 19 to petition the Convention: "Save yourselves, and you can save us! Such is the cry of France; will it not have been heard? Representatives of the People, we will tell you the truth: your divisions create all of our misfortunes. It is a Marat, a Robespierre, a Danton, who always occupy and agitate you, and you forget that an entire People suffers, worries, and awaits the solace of Laws." They went on to speak of the glory of France, of the one, great family that the nation should be, of the need to ignore disorganizing factions; and they closed with the following paragraph:

Elected of the people, you know it, France is not in Paris; she is formed by eighty-four Departments; if in one you are insulted, in another you will be respected, obeyed: there you will find a shelter from the furor and the plots of rascals; there you will enjoy your rights and Liberty; there you will live among the French, Republicans, brothers who will know how to ward off from you daggers and assassins. But before leaving the first cradle of Liberty, make a final effort; brave the storms; spurn the rumors of a few careerists; punish the conspirators; work to give sage Laws to a great People; save your country; obtain happiness for your fellow-citizens; above all, make yourselves respected; and if a few scoundrels again lift their blasphemous voices, think of us, speak, and you shall be avenged.[45]

In this address, one hears echoes of earlier messages to the Convention: the complaint against dissension; the denunciation of Marat, Robespierre, and Danton; a plea for the "solace of Laws." There remains hope that the Convention can rise above its disagreements to carry on its work, but there is the hint, again, that the Convention should be moved elsewhere and the promise to avenge the deputies if they should be attacked. Seven of the Calvados deputies wrote to the department lauding the letter and requesting additional copies to meet the enormous demand from other departments and popular societies. They reported a slight improvement in the situation in Paris.[46]

The amelioration of affairs in Paris proved illusory, however. In early May, Jean Baptiste Lomont wrote twice to his friend Lévêque, first on May 3 and again on May 10. He reiterated the praise of the Calvados delegation for the department's letter of April 19, but he also wrote of "the atrocious calumnies that people continuously heap upon the best deputies," of the threats that continued to hang over their heads, and of his fear that the Re-

45. A. D. Calvados, L10024 (Procès-verbaux du Conseil Général du département).
46. A. D. Calvados, L10125 (documents pertaining to federalism; letter of May 6, 1793, signed by Dumont, Philippe-Delleville, Lomont, Legot, Vardon, and Fauchet).

public might break into a thousand pieces. He remarked that he had encountered several of his "concitoyens" from Calvados in Paris. Bougon-Longrais, the *procureur-général-syndic* of the department, visited the capital in May; and Jean Adrien Lasseret, then a *notable* of Caen, had visited in late April, carrying a message from the municipal council to the Convention. While cautioning that circumstances might change quickly, Lomont closed his May 10 letter with an expression of guarded optimism.[47]

In subsequent letters, Lomont grew more pessimistic. On May 13, he railed against Bougon, with whom he said he had been "intimately tied . . . since the dawn of the revolution." Bougon, upon his arrival in Paris, had been accused by DuRoy (a Montagnard deputy who had been on mission to Caen in March) of having authored the Calvados letter of April 19. Bougon denied all knowledge of the letter and, after having read it, went so far as to say that he did not support it. This greatly dismayed the Calvados deputies. Although Lomont charitably blamed the incident on Bougon's youth and inexperience, he could not help but question his principles. He assured Lévêque that the entire Calvados delegation, except for the Montagnard Bonnet, continued to struggle for the principles of the Revolution and would die, if need be, for the liberty of France.[48]

Lomont next wrote to Lévêque on May 15, after the Convention had received a May 10 letter from the departmental administration. The administrators had denounced, without blaming either Montagnards or Girondins, the continued factionalism within the Convention and had once again implored the deputies to put aside their differences and get on with the business of drafting a constitution. Lomont was clearly disappointed in this letter. He wrote: "It seems, my dear fellow-citizen, that the more audacity the rascals show, the more the Calvados administration controls its vengeance and minces its words. I am a frank and plainspoken republican; I do not know, myself, how to speak with *Economy*. Your last address did not compare with the one before. Your last address speaks redundantly of passions, of rivalries, of the hatreds that trouble the peace amongst us, or speaks incessantly of our divisions, etc." This, said Lomont, was not acceptable; it was not precise. *Factions* did not exist within the Convention. One faction alone troubled the peace, and this was the Mountain. Lomont sug-

47. A. D. Calvados, L10276 (Lévêque correspondence).
48. A. D. Calvados, L10134 (documents pertaining to federalism); Grall, "La très courte carrière d'un procureur général syndic," 338.

gested more verve, a bolder tone in future letters and referred to the previous day's letter from Bordeaux as a model: "You will see, dear comrade, the address of Bordeaux—compare it. Simply compare your two addresses and decide for yourself. If I am wrong tell me your opinions as frankly as I tell you mine. Above all believe that my sincere devotion will end only with the life of your friend." Here, Lomont was virtually instructing Lévêque and the Calvados administration on the proper manner in which to write an effective letter to the Convention.[49]

Lomont sent his final letter of record, dated May 21, from Buges, where he was on mission to supervise the production of *assignats*. He expressed longing to return to Paris, where he could better defend the Republic with his life, and insisted that the attacks on individual deputies amounted to no less than attacks on the national sovereignty.

News of the Convention's tumultuous session of May 27 produced one final protest from Calvados before the drama in Paris reached its climax. This letter surely proved more pleasing to Lomont than did the address of May 10. The administrators reported the outrage of the people of Caen at reports of the disorderly May 27 session of the Convention and promised a departmental force to protect the national representatives. They concluded the address with a stern warning: "All the Departments, we have no doubt, will follow this example, and soon you will be surrounded by an imposing Army that will know how to make you respected. We declare a war to the death against Anarchists, Proscribers, and Factionists, and we will not put down our arms until we have returned them to oblivion."[50]

The months of April and May in the Haute-Vienne did not bring the flurry of correspondence that marked this period in Calvados. On March 19, the department had sent to the Convention a message in which it pledged its efforts against the Vendéan rebels and expressed its confidence in the Convention. Its one veiled criticism lay in calling for the rapid completion of a constitution that would unify the country.[51] Efforts to ready men and supplies to send to Niort and Poitiers occupied the next eight weeks. There is no

49. A. D. Calvados, L10276. This message is strikingly similar to two letters sent to the Bordeaux Popular Society on May 4 and 5 by Pierre Vergniaud, who implored his constituents to protest to the Convention and to come to the aid of their legislators. Lomont's counsel to Lévêque suggests that Vergniaud's entreaty was successful. For Vergniaud's letters, see F. A. Aulard, *Recueil des Actes du Comité de Salut Public avec la Correspondance officielle des représentants en mission* (Paris, 1891), IV, 196.

50. A. C. Caen, I34 (Adresses et députations à la Convention).

51. A. D. Haute-Vienne, L57.

record of further correspondence to or from the capital until the last week in May, when the situation in the Convention was becoming critical.

An explanation for the relative silence of the Haute-Vienne administrators during this period lies not only in their preoccupation with the Vendée revolt but also in the evolution of the attitudes of Limoges Jacobins during the first few months of 1793. Whereas the Caen club had broken its affiliation with the Paris Jacobins, the Limoges Jacobin club maintained its ties. But relations between the clubs in Limoges and Paris were marred by some stormy periods. On January 16, 1793, the Limoges club voted to draft a letter to the Convention in support of the Rodez club's petition requesting the expulsion of Marat from the Assembly. One week later, the club sent another address denouncing the factions in the Convention. It also voiced support for the Girondin minister Jean Marie Roland. On February 24, a letter arrived from the Paris Jacobins announcing the impending arrival in Limoges of Xavier Audouin, a native son who had recently relocated in Paris. The letter chided the Limoges club for not writing more regularly. Audouin—who had just married the daughter of Jean Nicolas Pache, the former minister of war and recently elected mayor of Paris—arrived in Limoges the next day. Club members questioned the recent behavior of the Paris Jacobins, particularly their attacks on Condorcet, but Audouin defended the Paris club and the people of Paris and offered to act as a special intermediary between the citizens of Limoges and higher administrative authorities. The club voted to re-establish correspondence with the Paris club and in subsequent months received regular letters from Audouin as well.

On March 18, Pardoux Bordas, an Haute-Vienne deputy to the Convention, passed through Limoges on a recruitment mission. He, too, talked with club members and stressed that though the Convention might occasionally appear divided, the great majority of deputies worked for the public good and were united in their votes on important matters.[52]

Reassured by these two visitors about the patriotism of the Paris club and the spirit of the Convention, the Limoges Jacobin club grew more radical in the weeks that followed. On April 1, still receiving the moderate Gorsas journal despite having canceled its subscription, the club voted to burn the most recent issue and send the ashes to Gorsas (who had once been a corresponding member of the Limoges club). On April 10, after some debate, the members voted to support the Paris Jacobin club's proposal for the recall of those deputies who had voted for the "appel au peuple" in the king's trial. Finally, in early May, the Limoges Jacobins congratulated Marat on his recent acquittal—a reversal of the attitude expressed in its January letter condemning Marat.[53]

The shift in attitude among the Limoges Jacobins could not have failed to restrain the actions of departmental officials. By late May, however, the situation in Paris had deteriorated, and on May 23, the Haute-Vienne administration sent another address to the Convention. Yet it conveyed neither the urgency nor the vehemence of the Calvados letters. The council expressed its profound appreciation for the honorable mention given the Haute-Vienne for its recent recruiting efforts. The administrators asked in recompense that the Convention forget its divisions, proceed quickly to the drafting of a constitution, and bring an end to factions and anarchy. In closing, they described the department's need for both arms and bread, which they implored the Convention to send.[54]

The following day, before this letter could have reached Paris, the majority of the Haute-Vienne delegation to the Convention reported to their constituents, in rather measured words, the confusion and disaccord in the capital, the difficult circumstances under which they debated, and the plots being uncovered by the Commission of Twelve. Only in their final paragraph did the deputies assume a more strident tone:

> Citizens! Paris is outraged by conspirators; it will avenge its glory. Respectful toward the national representation, sole rallying point of Frenchmen, friend of laws, it wants a constitution, the preservation of property and personal safety, order, peace, unity, the death of anarchy and all despotism. Under whatever form it appears this cry of all Good Frenchmen has struck it: Marseille, Bordeaux, Calvados and the Orne have made it ring out. It rings from all points of the Republic; would that it could be heard in our department. Paris has served its country well, and that which is in the hearts of its inhabitants is ready to be spoken. The country can only find help outside the abyss into which one would push it.[55]

Despite what he termed the "good intentions" of his fellow deputies, Gay-Vernon refused to sign this letter to the Haute-Vienne administration. He drafted a separate message, in which he played down the threat to the Con-

---

53. *Ibid.*, 99–124.
54. Fray-Fournier, *Le Département de la Haute-Vienne*, II, 261.
55. A. D. Haute-Vienne, L174 (correspondence from Haute-Vienne deputies to the Convention to the departmental administration).

vention: "Paris is excellent and the intriguers and malcontents will lose themselves in the crowd." He did not deny the existence of conspirators but expressed confidence that good citizens would be vigilant. He concluded, "I applaud the zeal of the deputation, but I do not share its opinion of the present circumstances. The diversity of sentiments proves that with the same desires one can employ different means in order to arrive at the same goal."[56]

The Limoges Jacobins, heeding the words of Gay-Vernon, issued a denunciation of the letter from the rest of the delegation.[57] But despite the arrival of an additional note from Bordas (who had also signed the earlier address), which dismissed "les menaces exagérées" and advised calm and restraint, the departmental administration, on May 30, drafted its strongest protest of the factions and dissension within the Convention. The administrators stated their hope that the Convention would finally have "vanquished the monster of disorganization, of anarchy, and of civil war." They denounced the scoundrels who talked of proscribing deputies, asserting that they spoke for all the people of the Haute-Vienne.[58]

Although the Haute-Vienne council did not go so far as to pledge a "war to the death," as administrators in Calvados had done, its May 30 message constituted a strong condemnation of the divisions and legislative paralysis that had developed in Paris in the previous months. Similar protests came from departments all over France. Indeed, the federalist revolt in June could be seen as the culmination of this long-term concern—as a simple, and final, reaction to the proscription of the Girondin deputies. On the other hand, many of the departments that sent protests to the Convention between January and June, like the Haute-Vienne, acquiesced in the revolution in Paris that confirmed the supremacy of the Montagnards.

The divergence of departments' reactions to the June revolt can be attributed in part to the composition of departmental delegations to the Convention and to the communication networks that developed between the deputies and their constituents. The delegations of Calvados and the Haute-Vienne both overwhelmingly supported the Girondins in 1793. But whereas in Calvados the sole Montagnard deputy was the disreputable former noble Bonnet de Meautry, who wrote only occasionally to his constituents in

56. Ibid.
57. Fray-Fournier, Le Club des Jacobins, 131.
58. A. D. Haute-Vienne, L391 (Adresses à la Convention).

Caen, the Haute-Vienne Montagnards Gay-Vernon and Bordas maintained regular contact with Limoges (almost incessant contact, in the case of Gay-Vernon) and consistently downplayed the divisions in Paris. By contrast, Lomont and de Cussy grew increasingly adamant in their denunciations of the factious Montagnards in April and May and exhorted the people of Caen to prepare for action.

The mediating role of the Limoges Jacobins also must be stressed, particularly in contrast to the negligible role of the Caen club. In Calvados, nearly all correspondence from deputies in Paris went to local administrations or to personal friends, such as Lévêque, who were also officials. The Caen Jacobin club had broken its ties with the Paris club and in 1793 fell into decline. The Limoges club, though, despite some temporary disillusionment with the mother society, maintained an active correspondence both with the Paris Jacobins and with Gay-Vernon and Xavier Audouin. This introduced to Limoges, and to the Haute-Vienne, a point of view to which Caen was little exposed. The people of Caen heard from their trusted deputies nothing but woeful reports and urgent alarms. Gay-Vernon counseled the Limoges Jacobins to ignore the well-intentioned, but exaggerated, reports of the other Haute-Vienne deputies, and the club faithfully carried that message to the local administrations.

It is important to note, however, that influence flowed not only from Paris to the departments but in the other direction as well. The departmental alignment in June, 1793, was not determined by instructions from deputies in Paris. The strength of the Jacobin club in Limoges gave Gay-Vernon a hearing in that town that he might not otherwise have enjoyed. Bonnet de Meautry had no comparable base of support in Caen, and this limited his influence. Gabriel de Cussy grew virulent in his denunciations of the "scoundrels" within the Convention and his calls for retribution, but he was encouraged in his statements by the strong expressions of concern and protest issued by authorities in Caen. The call for a departmental guard for the Convention came first from the Calvados administration and then from de Cussy.

A clear and consistent pattern emerges from the various protests and petitions registered by authorities in Calvados over this period. As early as July, 1792, the Calvados administration had denounced anarchy and factionalism, called for respect for the law, and particularly insisted that the nation resided not only in Paris but in all the departments of France. These themes were reiterated in all of the letters and protests sent from Caen to Paris over the next ten months: in October, in January, in April, and again in May. Calvados denounced factionalism and the excessive influence of Paris more frequently and consistently than any other department. In April, that aggressive posture earned the praise of moderate deputies in the National Convention. In June, it would lure to Caen many of the proscribed Girondins, anxious to find a secure haven from which to continue their struggle with the Montagnards.

Four

The Provinces Respond

June, 1793

The crisis within the National Convention reached its peak at the end of May, 1793. The heated session of May 27 ended with a late-night vote disbanding the Commission of Twelve. But the following day, the Girondin deputies attended in greater numbers, and the Convention voted to reinstate the Commission, although the Montagnards succeeded in preventing a full report of the Commission's findings. Nonetheless, this turn of events provoked the Paris sections into renewed activity. The Cité section called on all sections to send representatives the next day, May 29, to meet at the Evêché. That assembly became the Central Revolutionary Committee, a reincarnation of the Insurrectionary Commune that had been so important in the *journée* of August 10, 1792.

On that same day, Robespierre addressed the Jacobin club of Paris, delivering a speech that has been generally interpreted as a call to insurrection. Mobilization continued in the sections, and on the afternoon of May 31, a peaceful crowd surrounded the Convention. Representatives of the Commune delivered the sections' demands: the abolition of the Commission of Twelve, the proscription of twenty-four deputies, and the creation of an *armée révolutionnaire*. Girondin leaders countered this move by calling for an investigation of the brewing insurrection. After considerable discussion, this motion was carried. But Vergniaud, trying to secure the Girondins' temporary advantage, failed in an effort to lead his supporters from the hall.

Returning within minutes, he interrupted Robespierre, who, in a dramatic moment, accused Vergniaud and called for his impeachment. The Montagnards now took the offensive, and the session concluded with the final suppression of the Commission of Twelve.

Two days later, on June 2, the Convention again found itself surrounded, this time by eighty thousand armed national guardsmen led by François Hanriot. The crowd once more delivered a demand for the proscription of the deputies, and on the floor of the Convention a proposal calling for the resignation of those accused met with failure. Marie Jean Hérault-Séchelles, showing great courage, led the deputies out into the crowd, attempting to break the ring that surrounded them. The guardsmen stood their ground, however, forcing the legislators to return to the chamber. There, the deputies passed a decree ordering the provisional arrest of twenty-nine of their colleagues, as well as two ministers. Most prominent among them were the well-known deputies Vergniaud, Brissot, and Buzot, along with Barbaroux, Gorsas, Guadet, and Valazé. Also placed under guard, for his role on the Commission of Twelve, was the Calvados deputy Henry-Larivière.[1]

The proscription of the Girondin deputies produced an immediate, but varied, reaction in the departments of France. Many departmental administrations protested this violation of the nation's representatives, a few lauded the Montagnard victory, and the remainder maintained a generally silent neutrality. (See Table 1 for a breakdown of the protesting and nonprotesting departments.) Only a handful of departments engaged in prolonged resistance to the Montagnard Convention. That resistance centered geographically around the cities of Bordeaux, Caen, Lyon, and Marseille.

It is beyond the scope of this study to deal broadly with the federalist movement, but in order to place events in Caen and Limoges in a chronological context, Table 4 charts important developments in the several federalist centers. In both Lyon and Marseille, moderate elements in sectional assemblies had overturned radical municipal councils in April and May, 1793, and the federalist movement in those two cities grew out of their local political conflicts. Those conflicts in turn had been partially fueled by the meddling of Montagnard representatives on mission in local political affairs. In Lyon and Marseille, then, one sees in accentuated form a feature that characterized the federalist movement throughout France: a combination of local and national grievances that produced a revolt against Paris.

1. Soboul, *The French Revolution*, 309–11; Sydenham, *The Girondins*, 175–79, 215–16.

TABLE 4 Chronology of the Federalist Revolt

Date	Caen	Limoges	Marseille	Bordeaux	Lyon
May 29					Sections revolt against Jacobin municipality.
May 30	Commissioners leave for Paris; departmental force called for.				
June 3			Sections close Jacobin club.		
June 5		Departmental administration supports Côte-d'Or resolution.			
June 8				Departmental Popular Commission created; insurrection declared.	
June 9	General Assembly declares insurrection; Romme and Prieur arrested.				
June 11	Flow of foodstuffs to Paris cut off.		Insurrection declared; departmental force created.		

(continued)

TABLE 4 (continued)

Date	Caen	Limoges	Marseille	Bordeaux	Lyon
June 14		Limoges Jacobin club declares support for May 31 revolution.		Order issued for formation of departmental force.	
June 17		Departmental administration rebukes Lyon messenger.			
June 22	Departmental force leaves for Evreux.		Departmental force leaves for Paris.		
June 27		Departmental administration rejects Bordeaux entreaty.			
July 1–5					Departmental assembly declares insurrection.
July 12					Convention issues decree against Lyon federalists.
July 13	Departmental forces routed at Pacy-sur-Eure.				
July 17					
July 25	Calvados officials end insurrection.				Chalier executed.

July 27	Departmental force routed in Avignon.
July 31	Departmental force halts Paris march.
Aug. 1	Limoges prepares to resist Bordeaux federalists.
Aug. 2	"Army of pacification" enters Caen. Popular Commission dissolved; departmental force disbanded.
Aug. 14	Siege of Lyon begins.
Aug. 25	General Carteaux enters Marseille.
Sept. 18	Radical Club National overturns moderate municipality.
Oct. 9	Lyon succumbs to republican forces.
Oct. 16	National deputies enter Bordeaux.

In all four cities, local officials, principally departmental administrators, guided the organization of resistance to the National Convention, the outlines of which took shape during the first two weeks of June. Departmental forces assembled to march on Paris in all four cities. The federalist movement had disintegrated in Caen, Bordeaux, and Marseille by late July or early August, although Jacobins did not resume control of Bordeaux politics until late September. The federalist movement in Lyon gradually assumed a royalist character and only succumbed to republican forces on October 9, after a bloody two-month siege of the city.

The federalist revolt is a complicated historical event, varying both in intensity and in character from one region to the next. The revolt in Caen did not achieve the intensity or violence that it achieved in Lyon or Marseille, either in the rebellion itself or the repression that followed. In that respect, however, it was more the rule than the exception if one considers the federalist movement nationwide. As a guide to the character of the movement as a whole, federalism in Caen is particularly revealing because the rebels there, not only from Calvados but from other Norman and Breton departments, annunciated very clearly the aims of their rebellion and the grievances that had given rise to it. Study of the revolt in Caen, then, should yield considerable insight into the nature of the federalist movement. Comparison with Limoges will help to clarify why the revolt took root where it did.[2]

In Limoges, news of the events of May 27 through June 2 did not produce the heightened emotions and dramatic response that it would evoke in Caen. No special assemblies convened, and no urgent messages were sent to Paris. The departmental administration did express its concern over the proscription of the deputies, and it gave a sympathetic hearing to messengers from the Côte-d'Or who urged provincial protest. But letters from the deputies Gay-Vernon and Bordas, plus energetic input from the Limoges municipality, the Jacobin club, and officials in other districts, deterred the administrators from taking strong action. By the end of June, the department firmly

2. In writing this chapter, I relied primarily on archival materials, principally series L in the departmental archives of Calvados and the Haute-Vienne. For Caen, however, three published accounts were of great value in reconstructing the events of the revolt. See A. Goodwin, "The Federalist Movement in Caen during the French Revolution," *Bulletin of the John Rylands Library,* 42 (March, 1960), 313–43; Jeanne Grall, "Le Fédéralisme: Eure et Calvados," *Bulletin de la Société des Antiquaires de Normandie,* LV (1959–60), 133–53; and Vaultier, *Souvenirs.* Vaultier, a professor at the University of Caen, served as secretary of one of the Caen sections in 1793.

supported the Montagnard Convention; and by the end of July, the administration, along with the citizens of Limoges, stood ready to turn back the march of the Bordeaux force toward Paris.

The Limoges Jacobin club appears to have been the first local body to receive word of developments in Paris. This in itself is significant—the radical Jacobin club, not the more moderate departmental officials, first reported to the people of Limoges the Montagnard victory in the National Convention. Events in Paris therefore received a favorable interpretation. The journey from the capital to Limoges took longer than that from Paris to Caen—four days by coach instead of two. But as early as June 3, the Jacobin club read a letter from Xavier Audouin announcing that the people of Paris had risen and that great measures would soon be taken. The next day, Jean Baptiste Gay-Vernon, a departmental administrator, read to the club a report from his brother, the bishop. The assembly listened with great satisfaction to details of the current situation in Paris and unanimously voted its support of all measures taken by the Mountain. The members also sent a message to the bishop, thanking him for his regular bulletins, "without which the club might have been misled by the false reports that troublemakers never cease to spread." One club member, reflecting on the recent events, concluded that they had turned entirely to the profit of liberty and equality. The meeting closed with the reading of an address from the Convention and the decrees of May 31 and June 1, which reportedly produced great joy among those present.[3]

Up to this date, there is no evidence that the departmental administration even discussed these reports from Paris. On June 4, the Haute-Vienne council drafted an effusive address to its constituents, lauding their patriotism and sacrifices in sending volunteers to the Vendée and urging them to pull together in difficult times. The following day, the order of business changed after two messengers arrived from the Côte-d'Or bearing an urgent message. In a decree dated May 30, the Côte-d'Or proposed that the departments unite in sending an address to the Convention based on the principles of unity and indivisibility of the Republic, of the inviolability of national deputies, and of freedom of opinion. The message would state that the departments were prepared to rebel against any despotic authority that violated

3. Fray-Fournier, *Le Club des Jacobins,* 132–33. Fray-Fournier has compiled here a summary of the minutes of the Limoges club's meetings. The original registers have since disappeared from the departmental archives.

these principles. Commissioners from all the departments of France would deliver it to Paris, along with a fraternal message to the Parisians.

The Haute-Vienne administrators adopted the proposal after a brief discussion. The decree, it must be remembered, had been drafted in the Côte-d'Or before the proscription of the Girondin deputies. It did not propose active resistance to the National Convention; indeed, it offered no explicit course of action but rather espoused laudatory general principles and was in fact quite similar in tone to the message that the Haute-Vienne administration itself had sent to the Convention on May 30. The council named two of its members to carry the Côte-d'Or message to the Dordogne and the Corrèze and to inform those departments of its own adhesion.[4]

François Mathieu-Lachassagne relayed this message to the Dordogne, where officials in Périgueux gave him a warm reception. The department volunteered its support and sent its own messengers on to four other departments. The Corrèze, however, received Jean Baptiste Gay-Vernon less favorably. Officials there observed that events had changed since May 30, that the proposals of the Côte-d'Or could well produce a schism and federalism among the departments, and that the Convention was and should remain the only center of unity for France. They rejected the proposed address and sent a letter to the Convention denouncing the Côte-d'Or and the Haute-Vienne, a gesture that caused considerable embarrassment and difficulties for the Haute-Vienne in the following month.[5]

Little occurred in Limoges with respect to the national crisis until June 11, when two important letters arrived. The first came from four of the Haute-Vienne deputies, Faye, Lacroix, Rivaud, and Soulignac. Relatively subdued in tone, the letter congratulated the administrators for their addresses to the Convention of May 23 and 30 but made only veiled comments regarding the situation in the capital. The deputies wrote that those proscribed were demanding to hear the charges "that should have preceded and motivated their arrest." They also made a cryptic reference to the good citizens of Paris, whom they hoped would finally "tire of seeing themselves moved in a sense contrary to their own sentiments and to the public interest, and would surrender themselves to public indignation and the glory of the laws."[6] This

4. A. D. Haute-Vienne, L57 (Délibérations du Conseil Général, janvier-juillet 1793). The Côte-d'Or address is reprinted in Fray-Fournier, *Le Département de la Haute-Vienne*, II, 212–14.

5. A. D. Haute-Vienne, L181 (papers of the departmental council, correspondence).

6. A. D. Haute-Vienne, L174 (departmental correspondence with deputies to the Convention).

was far from a call to arms, but censorship of letters leaving the capital (to which they referred in the letter) may have made the deputies reluctant to express themselves more strongly.

The Haute-Vienne administrators responded to the deputies two days later. They noted that one paragraph had been scratched out and thus rendered illegible and further complained that a more detailed letter, to which the deputies had alluded in a postscript, had never arrived in Limoges. Nonetheless, the officials assured their representatives that they remained loyal republicans and desired only an end to factions and agitators and a speedy completion of the constitution.[7]

The second letter to arrive on June 11 came from Gay-Vernon. He described the "moral insurrection" that had occurred in Paris as a reaction to the slander that had been heaped on that city. He predicted that the Convention would now accomplish more in fifteen days than it had in the previous eight months. "The country is all, and individuals are nothing," he asserted, citing Lafayette and Dumouriez as former heroes who had proved to be traitors. The departmental administration as a whole, however, was not on the best of terms with Gay-Vernon, and its reply to the other four deputies suggests that it did not find completely convincing the bishop's reassuring account. Still, the administrators drafted a suitably ambiguous answer to Gay-Vernon calling, as had he, for prosecution of all traitors who plotted against liberty and equality.[8]

The Limoges Jacobin club, on the other hand, appeared persuaded by Gay-Vernon's regular bulletins. In addition to his first letter, the one received on June 4, the club received letters from the bishop on June 7 and June 13 and another note from Audouin as well. Inspired by these reports and by rumors of protest in other departments, the priest Foucaud proposed that an address be sent to affiliated clubs. He presented a draft on June 14, which the club quickly adopted. In stirring language, Foucaud lauded the patriotism Paris had displayed in its recent defense of the Revolution: "But your deputies have written that they are not free?" he asked rhetorically, answering that Louis XVI had made the same allegation and that Dumouriez, too, had questioned the Convention's freedom. As for the deputies' arrest, "We await in silence the terrible judgment that will soon be pronounced. If they are innocent, we will rejoice with display; but if they were guilty, dear friends,

7. A. D. Haute-Vienne, L391 (correspondence).
8. A. D. Haute-Vienne, L174 and L141 (correspondence of the departmental directory).

could republicans dare to regret it?" For those who proposed a march on Paris, Foucaud suggested the Vendée as a more appropriate gathering place. The Limoges Jacobin club remained loyal to the Convention, he added, and looked to it for guidance and a new constitution.[9] Jean Baptiste Gay-Vernon presented this address to the departmental directory, which refused to discuss it, but the departmental committee of public safety, composed of members from all three administrations, endorsed it without reserve.[10]

Two days later, the Jacobin club received another letter, this one from five of the Haute-Vienne deputies: Rivaud, Soulignac, Faye, Lacroix, and Lesterpt. Four of these deputies (all except Lesterpt) had already written to the departmental administration, and the letter to the Jacobins expressed many of the same sentiments as the earlier message. The deputies' views found a hostile audience among the members of the Jacobin club. Offended by the deputies' moderation and their alarm at the events of June 2, the Jacobins denounced them in a letter to the Convention (resulting eventually in their arrest) and expelled Faye and Soulignac from the club. If there had been any doubt about the Jacobin club's attitude toward the May 31 revolution, that doubt was now erased. Given the enormous influence of the Limoges Jacobins, both in the local administrative councils and on the local populace, the posture of the club with regard to the new regime in Paris must be considered a critical factor in steering the Haute-Vienne away from the federalist movement.[11]

On June 17, the Haute-Vienne administration clarified its own position under the watchful eyes of the Limoges municipality and Jacobin club. During the previous ten days, the departmental council had seemingly paid no attention to the crisis in Paris or the projects of other departments. It had devoted its meetings to the routine business of recruitment, grain supply, and fugitive émigrés. But on June 17, two commissioners arrived in town— one from Lyon and one from the Jura by way of Lyon. The council convened a special meeting, inviting district and municipal officials to attend, along with delegates from the Jacobin club. The messenger Tardi spoke first, setting the record straight on recent events in Lyon. Then Gauthier, the Jura commissioner, read a joint address from the Rhône-et-Loire and the Jura to

9. Fray-Fournier, Le Club des Jacobins, 134–38.
10. Most departments formed committees of public safety in April, 1793, assigning to them the inspection of foreign mail and the surveillance of suspicious individuals who might be agents of foreign powers.
11. Fray-Fournier, Le Club des Jacobins, 138.

the Haute-Vienne. It called for an assembly of *suppléants* to the Convention, much as the Côte-d'Or had earlier proposed, but further recommended the raising of departmental forces and the designation of centers of communication around the country to coordinate the provincial efforts. These regional centers would report to a central spot such as Bourges, where the Convention, or its *suppléants,* would be gathered. This plan, they insisted, did not favor schism or federalism but, in fact, supported the very opposite.

Yet the plan represented a qualitative step beyond the Côte-d'Or proposal, to which the Haute-Vienne administration had adhered just twelve days earlier. The Jura address spoke not of general principles but of concrete action in response to the proscription of the Girondin deputies. The assembly entered this address in the record, after which an unidentified member of the departmental committee of public safety rose to speak. These men, he said, had arrived in Limoges that morning and had been brought to his committee by a municipal officer who had questioned their passports. The two had initially claimed to be headed for Bordeaux on personal business, but a search of their papers had produced copies of a plan listing departments that might be induced to join the projects of Marseille, Lyon, and Bordeaux. Furthermore, their speech to the assembly made it clear that the Jura and the Rhône-et-Loire believed that the Convention was not free, despite the Convention's statements to the contrary and the fact that a majority of the deputies continued to deliberate in Paris. This member suggested that the proposals carried by the commissioners were more likely to cause trouble and sow civil war than to repair imagined wrongs and moved that the department take steps to halt the proposals' propagation. The Jacobin club delegates added their voices to this opinion and called for the arrest of the two commissioners.

A long discussion ensued. The opinions of other departments were introduced, including the response of the Seine-et-Oise to a similar entreaty from the Ille-et-Vilaine. The Seine-et-Oise administrators had rejected that entreaty, stressing the danger of schism within the Republic and the continued threat of internal and external enemies. After considerable discussion, a council member stepped forward to concur with the department's confidence in the wisdom and freedom of the Convention, which would soon deliver a new constitution. He moved that in response to the two commissioners' proposals a departmental declaration be issued recognizing the liberty of the Convention and the legitimacy of all its decrees since May 31. He further argued that to arrest the two would be pointless, because "people every-where know their rights and know how to maintain them." The assembly applauded loudly and adopted the proposed course of action unanimously.[12]

The two commissioners quickly left town and apparently went on to the Gironde, for five days later, on June 22, a special courier from Bordeaux arrived in Limoges, urging essentially the same measures that the Haute-Vienne had already rejected. A special assembly convened the next morn-ing and voted to release the courier with his passport. Messages addressed to the Creuse and the Corrèze would be returned to Bordeaux, along with a note stating that "pressing circumstances do not permit the Department of the Haute-Vienne to accede to the requests of the Gironde." Although clearly unwilling to join the protesting departments at this point, the Haute-Vienne administration remained characteristically cautious in its actions and pronouncements.[13]

Elsewhere in the department, reaction to the news from Paris was mixed. Pardoux Bordas, a deputy to the Convention from Saint-Yrieix, wrote to his district on June 2. He, like Gay-Vernon, sat with the Mountain; and in his letter, he spoke of the calm determination of the Parisians, of their devotion to liberty and respect for property even in the face of provocation, and of the "moral insurrection" that had taken place in the capital. A decree of accusa-tion against conspirators within the Convention would soon be passed, he said, although Brissot and others had reportedly already fled. Bordas coun-seled his constituents to take up arms and continue surveillance of conspira-tors at home.

Officials in Saint-Yrieix did not share Bordas' political views, and they interpreted his letter as evidence that a schism had developed within the Convention. The Saint-Yrieix Popular Society expelled Bordas from the club and on June 7 convinced the district to send a message to the departmental administration suggesting that a delegation to the Convention call for pri-mary assemblies to elect a new Convention.[14] The departmental administra-tion, which at first ignored this proposal, expressed its firm disapproval on June 24 but adopted no stronger measures, since Saint-Yrieix had taken no further action. The only other district to take a position was Saint-Junien,

12. A. D. Haute-Vienne, L57.
13. Ibid.
14. Fray-Fournier, Le Département de la Haute-Vienne, II, 215; Johannès Plantadis, L'Agi-tation autonomiste de Guienne et le mouvement fédéraliste des Girondins en Limousin, 1787–1793 (Tulle, 1908), 102.

which on June 22 berated the administration for having adopted the Côte-d'Or proposal without first consulting district councils.[15]

Deputy Gay-Vernon soon added his own reproach for the department's error in judgment on that occasion. By June 19, word had reached Paris of the Corrèze denunciation of the Haute-Vienne's actions. Gay-Vernon wrote to the department that he was confident of the administrators' pure intentions but hoped that they had by now seen the error in their action. He did not share the views of the other five deputies—for him, and he hoped for the department, principles were more important than individuals. Ten days later, the bishop scolded the departmental administrators more sharply. He lamented that they had violated their duty and responsibility by sending a deputy to the Corrèze with the Côte-d'Or proposal. He bemoaned their feebleness, saying he preferred strong and decisive men to those who claimed to believe in the freedom of the Convention and then did nothing to protect it from federalist plots. He felt they should have arrested the commissioners from the Jura and Lyon (a course of action that Limoges Jacobins had urged at the time), and he exhorted the administrators to be more diligent and energetic. The bishop closed by announcing that the new constitution would soon arrive.[16]

Official notification of the constitution's completion reached Limoges on July 2, and on July 4, the three administrative corps, meeting together, issued a declaration to their constituents. They recalled that for six months they had been imploring the Convention to complete the constitution. Now, at this difficult time, it was imperative that all citizens rally to the Convention and reject the federalist projects that threatened to divide the country. The administrators called on their constituents to gather in primary assemblies to consider and vote on the new constitution, delivered by their legislators after much debate and sage deliberation.[17]

Pierre Philippeaux, a representative on mission, formally delivered the constitution one week later, and voters throughout the department quickly approved it. But Philippeaux also brought grave reports from the Vendée and made an impassioned plea for renewed efforts to combat the rebels. The deputy asked that the Haute-Vienne send a contingent to join a gathering force in Tours. Despite their concern about the department's depleted man-

---

15. Fray-Fournier, Le Département de la Haute-Vienne, II, 225.

16. A. D. Haute-Vienne, L174 (letters of June 19 and 28).

17. A. D. Haute-Vienne, L57. The address is reprinted in Fray-Fournier, Le Département de la Haute-Vienne, II, 229–30.

power, the administrators unanimously voted to mount and equip a fifty-man cavalry corps. Expenses would be paid by a levy on the rich.[18]

As if this new strain on the department's resources were not enough, the administration soon received word that the National Convention had refused to allocate badly needed funds for the hospital in Limoges. Gay-Vernon wrote on July 19 that the department's failure to punish more severely the messengers from Lyon and the Jura, as well as the Saint-Yrieix officials, had caused this adverse decision. He blamed the departmental administrators for not heeding his advice but promised to see the minister of the interior about securing the funds. The other deputies, too, pledged to do what they could.

While awaiting resolution of this matter, the department received word from Toulouse that forces from Bordeaux were marching toward Paris and would pass through Limoges. Alarmed at this news, the authorities in Limoges united with the Jacobin club on July 23 to draft an appeal to "our brothers of Bordeaux." Announcing their recent acceptance of the new constitution, they implored the people of Bordeaux to do the same and to seek solutions to their grievances in that document rather than in actions that could only lead to civil war.[19]

A special courier from the Corrèze arrived one week later with news that the Bordeaux volunteers had not turned back. The Corrèze stood ready to block their path and asked the Haute-Vienne to join it. Eager to show their devotion to the Convention and the Republic, the administrators replied that they were of like mind and would, if necessary, send forces to unite with those of the Corrèze. The arrival on August 1 of the deputy Baudot raised patriotic spirits in Limoges to an even higher pitch, and the administration ordered the Limoges National Guard and all able citizens to prepare to take to the fields with guns, pitchforks, pikes, scythes—anything that would serve as a weapon—in order to prevent the Bordeaux forces from entering the department.[20]

Fortunately for the people of Limoges, the Bordeaux volunteers had gone no further than the borders of their own department before hearing that the forces from Normandy had been routed. They immediately turned back for

18. A. D. Haute-Vienne, L57.
19. A. D. Haute-Vienne, L203 (correspondence with the department of the Gironde).
20. A. D. Haute-Vienne, L58 (Délibérations du Conseil Général, juillet–décembre 1793), and L110 (Baudot mission).

their homes and had, in fact, probably dispersed even before Baudot arrived in Limoges. More good news reached the town in early August. The hospital funds had been withheld because of a misunderstanding, and the minister of the interior would soon release nineteen thousand *livres* for the aid of Limoges orphans.[21]

Between early June and late July, the Haute-Vienne administration had shifted from hesitant disapprobation of the May 31 revolution in Paris to firm rejection of the federalist entreaties issued by authorities in Lyon and Bordeaux. The department had reaffirmed its patriotism and dedication to the Republic and for that reason largely escaped the repression that followed the collapse of the federalist movement.

The departmental administration had taken no active steps to join a march on Paris, but its support of the Côte-d'Or resolution constituted an implicit recognition that such a measure might be necessary. In the following weeks, three factors combined to steer the department away from the federalist revolt. First were the roles of Gay-Vernon, Bordas, and Xavier Audouin, all of whom reassured the people of Limoges that the Convention continued to deliberate in freedom and that May 31 had been a victory for liberty and equality. This by itself would not have been enough. Gay-Vernon did not enjoy universal respect among departmental administrators, and the other five Haute-Vienne deputies sent more alarming reports of the situation in Paris. The Limoges Jacobin club, however, had confidence in the bishop and exerted considerable pressure on the departmental administration, both by regular attendance at general council meetings in June and July and because a considerable number of club members served as administrators. The municipal council, too, helped curb any departmental tendencies toward federalism by strongly protesting the administration's support of the Côte-d'Or resolution. Finally, the counterrevolutionary crisis in the Vendée and the precarious economic situation that prevailed in Limoges and the Haute-Vienne as a whole made resistance to the National Convention an unattractive option.

Whereas the Haute-Vienne's reaction to the Montagnard victory was slow and hesitant, the response in Calvados was swift and resolute. Even before the Paris sections mobilized on May 31, authorities in Caen had taken de-

21. A. D. Haute-Vienne, L174 (letter from Soulignac, Faye, Rivaud, and Lacroix, dated July 30, 1793).

cisive measures to protest and counter the political shift that began in the Convention on May 27. News of the May 27 dissolution of the Commission of Twelve arrived in Caen within two days.

The most likely carrier of this report was Antoine DeVic, *procureur* of the municipality. DeVic had been sent to Paris early in May to request an advance on the proceeds from the sale of national lands, which would relieve the penury of the *caisse des billets de confiance* in Caen. He returned to Caen in time for an evening session of the municipal general council on May 28.[22] Traveling by coach from Paris to Caen generally required two days, but it is possible that DeVic, bearing urgent news, left Paris on horseback after the May 27 evening session and arrived in Caen late the following day.

Other possible sources of information include the several deputies who maintained regular correspondence with officials in Caen. That one of these deputies may have relayed the report is suggested by an account in the *Affiches du Calvados*. In its issue of June 2, that journal stated that news of the dangerous situation in the Convention had arrived in Caen on May 29, though it did not identify the source, which may have been a letter or even a Parisian newspaper. The journal also reported that on the same day the Jacobin club, in a well-attended session, had petitioned the departmental directory to convene section assemblies in Caen.[23]

It was neither the departmental administration nor the municipal council that convoked section assemblies in Caen, however; it was Louis Caille, *procureur-syndic* of the district. Caille had been active in local affairs since early in the Revolution, particularly in the Caen Jacobin club, which he had helped found and over which he later presided. After a trip to Paris in early 1792, where he met Robespierre, he encouraged the Caen Jacobins to split with the Paris club. Caille was first elected to public office in September, 1792, when he was named *procureur-syndic*. Acting in that capacity, he issued two orders on May 30. The first ordered that the municipal council, given the danger to the *patrie*, convoke the sections in extraordinary assemblies. The second directed the municipal council to call a special meeting to consider what measures to adopt.[24]

22. A. C. Caen, D2 (Délibérations du Corps municipal et du Conseil Général de la Commune), May 4 and May 28, 1793.
23. *Affiches, Annonces et Avis Divers de la Basse-Normandie*, June 2, 1793, A. D. Calvados.
24. A. C. Caen, D2, May 30, 1793.

The municipal council met at ten o'clock that evening and immediately sent three delegates to the district and departmental administrations to request postponement of section assembly meetings so that bell-ringing, which might alarm the countryside and jeopardize the following day's market, could be avoided. (Despite the previous year's good harvest, grain was again in short supply in Caen.) Given the seriousness of the threat to the Convention, however, the superior authorities denied the municipal council's request. Even as the messengers returned to town hall, church bells rang out, and the assemblies began to gather. Each of the sections sent delegates to the departmental meeting hall later that night, where they joined representatives of the three administrative corps. This assembly drafted the final address sent by Calvados to the National Convention. The assembly also voted to form within the department, principally in Caen, an armed force to march to the aid of the Convention and issued an order inviting all good republicans to enroll at district *chefs-lieux*. It called on all the departments of France to adopt similar measures.

Two decrees of the Convention, registered by the departmental directory only one day before, may have impressed upon the assembly the gravity of the situation and convinced local authorities of the legitimacy of their actions. The first of these decrees, issued May 18, had established the Commission of Twelve, "charged with investigating all internal plots against liberty, and against the national representation." The second, dated May 24, placed under the safeguard of good citizens "la fortune publique, la Représentation nationale, et la ville de Paris." [25] These decrees made it clear that a threat to the nation existed and that all citizens had a responsibility to resist that threat.

To carry their address to the Convention, the assembly chose ten of its members, representative of the administrations, sections, and popular societies that were present. Most prominent in that delegation were Pierre Jean René Lenormand, then president of the departmental administration, and Louis Caille, from the district directory. [26] The contingent left the following

25. A. D. Calvados, L165 (Registre des procès-verbaux des séances du Directoire du Département à Caen, 16 mars 1793–10 septembre 1793); J. B. Duvergier, *Collection complète des Lois, Décrets, Ordonnances, Règlements, Avis du Conseil-d'Etat* (Paris, 1834), V, 294; *Réimpression de l'Ancien Moniteur,* XVI, 464–71.

26. A. C. Caen, I34 (Adresses et députations à la Convention, janvier–mai 1793). Also included in the delegation were Antoine Nicolas Marie, from the municipal council; another Lenormand, representing the Carabots; Legagneur, probably representing the Jacobin club;

day (minus one delegate, Legagneur, who had fallen ill) and arrived in Paris on June 2. In addition to the formal statement drafted by the assembly, they took a brief address reminiscent of previous calls for unity and a new constitution. But the changed circumstances they encountered in Paris prompted them to compose a more forceful discourse, which began as follows:

Representatives,
   You have just heard the Address sent to you by our Fellow-citizens at the time of the events of May 27. That which they feared has occurred, and other measures should be and will be employed. We have been the witnesses of new attacks upon liberty, by which a Faction has succeeded, through misleading armed Citizens, in proscribing thirty-four of your Colleagues and three Ministers, in placing them under arrest, and in temporarily dissolving the National Representation, which cannot exist without freedom of opinions. We would sacrifice our personal safety, even our lives, in order to complete the honorable Mission entrusted to us by our Constituents. The right that we exercise is a sacred right: Force can violate it; but it cannot prevent such attacks from becoming known in the Departments; they are already known in the Department of Calvados. From the banks of the Rhine to the Pyrenees, there is universal indignation, and its weight will crush the new Tyrants.[27]

The delegation closed its address by pledging that armies from throughout the country would soon join the majority of peace-loving Parisians to deliver the Convention from oppression, thus preserving the unity of the Republic and showing to all of France the true meaning of patriotism.

Unfortunately, the delegation did not gain admission to the floor of the Convention and therefore never delivered this message. The commissioners stayed on in Paris for several days, occasionally venturing out onto the streets but passing most of their time in the company of the Calvados deputies to the Convention. They left the capital on June 6, making stops in Evreux and Lisieux on their way back to Caen.

Several interesting letters arrived in Caen while the commissioners were carrying out their mission to the capital. Gustave Doulcet de Pontécoulant, former president of the Calvados administration and now a deputy to the

---

and Chappes, Feret, Levasnier, Mauger, and Tabouret, representing the five sections of Caen. Two local historians, Georges Mancel and Charles Renard, have suggested that Lenormand, president of the departmental administration, and Lenormand, president of the Carabots, were one and the same. All the evidence I have seen, however, including two different Lenormand signatures on a key insurrectionary declaration, suggests that there were two men of the same name, unrelated as far as I know, who played leading roles in the revolt.

27. B. M. Caen, Fn. B2634. Reprinted in Vaultier, *Souvenirs,* 174–75.

Convention, wrote the first of these. His letter, though undated, bore the heading "Samedy, à 7 heures du soir," and its tone clearly indicates that it was written on Saturday, June 1. Addressed simply to *citoyen* Lenormand, president of the Popular Society, at Caen, it read:

> Our dangers are by no means past, my dear fellow-citizen; the tocsin rings; the call to arms is sounded; and we are informed that Marat and the Revolutionary Committee of the Paris Commune have decided to renew the disturbances, and to continue what they call the insurrection of the people until the twenty-two, the twelve, and Isnard are indicted.
>
> I repeat that which I told you this morning, that which I will write to you in all possible ways until you acknowledge the receipt of one of my letters, that having neither crime nor weakness to reproach me, I await death without fear; that I leave to posterity the task of defending my memory; and that I bequeath my vengeance to my constituents and to all the true republicans of France.
>
> Your fellow-citizen and brother,
Gustave Doulcet[28]

Doulcet's despair and resignation are clearly registered in this letter. But more than that, he suggests that his letters were being prevented from reaching their destination, he asserts that he was guilty of neither crime nor weakness, and he implores his constituents to avenge the injustice being perpetrated on him and his colleagues.

Two days later, the nine commissioners sent to the capital wrote a note to the general assembly that had dispatched them. They announced the proscription and arrest of the deputies and described the public turmoil in Paris. They assured the Caen assembly that the majority of Parisians did not support these "scènes d'avillissement" and passed on the current rumor that a great deal of money had been distributed to incite the people against the deputies. They wrote of the general indignation of the other departments and urged even greater fortitude in the face of this grave danger to the Republic.[29]

One of the nine, Antoine Nicolas Marie, exhibited a calmer attitude in a brief letter he sent on June 6 to Jean Le Goupil Duclos, mayor of Caen. He opened, "Do not worry on our account," related the commissioners' intention to address the Convention, and closed with the observation that "Paris

28. *Brochures Normandes: Caen sous la Révolution*, B. M. Caen, Rés. Fn. Br. D156–209.
29. A. C. Caen, I35 (Révolution du 31 mai 1793).

is tranquil in appearance, and we count upon the friendship of our fellow citizens." Marie expressed none of the alarm or exhortation contained in the previous letter.[30]

The gravity of the situation in Paris, however, was confirmed in a letter dated June 8, sent from the deputy Lomont to Pierre Jean Lévêque, who had replaced the absent Lenormand as president of the departmental administration. In the letter, Lomont lauds Lévêque's character and warns him of the need for renewed patriotism:

Brother and friend,

Your tactfulness and exquisite honesty have earned my esteem beyond all expression; may your fellow-citizens always do you the justice that you deserve! I have not replied to your excellent letter of the seventeenth, because I was at Buges acting as the Convention's commissioner to the paper factory there. But how times have changed since that period! We must close ranks if we are to triumph over the enemies of the country! No more small measures, or the liberty with which brave republicans should perish will be finished.

I will say no more to you; you know what is happening . . . courage, and again more courage!

Greetings and good health,

Lt

I send this to your home: the secrecy of the mails is violated with impunity, etc. . . . by not including your official title in the inscription it will be less suspect (this letter) and more likely to reach you.[31]

Again, we see expressed the fear that the mails were being searched, with Lomont even so cautious as not to sign his full name.

In spite of the alarming news that continued to arrive from Paris, business went on much as usual in Caen during the first week of June. Both the municipal and district councils, as well as the departmental administration, concerned themselves principally with ensuring an adequate grain supply. On June 2, Bougon-Longrais, the *procureur-général-syndic,* scolded the *comité de subsistance* for its slow enactment of the *maximum* on barley, rye, and oats. That same day, Bougon noted the importance of maintaining correspondence with the representatives on mission to the 14th Military Division, commanded by General Félix Wimpffen and headquartered in Bayeux. Two days later, the council sent two of its members, Pierre Mesnil and Barnabé Cauvin, to warn the two representatives on mission of a possible

30. *Ibid.*
31. A. D. Calvados, L10276 (Lévêque correspondence).

arms shipment from England to the Manche coast and to invite them to confer with the Calvados administration. The two representatives, Charles Romme and Claude Antoine Prieur (of the Côte-d'Or), arrived in Caen on June 5 and met with all three of the local administrations. They engaged in an amicable discussion regarding issues of military defense and grain supply and left the next day for Bayeux.[32]

On June 7, the departmental directory read two decrees of the Convention into the official minutes. The first, dated May 31, announced the suppression of the Commission of Twelve. The second, dated June 1, contained an official account of the events of May 31, stressing that debate continued freely within the Convention and that only liberty had triumphed by that grand *journée*.[33]

Caen remained calm until Saturday, June 8, when the nine commissioners returned from Paris. At this point, the sequence of events becomes somewhat clouded. At least three versions exist of the twenty-four hours that culminated, early on June 9, in a declaration of insurrection.

The following account is the one most strongly supported by the record. The precise time at which the commissioners arrived in Caen is not known; but late in the morning or early in the afternoon, the departmental council convened a special session, inviting members of the district and municipal councils, members of the civil and judicial tribunals, and delegates from the sections of Caen. At this meeting, one of the nine commissioners, Dom Mauger, a former Benedictine monk recently appointed physics professor at the University of Caen, delivered their report.

According to the commissioners' account, they had arrived in the capital on Sunday, June 2, only to discover that the sections of Paris had already risen. They had met, as they entered the city, an unnamed Calvados administrator returning to Caen, who had told them that the Commission of Twelve and twenty-two others would soon be arrested. Reaching the heart of Paris late that night, the nine had passed 100,000 armed men with cannons trained on the Convention. On arriving at their hotel, they had learned the details of that day's events. They had been told of a man, posing as a municipal officer, who had roused the faubourg Saint-Antoine that morning, of the bravery of the deputies as they marched into the crowd, and of

---

32. A. D. Calvados, L160bis (Conseil Général du Département, procès-verbaux des séances, 2 juin 1793–31 juillet 1793).

33. A. D. Calvados, L165; *Réimpression de l'Ancien Moniteur*, XVI, 540.

Marat leading a band of paid scoundrels. The Girondin deputies had reportedly been proscribed under the threat of the men and cannons of Hanriot.

The following morning, Mauger continued, they had visited a few of the Calvados deputies, as well as Pétion, Jean Denis Lanjuinais, Barbaroux, and Valazé, all of whom had described the commissioners' mission as pointless. The deputies had cited the example of the commissioners from the Seine-Inférieure, who had been battered and spit upon in the Convention. Undaunted, the delegation had gone on June 4 to visit the deputy Vardon, where they had again encountered the majority of the Calvados representatives. The nine had decided to send six of their lot back to Caen with a report, leaving three in Paris to deliver their message. Just then, a deputy had burst in with news of an order for the arrest of those in Paris who had not supported the June 2 insurrection. Ten thousand people had already been jailed, he had claimed, and an arrest order had been issued for the commissioners from Caen. Faced with this great peril, all nine had decided to remain in Paris and to go to the Convention the next day!

This they had done, only to be told that the Committee of Public Safety now dealt with petitions such as theirs. Gustave Doulcet had tried unsuccessfully to gain them admission to the assembly. Discouraged, they had left, followed through the streets by "groupes de furieux." The nine had departed Paris late that afternoon "under the eye of a thousand spies," who had followed them to the edge of town.

Arriving in Evreux on June 6, they had met a man named Beaumier who had allegedly been paid 3,600 *livres* by Joseph Garat, the minister of the interior, to sound out the departments of Lower Normandy. Beaumier had told the nine of Garat's plan to become dictator. After peace had been restored and the Girondins eliminated, Garat, presumably in league with Robespierre and Marat, would fix a "maximum des propriétés" at 6,000 *livres* annual revenue. The domination of Paris would be assured. Shocked by this tale, the delegation had turned Beaumier over to the Eure authorities. That evening, they had met with a Eure general assembly, which, they reported, had already taken insurrectionary measures. The commissioners had stopped the following day in Lisieux, where they had also met with local authorities, and had traveled directly from there to Caen on June 8.[34]

---

34. A. C. Caen, I36 (Insurrection et actes des administrations insurgées, mai–juillet 1793). A major portion of the commissioners' report is printed in the notes to Vaultier, *Souvenirs*, 170–73. The true status of Beaumier is unclear. He was apparently a *commissaire observateur*

Mauger's report made a strong impression on the assembly, and Lévêque, now president of the departmental administration, proposed an oath declaring eternal war against agitators, rebels, and the *maratistes* who divided the Convention. All those present swore the oath, "with all the energy and enthusiams of which a free people is capable." The minutes of the meeting and the report were ordered printed and sent to all departments and to the sections of Paris. As the meeting drew to a close, those present voted to convene section assemblies that evening. The assemblies would be visited by departmental administrators and by members of the commission to Paris. It was further agreed that future departmental meetings should include the district and municipal councils, along with the tribunal, section, and club representatives who had attended this session. This marked the first instance during the Revolution in which meetings of the Calvados administration were in any sense opened to the public.[35]

In this version of the events of June 8, the report of the commissioners sent to Paris plays a central role. The report could hardly have been more inflammatory—it spoke of spies and armed legions in the capital, recounted the abuses and threats suffered both by the commissioners themselves and by the Calvados deputies, and told of secret agents roaming the provinces, sent by men who hoped to rule over France as dictators. The people of Caen now had direct confirmation of the woeful tales that the Calvados deputies had told in recent letters.

That this report embodied a degree of exaggeration is hardly surprising. Some evidence suggests, though, that not all of the commissioners to Paris viewed the situation so urgently. Nicolas Marie's early letter to Le Goupil Duclos described the capital as calm. Another of the commissioners, Guillaume Feret, testified after the revolt that the armed soldiers he had seen in Paris were patrolling the streets peacefully. Feret had never visited the capital before, and a bad leg kept him in his hotel room during the entire stay. He later claimed that René Lenormand, Louis Caille, and Dom Mauger had made nearly all of the decisions for the group, had arranged their meet-

---

for the department of Paris in May, 1793, and wrote to Garat on May 25 requesting employment in his service. There is no record that Garat gave him such a mission, and Pierre Caron does not list him as one of Garat's agents. Beaumier's run-in with the Caen commissioners did create problems for another Garat agent, Bouisset, who was detained and harassed in Calvados as he passed through on his way to Brittany in June. See Pierre Caron, *Rapports des Agents du Ministre de l'Intérieur dans les départements (1793–an II)* (Paris, 1913), I, 108–109.

35. A. D. Calvados, L160bis.

ings with deputies, and had taken responsibility for drafting the report.[36] If Feret can be believed, and he admittedly was writing in his own defense, both the trip to Paris and the later report were managed by men already predisposed to insurrection; in that case, the representatives of the Caen sections made very minor contributions to both the mission and the report.

Frédéric Vaultier gives an account in his *Souvenirs* that minimizes the importance of the commissioners' report, suggesting instead that the section assemblies declared their insurrectionary intention on June 8 before hearing from the men sent to Paris. He seems to ignore the fact that earlier that day Mauger had read the report to the special session, which section representatives had attended, but his chronicle of the events of that evening is interesting in other respects. As secretary of the section Liberté, Vaultier received an address that a prominent citizen wished to have read to the section assembly on the evening of June 8. This citizen insisted on anonymity, and only after Vaultier himself had taken credit for the address did the assembly allow him to read it aloud. He did not reprint it in his memoirs but described it as written "in a most pronounced spirit of insurrection." Those in attendance greeted the speech with acclamation, and the section declared itself in insurrection "en principe." Liberté sent Vaultier to deliver his address to the other sections in order to secure their adhesion. Only when he wrote his recollections, over thirty years later, did he identify the true author of the speech as Pierre Jacques Samuel Chatry *l'aîné*.[37]

It is possible that Vaultier is indulging his memory to gain his own small bit of revolutionary glory. But despite the absence of strong corroborating evidence (which, given the nature of the episode, one would hardly expect), this account sounds plausible, and we cannot dismiss it out of hand. Chatry did, in fact, live on the Place de la Liberté and would have been a member of Vaultier's section. It has already been pointed out that he had played an active role in municipal politics since 1789, first as a member of the Caen General Committee and then as a municipal officer and *notable*. He belonged to a wealthy, commercial, Protestant Caen family. In 1793, he held public office as a *notable* and as president of the Tribunal of Commerce. Although clearly influential in local affairs, Chatry preferred not to exercise a promi-

36. A. D. Calvados, L10136 (documents pertaining to federalism). This information is contained in a letter dated March 10, 1794, sent by Feret to the representatives on mission Bouret and Frémanger.
37. Vaultier, *Souvenirs*, 12–13.

nent leadership role. In 1791, he declined election as mayor because he felt it would be imprudent for a Protestant to hold that position at a time when religious opinions were a political issue. Drafting an inflammatory speech and then giving it to Vaultier to deliver would have been consistent with his sense of discretion, with his concern for political affairs, and also with his later, active participation in the revolt.[38]

In addition to this circumstantial evidence, Vaultier's story is partially supported by Jean Baptiste Leclerc, a departmental administrator in 1793. Interrogated in August, after the revolt had failed, he acknowledged that he had accompanied several of the commissioners who had been sent to Paris as they reported to section assemblies on the night of June 8. Leclerc noted that people in the sections were already calling for revolt and that the section Liberté, in fact, had declared itself in insurrection before the commissioners arrived. This confirms Vaultier's recollection of the sequence of events, though not the role of Chatry.[39]

A final possible amendment to the official record of the events of June 8 accords a position of prominence to the Carabot club. One of the commissioners to Paris, Lenormand (not René, but a second Lenormand), had been sent explicitly as a representative of that club, and the delegation may have included other Carabots as well. Georges Mancel, in his notes to Vaultier, claims that on their return from Paris two of the commissioners reported immediately to their fellow Carabots. Taking the initiative, the club sent twelve of its members to the assembled authorities with a petition, proposing that all Calvados deputies to the Convention be recalled; that local authorities recognize no measure issued by the Convention, or by the "so-called Executive Council," after May 27; that a court be created to judge *maratistes* and other "factieux"; that the Calvados authorities create a cavalry force of two hundred men for public security; and finally, that all couriers sent by the Convention be arrested and their packets seized, inspected, and burned. The fact that a general assembly adopted several of these measures early on the morning of June 9 supports the veracity of this account.[40]

The meeting of June 9 was of singular importance for two reasons. First, on that morning, the people of Caen confirmed their intention to pursue an

38. A. D. Calvados, L10074 (Elections et actifs, 1790–92); A. C. Caen, D1, D2, and K34 (Mairie, 1790–an II).

39. A. D. Calvados, L10125 (interrogations of federalist suspects).

40. A. D. Calvados, L10136; Vaultier, *Souvenirs*, 138–39. The handwritten copy of the Carabot petition in the Calvados archives is undated.

insurrection against the Montagnard Convention. Second, more than any subsequent event or action, the oath sworn on June 9 and the assembly's decision to arrest and imprison the deputies Romme and Prieur would provide damning evidence against the Calvados federalists after their revolt collapsed.

A variety of documents enables us to reconstruct the events of that day and identify the leading figures in the drama. From the official *procès-verbal* of the June 9 meeting, we learn that representatives from all of the local administrations, courts, and clubs attended the session. However, many who might have come stayed away. Only thirteen of thirty-seven departmental administrators were present, though this was not unusual. Early in the year, as many as thirty administrators had attended council meetings with some regularity; but in recent weeks, attendance had never reached even 50 percent. Caen district officials showed slightly greater diligence—seven of the thirteen council members were present at the meeting. Surprisingly, the Caen municipal council had proportionally the fewest representatives in attendance. Of the forty-four current council members, only ten were present. Although eight of the fourteen officers came, both the mayor and the *procureur* were absent.

Pierre Jean Lévêque presided over the assembly, which began with a discussion of proposals made by the sections and the popular societies. Those present unanimously declared themselves in a state of insurrection and resistance to oppression until that time when the Convention should recover its liberty. Two messengers from the neighboring department of the Orne reported that the administration of that department was preparing an armed force and called on Calvados to do likewise. This proposal was referred to a committee. Then, in its most decisive action, the assembly named Lenormand (not René, but the second Lenormand) and a few of his fellow Carabots to go to Bayeux to arrest the two deputies Romme and Prieur. They were to bring the two back to Caen, where they would be held in the Château as hostages against the safety of the deputies arrested in Paris. An additional messenger traveled to the neighboring department of the Manche to request its support for the Calvados position.

Acting on the recommendations of the Carabots, those assembled ordered the postal service to redirect to the Calvados administration all letters addressed to the representatives on mission. All local *payeurs généraux* were instructed to disburse no funds whatsoever without an order from the departmental or district directory. The assembly also ordered that all munitions and military convoys intended for the coast be held in Caen (so that the populace would not be disquieted!). General Wimpffen, commanding the 14th Military Division, was invited to Caen to confer with officials. The session closed with the appointment of a provisional insurrectional committee, composed of one representative from each local corps: René Lenormand, from the departmental administration; Louis Caille, from the Caen district council; Samuel Chatry *l'aîné,* a municipal *notable;* Pierre Michel Picquot, the public prosecutor for the Criminal Tribunal; Pierre Costy, a judge on the district tribunal; François Anne Pierre Tabouret, from the section Liberté; François Le Carpentier, a municipal *notable* representing the Jacobin club; Jean Michel Barbot, from the Carabot club; and Charles L'honoré, a judge on the Caen Tribunal of Commerce.[41]

There is much, however, that the official record omits or distorts. For one thing, it exaggerates the single-mindedness of those present. The *procès-verbal* records the unanimous declaration of a state of insurrection, followed by the signatures of all those present, as well as the names of a number of other officials who signed at a later date. But some of those present opposed this declaration—in particular, Robert Tirel, an *homme de loi* and district director. Tirel questioned the advisability of insurrection and especially objected to the proposal to arrest Romme and Prieur. However, the assembly shouted him down and passed a clause that labeled as suspect and traitorous anyone who refused to support and sign the declaration of revolt. The heated emotions, fueled by the report from Paris, clearly made public opposition to the insurrection a dangerous proposition.

A number of individuals claimed in their interrogations, perhaps for reasons of self-preservation, to have been intimidated into signing the June 9 minutes. One of these was Gilles Fleury, a saddle maker and town *notable.* He, too, claimed to have opposed the arrest of the two deputies. He had been shouted down along with Tirel and had signed the *procès-verbal* out of fear for his safety, he said. At a meeting eight or nine days after June 9, the deputy *procureur* had observed that the menacing clause rendered the deliberation of June 9 legally null. Those present had voted to strike it from the record, and the offending words had been scratched from the original minutes. Fleury claimed in his interrogation to have argued that since some had

41. A. D. Calvados, L189 (Registre des arrêtés du Conseil Général du département du Calvados, 11 août 1792–26 juillet 1793).

signed under coercion, the questions and orders should be reopened for discussion. This motion had been quickly dismissed, but two days later Fleury had discreetly scratched out his signature in the presence of the secretary.[42]

The official record also leaves unexplained the curious absence of the Caen mayor from the June 9 meeting. Again, it is the later interrogation transcripts that provide information. Le Goupil Duclos claimed that work had detained him at the town hall on June 8 and that he therefore had not been able to attend the section assemblies or hear the report from Paris. He had gone to the Abbaye-aux-Hommes, where the departmental council met, at nine o'clock that evening, stayed until midnight, and returned home when informed that a general meeting would not be held until the following morning. The next day, he had been astounded to learn that the meeting had convened at 4 A.M.! It appears that the mayor of Caen, who remained aloof from the revolt throughout June and July, was not absent by choice on the morning of June 9 and that this critical meeting took place at a most unusual hour. Indeed, the time may have been largely responsible for the generally low attendance at the meeting.[43]

The assembly met again that evening to prepare further for resistance against Paris. The session had scarcely opened, however, when Henry-Larivière and Gorsas, two of the proscribed deputies, arrived in the hall. Each addressed the assembly, and those present were "seized by horror" at their description of events in Paris. The assembly ordered that the bulletin of the Convention no longer be printed and further voted to disregard all orders issued by the Convention after May 27 and to suspend all correspondence with the Executive Council. It invited the other five districts of Calvados to send representatives to Caen and voted to form five committees, each to be composed of five members.[44] One committee was assigned to draft an appeal to the citizens of Calvados to volunteer for a departmental force to march to

42. A. D. Calvados, L10125 and L189. The incident involving Tirel was attested to, under interrogation, by Leclerc, Fleury, the departmental administrator Cauvin, and Le Goupil Duclos, the mayor of Caen. The original minutes of the meeting do show the controversial clause, barely legible, to have been crossed out. The signature of Fleury is also faintly visible.

43. A. D. Calvados, L10125 (interrogation of Le Goupil Duclos). Mancel, in his notes to Vaultier's memoirs, reports the time of the meeting to have been 2 A.M., hardly a more hospitable hour. If this was indeed the correct time, it would seem even more likely that Le Goupil was deliberately misled when told at midnight that the assembly would take place the next morning.

44. The five committees were *comité de résistance à l'oppression, comité de militaire, comité des finances, comité des subsistances, comité de rédaction et de correspondance.*

Paris. In addition, the delegates voted to name sixteen commissioners to travel in pairs to the sixteen surrounding departments to invite them to join Calvados in selecting a town from which a central committee could direct their efforts.[45]

Late in the meeting, two messengers from Evreux arrived to inform Calvados officials that the Eure was organizing in protest. These men announced that they had passed through Lisieux, where officials and citizens were prepared to enroll in a departmental force. Inspired by this news, René Lenormand, Adrien Thiboult, Louis Caille, and Antoine Nicolas Marie immediately stepped forward as the first volunteers for the Calvados battalion.[46] The session closed with an order that each district council open registers for the enrollment of volunteers.

New developments followed in quick succession during those hectic days. Before going on, we would do well to briefly assess what had occurred thus far. In the span of two days, the department of Calvados, principally the *chef-lieu* of Caen, had shifted from a state of concern and alert to one of open insurrection. Emotions had run high following the report of the commissioners returned from Paris and had been heightened by the words of Gorsas and Larivière. Fateful steps had been taken in the decisions to form a departmental force and to arrest the deputies Romme and Prieur. A general assembly (composed largely of departmental administrators but including representatives from the district, the municipality, and the sections and clubs of Caen) had been formed to coordinate resistance efforts. But one must question, particularly in light of later events, the extent of popular support for these actions, even at this early, exhilarating stage of the revolt.

Virtually all of the men named to the provisional insurrectional committee had extensive experience in local administration. Administrators with clear ties to individuals in Paris had played the most active roles to this point. René Lenormand, president of the department from January through May, came from the same area as Doulcet de Pontécoulant and maintained

45. The departments to be visited were the Eure, Seine-Inférieure, Somme, Orne, Sarthe, Indre-et-Loire, Mayenne, Maine-et-Loire, Eure-et-Loir, Loir-et-Cher, Manche, Ille-et-Vilaine, Côtes-du-Nord, Morbihan, Finistère, and Loire-Inférieure. The commissioners were not named until the following day.

46. Lenormand was a departmental administrator. Adrien Thiboult was also a departmental administrator, representing Lisieux, who thus might have been expected to step forward. Caille, of course, was *procureur-syndic*, and Antoine Nicolas Marie was a Caen *notable*. Lenormand, Caille, and Marie were three of the nine commissioners who had just returned from Paris.

contact with the deputy; Lévêque, the newly elected departmental president, regularly corresponded with the deputy Lomont; Caille, a district administrator, had traveled to Paris in January, 1792, to seek information regarding the split between Feuillants and Jacobins and since that time had reportedly maintained regular communication with several of the Girondin leaders, especially Barbaroux; Chatry *l'aîné*, who perhaps played a key role with the volatile speech delivered by Vaultier to the Caen sections, was a *notable* and had previously served for two years as a municipal officer; and Marie, sent to Paris as a commissioner and one of the first to volunteer for the departmental force, sat in 1793 as a Caen *notable*.

The one exception to this pattern is the second Lenormand, a member of the delegation to Paris and later of the group sent to Bayeux to arrest the two deputies, who can only be identified as having been president of the Carabots. This group constituted a potential source of popular input to the general assembly, but it is difficult to estimate the size of the Carabot membership. Vaultier says that it grew after May 31, but he also suggests that the new members (he mentions General Wimpffen by name) already held positions of authority and may have joined in order to exercise a more direct influence over the club.[47] As for the sections, another possible source of popular input, no record of their regular sessions during this period exists; therefore, we do not know the attendance at the meetings of June 8, nor do we know if they continued to meet throughout the revolt. It should be noted, however, that the church bells, the regular means of summoning citizens to these assemblies, were not rung on the evening of June 8 for fear that ringing them would alarm the countryside. In addition, these meetings were held late at night, an inconvenient time for many, as was the early morning hour of the important general assembly on June 9. Finally, both Esnault and Dufour, the diarists, noted a general lack of public enthusiasm among the people of Caen during this period for the protest being marshalled against Paris and the Montagnards.[48]

On June 10, Lenormand and the Carabots returned to Caen with their prisoners, Romme and Prieur. The two deputies appeared before the general assembly, where Lévêque assured them of the Calvados citizens' respect for their persons and office, while declaring the assembly's determination to

47. Vaultier, *Souvenirs*, 97.
48. Lesage (Esnault), 108, and (Dufour), 120.

hold them as hostages for the arrested representatives in Paris.[49] Delegates from Bayeux accompanied the Carabots and reported their city's adherence to the state of insurrection. Six more departmental officials and one district administrator stepped forward to enroll in the departmental force, and the assembly ordered the Caen National Guard to gather that evening so that its members could volunteer for the force as well.[50]

A more important meeting of the general assembly took place that afternoon, with General Wimpffen in attendance. The general swore his devotion to the insurrection and requested that military supplies intended for the coast be allowed to continue to their destination. The assembly willingly granted the request. Although Louis Caille questioned the dependability of Wimpffen and the advisability of his appointment as commander of the rebel forces, the matter was quickly passed over. Wimpffen's royalist sympathies and later recalcitrance in leading the march on Paris supported, in retrospect, Caille's reservation.

The assembly then ordered the reconvening in Bayeux of the administrative council of the 14th Military Division, composed of five commissioners from neighboring departments. The council was to commence making plans for raising an army to march to Paris. This order is noteworthy, for it was the first action by Calvados officials that could be interpreted as a direct reaction to a recent order from the capital.

Since early in 1793, the Calvados administration had expressed its concern to the minister of war, the minister of the interior, and the Convention regarding the need for stronger defenses along the Channel coast to repulse a possible attack from England. Some local officials, no doubt, recalled the frequent British attacks, and the consequent disruption of commerce, during the Seven Years War (1756–1763). The declaration of war against Britain on February 1, 1793, increased the current danger, and one week later the departmental council wrote to the minister of war to request that Wimpffen be assigned to command the troops of the 14th Division, also known as the Army of the Coasts of Cherbourg. The minister acknowledged the request

49. *Affiches, Annonces et Avis Divers de la Basse-Normandie,* June 13, 1793, A. D. Calvados.
50. A. D. Calvados, L189. The departmental officials were Jean Charles Hippolyte Bougon-Longrais; Pierre Mesnil, a Caen merchant; Jean Jacques Petit, a merchant from Falaise; Jean Baptiste Leclerc, a *juge de paix* from Cambremer; Nicolas Lenoble *l'aîné;* and Germain Dubosq, president of the Criminal Tribunal, originally from Vire. The district official was René François Lahaye, a property owner and former mayor of the small town of Audrieu.

but took no immediate action.[51] The administration apparently then sought the intervention of Fauchet, who wrote to Calvados on February 24 that the Executive Council had decided to transfer Wimpffen to the 14th Division. Delays followed, however, and the Calvados authorities remained dissatisfied with the defense of their coast. On April 7, the departmental council sent Bougon-Longrais to Paris to press more forcefully their demands for a stronger defense before the Executive Council and the Convention.[52] Whether as a result of this mission or not, the manpower of the 14th Division increased in April, and in mid-April, the Convention issued an order for the creation of an administrative council attached to the 14th Division. This council, to be headquartered in Bayeux, was to be composed of one representative each from Calvados, the Manche, the Orne, the Eure, and the Seine-Inférieure. The Calvados administration named André Bresson as its representative, and he left Caen to assume his position on April 18. Finally, on May 15, the minister of the interior, Garat, confirmed the appointment of Wimpffen as commander of the 14th Division.[53]

It must have come as a rude surprise to the Calvados authorities, then, when Romme and Prieur arrived on mission from the Convention in late May and, as one of their first actions, ordered the dissolution of the administrative council in Bayeux. Deputies on mission were to assume its former role, and the representatives of the five departments would now become a committee of correspondence with no deliberative powers. After struggling for half a year to secure an adequate defense, local officials now saw full control of the Cherbourg army returned to the central government, which had seemingly ignored for so long the threat to their coast. The Convention's decision at this time was probably motivated by a distrust of General Wimpffen, whose royalist sympathies were well known. Wimpffen expressed his disapproval of this action to the representatives on mission; but on May 27, the administrative council held what it believed to be its final session.[54] On June 10, however, with Romme and Prieur safely in custody, the Calvados general assembly restored the council to its former powers.

The following day, the general assembly adopted another measure directed against the capital. It ordered the suspension of all transport to Paris of "denrées de première nécessité," principally foodstuffs. The municipality

51. A. D. Calvados, L10550 (documents pertaining to Wimpffen).
52. A. D. Calvados, L165.
53. A. D. Calvados, L10550.
54. A. D. Calvados, L10551 (documents pertaining to Wimpffen and federalism).

enacted this order immediately, and goods destined for Paris were stopped in Caen to be stored in the former house of the Carmelites. Two considerations inspired this action. The first was long-standing resentment of the capital's voracious appetite for both food and tax revenues. One finds expressions of this resentment throughout provincial France, not only in Caen. The second was the current shortage of grain in the Caen market, a problem since early spring. In the minds of many people in Caen, the shortage could be attributed to the export of grain to Paris (though it was more likely due to the reluctance of local farmers to send grain to the market, despite an abundant harvest).[55]

On June 21, the mayor of Paris, Jean Nicolas Pache, sent a letter to the Caen district council protesting the boycott on goods to the capital. Pache wrote eloquently of the threat of anarchy that this might pose, of the aid it would give to Cobourg and Brunswick, and of the sacrifices already made by Parisians for the liberty of the nation. He implored the people of Caen to send a prompt disavowal of this barbarous project. Three days later, the general assembly replied, noting its affront at Pache's decision to send his appeal only to the district council—an obvious attempt to sow division among the local authorities. The assembly's letter spelled out the usual grievances against factionalism in Paris and the violation of the National Convention and reiterated the determination of Calvados citizens to resist oppression and dictatorship. But it also bitterly denounced the parasitism of Paris:

> Do you wish continually to mislead us with trivial phrases, when they are contradicted by the facts? As if it were not sufficiently notorious that, under the plausible pretext of supplying the city of Paris, you have wickedly exceeded the bounds of prudence with the criminal intention of reducing a generous and magnanimous people to famine. . . .

> Does the administration of the Department of Calvados not have reason to wonder at the reproach directed against it by the municipality of Paris, when, from all parts of France, objections ring out over the enormous sums that the Commune has swallowed up through the squandering of monsters who have embezzled from the public Treasury.

The Calvados assembly further accused the Paris municipality of paying the instigators of the recent disruptions and charged that the Parisian battalions

---

55. A. D. Calvados, L189; A. C. Caen, D2. See also A. D. Calvados, L1923. In mid-April, the Calvados *comité de sûreté général* had investigated an allegedly illicit shipment of foodstuffs to Paris. Members of the committee observed that while such a shipment could not possibly benefit the well-provisioned capital, it had appreciably harmed Caen.

sent to combat the Vendéan rebels had in fact gone to aid the revolt and spread chaos. The assembly had no intention of moderating its position, and the boycott remained in effect until early July.[56]

Fortunately for Paris, the efforts of Calvados to blockade the capital did not receive universal support. The northwestern departments in Lower Normandy and Brittany joined in the boycott, but grain continued to travel up the Seine from Le Havre and Rouen. Still, by early July, the bakers of Paris were in serious straits; and on July 14, Pache wrote a confidential letter to Robert Lindet and Jean Michel DuRoy, representatives on mission who had been sent by the Convention to pacify the Norman departments. He begged them to make their first priority the reopening of trade routes, so that grain from that region could again reach the capital. Pache stressed the gravity of the situation by reminding the two representatives that famine in Paris might bring the downfall of the Republic. Indeed, the boycott on grain appears to have been a far more potent weapon than the small armed force that the Calvados rebels eventually sent toward Paris.[57]

During the second week of June, officials in Caen proceeded to consolidate their organization and to seek wider support for the insurrection. On June 11, the same day the grain boycott began, the general assembly made appointments to the five committees created on June 9. Twenty-one of the twenty-five appointees already held official positions at the departmental, district, or municipal level; thus, the appointments preserved the predominant role played by elected officials in leading and organizing the revolt. These committees, under the supervision of the general assembly, would guide the local revolt for the remainder of June.

To generate support for the resistance effort, the assembly prepared an address to the citizens of Calvados. It began by denouncing as a fabrication the recent proclamation of the National Convention that reported the freedom of that body and the tranquility of Paris. It recounted the terrifying scene that the Calvados commissioners had encountered in the capital and called all citizens to arms so that Calvados might join the other departments in defeating this assault on the nation's sovereignty. Despite this bellicose appeal and the supposed gravity of the threat to the nation, the general assembly promised that not a drop of blood would be shed, since the majority of

56. A. D. Calvados, L10134 (addresses and proclamations during the federalist revolt).

57. A. D. Calvados, L10119 (Lindet mission, correspondence). See also Goodwin, "The Federalist Movement in Caen during the French Revolution," especially pages 327–43.

oppressed Parisians would welcome their liberators with open arms. The reputation of the brave Norman warriors was already intimidating the new tyrants in Paris.[58]

The general assembly also sent letters and messengers to surrounding departments. The first of these went to Rouen, for the importance of securing the support of the Seine-Inférieure was clear. With grain supplies running short, Caen would be turning to Le Havre for emergency shipments. Rouen, located on the Seine, could easily block supplies traveling up the river to Paris and would be a vital component of any blockade effort. Moreover, long-standing ties, both commercial and juridical, joined the capitals of Upper and Lower Normandy. Thus, as early as June 9, the members of the general assembly sent a letter to Rouen explaining to the departmental council their alarm at the violation of the Convention, their determination to resist oppression, and their declaration of insurrection. They expressed hope that the Seine-Inférieure would support their actions and requested the shipment to Caen of any available grain. Finally, they informed the Seine-Inférieure that they had ordered the arrest of Romme and Prieur, referring to the deputies as "Proconsuls Nationaux."[59]

Despite their own misgivings regarding the recent turn of events in Paris, the administrators of the Seine-Inférieure were not prepared to follow the drastic steps marked out by their counterparts in Calvados. In a return letter dated June 18, written after the officials in Rouen had conferred with a messenger sent by the Calvados general assembly, the Seine-Inférieure administration maintained that officials in Caen had exceeded their legal powers in ordering the arrest of Romme and Prieur and in freezing public funds. As administrators, they could register their disapproval through letters of protest, but the constitution would not justify the arrest of national representatives or the rejection of the authority of the Convention. In sum, the Seine-Inférieure administrators viewed the Calvados actions as a more serious threat to order than the violations they sought to remedy.[60] The attitude of the Seine-Inférieure administration illustrates the dilemma facing provincial moderates. Although they deplored events in Paris, their own commitment to constitutional legality prevented them from taking decisive action,

58. A. D. Calvados, L189. A signed copy of the address, dated June 10, 1793, can also be found in dossier L10134.
59. A. D. Calvados, L10134.
60. The main portion of this letter is reprinted in Mancel's notes to Vaultier, *Souvenirs,* 192–93.

lest they be guilty of precisely the transgression of which they accused the Montagnards.

The general assembly enjoyed greater success in securing the support of other departments. The Eure and the Orne, of course, had already sent messengers to Caen declaring their intentions. On June 12, sixteen commissioners left Caen to visit other neighboring departments and inform them of Calvados' actions. Most of those chosen were minor figures, representatives from the Caen sections and clubs, but the assembly named several familiar officials to visit key departments. Louis Caille and Chaix-d'Estanges left for the Manche, which had expressed some apprehension over the arrest of Romme and Prieur, and for the Ille-et-Vilaine, where delegates from other Breton departments were known to be already gathering in Rennes. Bougon-Longrais departed for the Seine-Inférieure and the Somme, while Lenormand, the Carabot president, and Caille *le jeune* journeyed to the departments of Finistère and the Côtes-du-Nord. On that same day, Charles François Duhamel-Levailly, a departmental administrator from Bayeux, informed the assembly that urgent business required his presence in Bordeaux, and he was delegated to carry news of the insurrection to the Indre-et-Loire, the Indre, the Haute-Vienne, the Dordogne, and the Gironde.[61]

In Caen, the general assembly began preparations for the formation of a departmental force. On June 14, it ordered a contingent of four hundred infantrymen with two cannons, one caisson, and a half company of cannoneers sent to Evreux to be put at the disposition of that department. Soldiers were to be drawn from Caen, Lisieux, and Falaise. Two days later, with the Caen contingent still incomplete, the military committee ordered the Lisieux and Falaise troops to leave as a vanguard, to be followed on June 19 by a full company of two hundred from Caen. The departmental officials Lenormand and Mesnil accompanied the vanguard as civil commissioners. Officials instructed the *chef de légion* in Caen to fill the ranks of that company from the National Guard. Even this did not suffice to complete the company, however; and on June 19, the general assembly ordered the sounding of a call to arms after that day's parade, to attract more recruits. Those who signed up were to prepare to leave on Friday, June 21.

The Carabots appeared in the June 19 parade, fully armed and prepared

61. A. D. Calvados, L189. The diligence with which Duhamel performed his mission is open to question. I found no record whatsoever of his stopping in the Haute-Vienne.

to march toward Paris. This public demonstration as well as an assurance from the general assembly that the wives and children of those who volunteered would be protected by the authorities, may have helped to generate enthusiasm. Yet the contingent was finally filled only by the conscription of five men from each company of the Caen National Guard. In a town of roughly thirty thousand, it had taken a full week to assemble two hundred volunteers for this venture. Finally, on June 22, the company embarked on the road to Evreux, led by a departmental banner entrusted to the Carabots and the Jacobin club. The Caen volunteers took as their motto that of the Carabot club: "L'exécution de la loi, ou la mort." The departmental administrators Lévêque and Bougon accompanied the contingent.

The addition of the 6th Battalion of Calvados volunteers, previously assigned to combat the Vendéan rebels, boosted this small force. Lieutenant Colonel LeRoy appeared before the general assembly on June 20 to report that his battalion, fighting alongside "Parisian brigands," had grown disillusioned and dispirited. Fearing desertion, LeRoy had ordered his men back toward Calvados. They now awaited new orders in Alençon. The assembly could scarcely ignore this stroke of good fortune and ordered the battalion to proceed immediately to Evreux.[62]

For the first Caen force, however, problems continued. Only hours after the troops had left the city, the newly appointed quartermaster, Edouard LeGrix, dashed off a letter to Pierre Jean Lévêque. The departmental treasurer, St. Firmin, had refused to release funds for the supplies and lodging of the troops on their route to Evreux. LeGrix wrote that the assembly, "disorganized, so to speak," had put off until the following day a resolution of the problem. The quartermaster was therefore trapped in Caen waiting for funds. LeGrix advised Lévêque to conceal the present predicament from the troops, in order to avoid hostile rumors. He also noted the recent arrival in Calvados of copies of the new constitution.[63]

The general assembly resolved the temporary crisis the next day by ordering St. Firmin to disregard prior obligations and normal procedures and to release the money immediately to LeGrix. To discourage similar recalcitrance in other quarters, the assembly issued an order requiring all civil, judicial, and military officials in Calvados to swear an oath, pledging to: "maintain with all one's power liberty and equality, to uphold the unity and

62. *Ibid.*
63. A. D. Calvados, L10276 (Lévêque correspondence).

indivisibility of the Republic, to wage war against tyrants and anarchists, to not lay down arms until the National Convention is free and France avenged for the attacks committed against the sovereignty of the people."[64]

During this same period, the third week in June, the officials who had gathered in Caen took steps to more actively involve the rest of the department in the revolt. On June 18, the general assembly convoked all cantonal primary assemblies for the following Monday, June 24. These assemblies were to swear the oath of loyalty cited above and to elect one delegate apiece to join the assembly in Caen. This order produced mixed results. The district council of Falaise refused to call primary assemblies until a second, more sternly worded, order was sent to the district officials. Scattered reports filtered in of individual cantons' refusing to proceed as ordered. But many assemblies did meet, and on June 25 and 26, some thirty-seven cantonal delegates appeared before the assembly for ratification. The enthusiasm of these new delegates, however, appears to have been short-lived. No record of attendance exists for the general assembly, but it voted on July 3 that those members wishing to be absent must present their reasons to the *comité de salut public*. The assembly also ordered district councils to invite cantons to choose substitute delegates to confer with primary delegates, so that one of the two would always be present. Furthermore, some cantons had still not elected any delegates. On July 9, the assembly instructed district officials to forward the names of individuals who were obstructing the convocation of primary assemblies. Primary assemblies never convened in Caen, since section assemblies had already sent delegates to the general assembly.[65]

The general assembly also took steps to increase the size of the departmental force. As reports came in of the creation of volunteer forces in other departments—ranging from the Gironde and the Bouches-du-Rhône to Finistère, Morbihan, and the Ille-et-Vilaine in Brittany—it became clear that Calvados would have to bolster the 400-man vanguard that had left for Evreux on June 22. Thus, on June 27, officials called for more volunteers to march to Paris. The assembly proposed to raise a force of more than 1,000 men, with Caen furnishing 405 volunteers and the other major towns providing the remaining 600 in proportion to their population. Companies were to be formed immediately and made ready to leave for Evreux by July 4. Although people of the countryside would not be asked to join, because of

64. A. D. Calvados, L189 (minutes of June 23, 1793).

65. A. D. Calvados, L189 and L160ter (Assemblée Générale des autorités constituées réunies au chef-lieu du département, 1 juillet 1793–26 juillet 1793).

the upcoming harvest, they could do so if they wished. All volunteers would be paid forty *sous* per day. Once in Evreux, volunteers could terminate their service with one month's notification. The force, whose only objective was to "cooperate with our brothers, the good citizens of Paris, in restoring the freedom of the National Convention," could not be required or ordered to perform any other service. Although the general assembly ostensibly issued this order, only departmental officials signed it.[66]

Again, as with the formation of the vanguard, this appeal for popular support of the patriotic insurrection against the new tyrants in Paris did not receive an enthusiastic response. On July 2, because of resistance to recruitment, the assembly ordered all able-bodied men under the age of fifty who did not have young children to join the force, adding that those who refused would be fined and imprisoned in accordance with the law of April 19, 1793. This order was posted in Caen on July 4, over the objection of the mayor, Le Goupil Duclos. But according to Victor Dufour, most people still refused to enroll.[67]

To overcome this apathy, officials scheduled a public parade and review in Caen for Sunday, July 7. Music, speeches, and a parade of the National Guard regaled a sizable crowd. After the festivities, General Wimpffen, accompanied by members of the insurrectionary assembly, passed before the ranks and called forward those who had volunteered to march to Paris. Seventeen brave Normans stepped forward—a very disappointing response.[68]

One day later, whether because of objections to the illegality of requiring citizens to enroll in the force or because of apprehensions that reluctant "volunteers" would damage troop morale, General Wimpffen, with the approval of the assembly, rescinded the order constraining all able-bodied citizens to join the force. All those whose health or business might impede their wholehearted participation in the campaign could retire, as could those who simply regretted having joined. Battalion leaders were instructed to dismiss those men whom they considered unfit.[69]

Even if the majority of Calvados citizens refused to believe that the recent

66. A. D. Calvados, L189; *Brochures Normandes: Caen sous la Révolution*, B. M. Caen, Rés. Fn. Br. C980.

67. Lesage (Dufour), 120; see A. C. Caen, I42 (L'Armée Libératrice, mai–juillet 1793) for a copy of the decree.

68. Vaultier, *Souvenirs*, 23–24. Charlotte Corday, a native of Caen, is reported to have been in attendance on this occasion, and it has been suggested that it was this pathetic response to the federalists' call to arms that convinced her to go to Paris and do her own part in combating the anarchists.

69. A. D. Calvados, L160ter (minutes of July 8, 1793).

events in Paris posed a threat to their life and liberty, the members of the general assembly remained convinced of the rectitude of their actions. Early in June, letters demanding a protest of the proscriptions had arrived from many departments, giving the impression of nationwide support for a march to the capital. Most of these departments, of course, took no further action, but this would not be apparent to authorities in Caen until much later.

A more important factor in encouraging the insurrectionary attitude of the general assembly was the almost continuous stream of proscribed deputies into Caen in the weeks after June 8. Every two or three days, a new Girondin face appeared in town. By mid-July, at least eighteen deputies had reached Caen, and most remained there until the end of the month. The first to arrive were Henry-Larivière and Gorsas, who attended the evening session on June 9. Three days later, François Buzot, Jean Baptiste Salles, and Denis Toussaint Lesage arrived, followed on June 15 by Barbaroux, Bergoeing, J. P. Duval, and J. C. G. Lahaye. Gabriel de Cussy, who may have encouraged his colleagues to choose Caen as a refuge, reached Caen on June 18 and announced the imminent arrival of several more. The rest were somewhat tardy, but Guadet and Louvet appeared on June 26, Pétion on June 28, Lanjuinais on June 30, and Kervélégan on July 2. E. Mollevaut, former president of the Commission of Twelve, arrived on July 4, and Gaspard Severin Duchâtel straggled in six days later.[70]

Vaultier discounts the influence of these deputies on the atmosphere in Caen, insisting that they kept to themselves and did not attempt to incite the population. Certainly, the miserable turnout on July 7 for the volunteer force indicates that their presence was not profoundly felt. But most other evidence suggests that the deputies were fairly active during their stay, even if their efforts did not produce an outpouring of support. J.-B. Renée noted in his recollections of the Revolution that "the arrival of these representatives, the eloquence of most of them, and principally that of Buzot, the famous lawyer from Evreux, and of Barbaroux, the young and brilliant

70. A. D. Calvados, L189. Vaultier lists four other deputies (Boutidoux, Giroust, Valady, and Meillan) but excludes Duval, Lahaye, and Lanjuinais. Boutidoux did reach Caen but was a former *constituant,* not a *conventionnel.* Mancel, in his notes to Vaultier's memoirs, disputes the presence of Giroust, Valady, and Meillan. Vaultier, however, claims to have become personally acquainted with Valady, and it would seem reasonable to accept his word in at least this case. The official *procès-verbal* records the arrival of Guadet on June 26 "with several of his colleagues," and it is possible that the four deputies mentioned by Vaultier arrived in this group. Louvet is mentioned by name later in the June 26 minutes. See Vaultier, *Souvenirs,* 18, 63, 208–209.

Marseille orator, redoubled the ardor of the *fédérés*."[71] Nearly all of the fugitive deputies did address the general assembly, and several appeared in that forum on more than one occasion.

The reasons that the deputies chose Caen as their refuge are probably several. Vaultier suggests that de Cussy urged this option upon his colleagues, and that is certainly possible.[72] It is also clear that after the arrival of the Caen commissioners in Paris on June 2, the Girondin deputies believed that considerable support for their cause existed in Caen. Over the past eight months, the Calvados authorities had been extremely vocal in their calls for an end to factionalism and for respect for the Convention. The reaffirmation of these sentiments by the June delegation made Caen a more promising haven than, say, Rouen. Caen was reasonably close to Paris—an easy two-day journey—and near the sea, should more drastic flight become necessary (though it is clear that very few of the deputies seriously considered this option). The deputies sought, more than their own personal safety, a base from which they could continue their fight against the Montagnards and the centralist tendencies fostered in Paris. Twice in the past six months—first in March and again in June—the Parisian presses of Gorsas and other moderate journalists had been attacked and ransacked. The proscribed deputies and their supporters needed a hospitable location from which they could publicize their opinions and appeal for help.

This they found in Caen. The town warmly welcomed the deputies, and the authorities put at their disposal the Hôtel de l'Intendance for the duration of their stay. On June 28, the general assembly even voted that each *conventionnel* in Caen be paid from the departmental treasury his usual monthly indemnity. Messages from Pétion and Barbaroux to their constituencies were printed and distributed at departmental expense. Buzot arrived in Caen with his own *compte-rendu* of the events of May 27–31, and other deputies brought official papers from the Commission of Twelve. The deputies entrusted these papers to the general assembly for verification and publication. When Gorsas and Guadet delivered particularly stirring speeches to the assembly on June 26, these were ordered printed and circulated. Buzot's appeal for an armed force to be sent to Evreux, delivered to the general assembly on June 21, offers another example of the active efforts of the deputies to encourage resistance to the Montagnard Convention. The mayor, Le

71. Sauvage, "Les Souvenirs de J.-B. Renée," 21.
72. Vaultier, *Souvenirs,* 17.

Goupil Duclos, whose support of the revolt was at most lukewarm, insisted in his later interrogation that he had never aided or consulted the proscribed deputies, that he in fact had hated to see them in Caen and had been convinced that they were misleading good citizens with their speeches and writings.[73]

Further support and encouragement for the Calvados insurrection came from representatives of the Breton departments who were gathering in Rennes. One of the early decisions of the general assembly in Caen had been to consult with other departments regarding the choice of a central town from which their efforts of resistance to oppression could be directed. The assembly named commissioners to visit these departments, and Antoine DeVic and Maurice Renouf la Coudraye, a Caen *juge de paix*, left on June 12 for Morbihan and the Loire-Inférieure. They passed through Rennes on their route toward Nantes, and DeVic wrote back to Caen on June 19 of the decision made by authorities there to form the Central Committee of Resistance to Oppression.[74] A special courier from Rennes delivered DeVic's letter to Caen, bearing an additional announcement that this committee would convene in Caen. Two commissioners from each of the five departments—Finistère, Morbihan, Côtes-du-Nord, Loire-Inférieure, and Ille-et-Vilaine—would shortly depart for Calvados. The general assembly ordered copies of both of these letters sent to the Orne, the Eure, the Manche, and the Seine-Inférieure, hoping that this news might encourage the latter two to lend their support to the insurrection.[75]

The Central Committee began to assemble in Caen during the last week of June. The first to arrive, on June 23, were two delegates from the Mayenne, a department that had not even sent representatives to Rennes. Two commissioners from the Maine-et-Loire arrived on June 26, joined the next day by commissioners from the Côtes-du-Nord. Delegates from the other four departments that had been represented in Rennes arrived in short order. No official record of the Central Committee's meetings exists, but the minutes of the Calvados general assembly indicate that the first session took place on June 28.[76] In addition to the departments already mentioned, the Orne and

73. A. D. Calvados, L189 and L10125 (interrogation of Le Goupil Duclos).
74. A. D. Calvados, L10134 (addresses and proclamations during the federalist revolt).
75. A. D. Calvados, L189. The Central Committee, after it convened in Caen, continued to woo the Seine-Inférieure, but authorities in Rouen persisted in their conviction that it was beyond their authority to declare the department in revolt. The Manche wavered throughout June and July but never became actively involved in the revolt.
76. A. C. Caen, I43 (Mission Lindet, Oudot, DuRoy, et Bonnet).

the Eure sent delegates. The Calvados general assembly named Louis Caille and Samuel Chatry *l'aîné* as its representatives to the committee, thereby bringing to ten the number of departments joining that assembly. Of these, however, only seven truly supported the insurrection. Administrators in the Orne soon withdrew their commitment to the movement, while the Loire-Inférieure and the Maine-et-Loire were absorbed in the battle against the Vendéan rebels.[77]

The convocation of the Central Committee altered somewhat the situation in Caen. That body now took responsibility for propaganda efforts, drafting letters to other departments, proclamations to the nation, and messages to the citizens of Paris. It also undertook to coordinate the forces gathering to march to the capital. Very soon after the committee had first met, word arrived from officials who had remained in Rennes that the Ille-et-Vilaine volunteers would soon arrive in Caen, that the Morbihan troops would leave the next day, and that a battalion from Finistère would depart on July 3. A contingent from the Mayenne was also reportedly in transit.[78] This news certainly inspired greater optimism than did the size of the Calvados force at that time.

Without complete documentation from the Central Committee meetings, it is impossible to say much regarding the committee's internal organization; but the majority of letters and statements that it issued bore the signatures of L. J. Roujoux (a departmental administrator from the Finistère), as president, and Louis Caille, acting as secretary. The most important of the declarations issued by the committee was a twenty-seven-point program outlining the grievances of the federalist rebels and their proposals for the reorganization of political life in Paris. This program was debated in Rennes from June 19 to 23, but it was not officially printed until after the committee had convened in Caen, and it seems certain that it received the approval of departmental representatives there who had not been present in Rennes. Its importance lies in the fact that it represents the views of a region, not just one department, and that it reveals something of the fears and resentments that inspired the federalist revolt.

The declaration was divided into four sections. The first, which addressed the role of Paris in national politics, included the following notable pro-

77. For an account of the federalist activity in the Orne, see Nicolle, "Le Mouvement fédéraliste dans l'Orne en 1793," XIII (1936), 481–512, XIV (1937), 215–33, XV (1938), 12–33, 289–313, 385–410.
78. A. D. Calvados, L10134 (letter dated June 30, 1793).

posals: that a constitutional decree establish a departmental guard for the national assembly; that the proscribed deputies be returned to their functions; that the *comités révolutionnaires* in Paris be abolished; that the sections of Paris no longer be permitted to meet *en permanence;* that the Revolutionary Tribunal be suppressed; that the Commission of Twelve be reinstated; that the assassins of September 2 be prosecuted; and that the Jacobin and Cordelier clubs of Paris be abolished. These proposals would have done away with organizations and measures that became the order of the day during the Year II.

The second section concerned the powers and responsibilities of the National Convention. It suggested that the Convention itself be limited to the role of a legislative assembly; that the Committee of Public Safety be deprived of its dictatorial powers; that the deputies sent on mission to the armies and the departments be recalled to their posts in Paris; and that the Executive Council be given sufficient authority to run the government.

Turning to issues of finance and the treasury, section three demanded that a commission formed of capable men be charged with examining the accounts of former ministers and the Commune of Paris, researching the source of the huge fortunes that had blossomed since August 10, 1792, and restoring order to national finances; that no more funds be advanced to the municipality of Paris from public funds and that Paris be required to pay its back debts; and that there be no more *assignats* created and that a means be found to diminish the number in circulation.

A final section addressed the need for a constitution and for a renewed commitment to national unity. It called for a constitution to be issued within two months after the Convention had regained its liberty; for the laws that had not been freely enacted to be submitted for debate once again; and for primary assemblies to be convened to elect new legislators if the divisions and animosities within the Convention could not be overcome. A postscripted article demanded the prompt reorganization of the Paris National Guard, with care taken to appoint officers who had not been leaders on May 31.[79] (Appendix I gives a complete list of the Central Committee's demands.)

This petition is noteworthy for several reasons. Much of what it expresses—the suspicion of the municipality of Paris, the demand that the in-

---

79. *Brochures Normandes: Caen sous la Révolution,* B. M. Caen, Rés. Fn. Br. B2634. See also Jeanne Grall, "La France au lendemain du 31 mai 1793," *Bulletin de la Société des Antiquaires de Normandie,* LV (1959–60), 513–24, for a summary of this declaration.

tegrity of the Convention be respected, and the wish that a constitution be quickly prepared—is reminiscent of previous statements from Calvados. The demands for suppression of the revolutionary committees, the section assemblies, and the two most radical Paris clubs show a strong preference for "representative" democracy, a political vision that had already triumphed in Caen a year and a half earlier. But there are new elements here as well, such as the call for abolition of the Jacobin club, the demand that the powers of the Committee of Public Safety be limited, and the insistence that representatives on mission be recalled. Most interesting of all is section three, which proposes an investigation of recently created private fortunes, an end to the use of national funds for Parisian expenses, and a reduction in the circulation of *assignats*. These are economic issues, not explicitly political issues, and they give an indication of the social background of the federalist rebels. They did not belong to the popular classes, the laboring poor, the sansculottes—no demand is made for more stringent enforcement of the *maximum*. These were wealthy landowners and merchants, exasperated with the inflation and the worthless *assignats*. They were suspicious of fortunes that had been made during the Revolution, and they were tired of paying taxes for the support of Paris radicals.

This last grievance, in particular, is consistent with previous Calvados protests and with the general resentment of the undue influence of the capital. In another declaration of its objectives, the Central Committee made clear that it intended to punish the usurpers in Paris. It accused them of nepotism and corruption; of bungling the war effort; of supporting Pache, who was monopolizing grain supplies at the expense of the departments; of insulting public justice in the trial of Marat; and of supporting the power of Paris.[80]

Yet for the citizens of Paris, the officials gathered in Caen expressed nothing but compassion. In one of its final proclamations, addressed to all Frenchmen, the Central Committee stressed the peaceful intentions of the troops headed toward the capital but issued a subtle warning:

The departmental force that is progressing toward Paris does not go in search of Enemies in order to fight them; it goes to fraternize with the Parisians, it goes to make an impression on the Factious elements by its firm and tranquil countenance; it goes to strengthen the tottering statue of Liberty. Citizens, who will see pass within your walls, into your Hamlets, these friendly Armies, fraternize with them: do not

80. A. C. Caen, I36 (Insurrection et actes des administrations insurgées, mai–juillet 1793).

allow bloodthirsty Monsters to settle amongst you, with the aim of stopping those Armies in their march: do not allow mobs to form at the dismal sound of the tocsin; mingled in amongst our Enemies, we will not be able to distinguish you.[81]

The arrival of the Central Committee in Caen brought a reorganization of the Calvados general assembly. Up to this point, the assembly had been a rather ad hoc organization dominated by departmental and district officials, but now it became a more formal body, incorporating the cantonal delegates who arrived at the end of June. On July 1, to permit departmental administrators to return to their normal duties, the assembly elected new officers and appointed new committees. Chaix-d'Estanges, the former vicar of Fauchet and now curé of the parish Saint-Etienne, was elected president. As vice-president the assembly chose Charles Debaudre, a priest from Bayeux who may also have been a supporter of Fauchet.[82] Dom Mauger, one of the nine commissioners to Paris, became *procureur-syndic* until that position was abolished as superfluous. Nicolas Marie Quetil de la Poterie, a clerk for the department and president of the section Union in Caen, was elected secretary; Mariette, another priest from Bayeux, was chosen as his assistant. It is curious that at least three of these five officers, and possibly Dom Mauger, were clergymen who had been in some fashion affiliated with the deputy Claude Fauchet.[83]

The newly constituted general assembly issued the order threatening jail terms for those who refused to join the departmental force. On July 1, it decreed that departmental administrators who failed to appear at their posts within three days would be declared traitors to the cause, denied their salaries, and replaced.[84] The assembly further attempted to consolidate its power and generate popular support for its cause by calling for the confiscation of

81. A. D. Calvados, L10135 (documents pertaining to federalism). This declaration was issued on July 5, as the departmental forces were preparing to leave Caen for Evreux.

82. Debaudre arrived as a delegate to the General Assembly on June 25. He is identified as a priest by Hufton, *Bayeux in the Late Eighteenth Century*, 197.

83. This is interesting in light of Olwen Hufton's claim that Fauchet, during his brief time in Calvados, attempted to carve out his own local power base. This is clearly supported in the religious sphere by Fauchet's ordainment of several hundred allegedly ill-prepared priests in Calvados. But while the bishop was certainly active in political affairs, there is little evidence of a conscious effort to place his supporters in political office. Hufton describes Chaix as Fauchet's mouthpiece in the Caen Jacobin club, which is entirely possible, and Fauchet was apparently on good terms with Louis Caille and Bougon-Longrais. This hardly constitutes a power base, however, and I would not describe Fauchet as the dominant figure in Calvados politics. Caille and Bougon, themselves, were at least as ambitious as the bishop. See Hufton, *Bayeux in the Late Eighteenth Century*, 180–95.

84. A. D. Calvados, L160ter.

newspapers opposed to the principles of the insurrection and by issuing its own journal, the *Bulletin des Autorités Constituées*. Nine issues of the *Bulletin* appeared between June 25 and July 17, with 1,500 copies of each issue printed in Caen and distributed throughout the department. The journal summarized the proceedings of the general assembly, recorded news from Paris, and printed addresses from other towns and departments. Its first issue reported that sixty-nine departments supported the protest movement. The journal gave the most optimistic account possible of resistance to Paris in an attempt to encourage support within the department and counter the Montagnard propaganda emanating from the capital.[85]

After July 1, departmental officials played a much smaller role in the general assembly, perhaps worried by the recent decrees of dubious legality but perhaps also chastened by the Seine-Inférieure's suggestion that they had exceeded their authority by declaring the department in a state of insurrection. Each new committee included one departmental official, but the administrators could now argue with some justification (and they did precisely this after the revolt had collapsed) that the general assembly reflected the wishes of the people through the delegates they had chosen in primary assemblies. It is important to remember, however, that primary assemblies never convened in Caen, at least not until after the revolt.

The departmental directory now began to meet more frequently in order to deal with affairs that had gone largely unattended since the first of June. But the administration was understaffed, since many clerks had apparently been persuaded by the arguments of elected officials and had left for Evreux with the departmental force. The leaders of the council were also absent. Lenormand, Lévêque, Mesnil, each of them a director, and Bougon-Longrais, the *procureur-général-syndic*, had left for Evreux with the departmental forces, along with the administrator Thiboult.

Mindful of the need for leadership in Caen, the general assembly ordered Lévêque and Bougon to return to their administrative duties on June 27, "considering that much business remains stagnant at a time when it is essential not to add to the number of malcontents." The general assembly sent another appeal to Lévêque on July 1, insisting that "the sections, the dragoons of Calvados, the carabots, the popular societies, all of your constitu-

85. A. C. Caen, I37 (*Bulletin des autorités constituées*, vols. 2–9, juin–juillet 1793). The missing copy can be found in B. M. Caen, Rés. Fn. B402. All nine issues were collected, edited, and published by Charles Renard in 1875. The issues are numbered but not generally dated, and the precise date of publication is therefore difficult to ascertain.

ents are clamoring for your presence." The next day, Benard, secretary of the department, sent Lévêque a list of the new general assembly officers and pleaded, "Come to our aid, the sections are mutinying. We are in need of prudence and foresight. Even to the degree that one possesses the one and the other, it remains to be feared that we will not be able to preserve the peace."[86]

Lévêque and Bougon, however, considered their efforts more urgently needed in Evreux, where they and their colleagues were struggling to maintain the wavering support of the Eure administration. They refused to return to Caen, and some people in Caen endorsed that decision. Chatry *l'aîné* wrote to Lévêque on July 6 that although the commmissioners' talents would be of greater use in Caen, to return at that difficult time would serve as a pretext for "les malveillants" to prevent other citizens from marching to Paris. These types had done all they could in recent days to do precisely that, but happily without much success, wrote Chatry.

That the "malcontents" and "troublemakers" ultimately prevailed is amply evidenced by the seventeen volunteers who stepped forward for the public inspection on July 7. This miserable demonstration, however, was not reported to the commissioners in Evreux. On the contrary, Charles Cailly, a member of the general assembly correspondence committee, wrote to the civil commissioners in Evreux on July 8 that the previous day's recruitment effort had been a complete success: "Yesterday's maneuvers of the Caen national guard have produced the most favorable effect. There is a constant procession of citizens coming forward to join. There is reason to hope that the battalion will be more than full." Cailly went on to report, erroneously, that Rouen now supported the insurrection, a development that would have alleviated the pressing grain situation. Authorities had already been forced to release military supplies in order to feed the population of Caen. Cailly also noted that Louis Caille had departed for Evreux, with Dom Mauger replacing him on the Central Committee of Resistance to Oppression.[87]

The arrival in Evreux of contingents from other departments soon reinforced for the Calvados commissioners the optimism engendered by Cailly's misleading letter. On July 3, a battalion from the Ille-et-Vilaine reached Caen and proceeded to Evreux. The Morbihan contingent arrived in Caen

86. A. D. Calvados, L10276.
87. *Ibid.*

on July 8, followed the next day by a company of 200 from the Mayenne. Reinforcing these troops were two regiments of cavalry from the army of the 14th Division—the dragoons of the Manche and the chasseurs of La Bretèche—fortuitously under the command of Wimpffen. All of these had congregated in or near Evreux by July 10. Vaultier estimated their total number at 1,900—400 cavalry, 900 Breton troops, and 600 volunteers from the Eure and Calvados.[88]

The arrival of these troops in Evreux presented problems along with promise. They had to be housed and fed, and the populace of the town showed signs of growing restive and disenchanted with the movement. This attitude worried the Eure administrators, whose resolve may have been maintained only by the enthusiasm of the Calvados commissioners. Jean Capdeville, one of Garat's agents in the departments, wrote in a report that Bougon-Longrais presided over the administrative assembly in Evreux. Capdeville, sent with copies of the new constitution, addressed the assembly and tried to explain that the Convention was working diligently and had drafted a constitution that would unite the country. But Bougon and Lenormand dominated the proceedings and persuaded the officials to arrest Capdeville and send him to Caen. Two Eure administrators spoke to the agent later, expressing their regret at the actions of the assembly, which they claimed to be under the sway of the Calvados commissioners.[89]

Lack of military leadership was another grievous problem for the insurrectionary force. On July 10, urgent letters went from both Lévêque and the military committee in Evreux to General Wimpffen, who remained in Caen. Lévêque wrote that there existed neither harmony nor a plan of defense in Evreux: "Send to us, therefore, in the name of God, the one and the other; or provisionally authorize someone, with sufficient military talents, who could direct the military operations. Moreover, your presence is indispensable in order to organize the public forces that are here." The committee's letter emphatically seconded Lévêque's plea: "We have men, but without a leader. Much courage, but nothing to direct it. If you delay any longer to

---

88. A. D. Calvados, L189; Vaultier, *Souvenirs*, 19, 61. Many estimates made at the time were wildly inaccurate, ranging from a low of five hundred to a high of five thousand. Vaultier's figure is supported by both the deputy Louvet and the representative on mission Lindet. Volunteers from the Finistère, numbering several hundred, did not reach Caen until July 13 and never went on to Evreux.

89. Caron, *Rapports des Agents du Ministre de l'Intérieur*, I, 180–190. See also Léon Dubreuil, "Evreux au temps du fédéralisme," *Révolution Française*, LXXVIII (1925), 322–28.

send someone who can conduct in a prudent and active manner the military operations, the goal will be missed." [90]

Wimpffen responded immediately by sending General Joseph Puisaye to command the troops in Evreux. Puisaye arrived on July 10 and within two days had prepared to mobilize his forces. Given the crumbling of what little popular support had once existed in Caen, plus the disorganization and confusion rampant in Evreux, it is hardly surprising that the march of the federalist forces toward Paris would culminate quickly in a total fiasco.

On arriving in Evreux, Puisaye consulted with the Calvados commissioners, and they agreed on the need to secure Vernon, strategically located on the route to Paris. Reports had come in that the Convention was sending Parisian battalions to repel the departmental forces, and Vernon would be a vital link in the defense against such a charge. Word had also been received that Bonnet de Meautry, the lone Calvados deputy who sat with the Mountain, had been sent on mission to undermine the revolt. On July 7, Lenormand forwarded news to Caen of six other "maratistes," allegedly posing as haberdashers and peddlers, on their way to Normandy under orders of the Executive Council. He provided more detailed descriptions for two of these imposters. The first, Dufour, aged between thirty and thirty-five, stood five feet three inches tall, had black hair and a long nose, and was pockmarked and toothless. The other, named Le Cinque, was big and around thirty years of age. Lenormand urged renewed vigilance so that these troublemakers might be apprehended. [91]

Puisaye, assisted by Lieutenant Colonel LeRoy of the Calvados 6th Battalion, decided to gather his forces in Pacy-sur-Eure on July 12, electing to lay over one night before moving on to Vernon the following day. Colonel Alexandre Puisaye (no relation to the general) headed one of the contingents, along with Lévêque. LeRoy, of course, commanded his battalion, and Bougon and Caille led the largest segment of the departmental forces. The

90. A. D. Calvados, L10136 (documents pertaining to federalism). There is some irony in the phrasing of the committee's plea. In April, after Wimpffen's assignment to Calvados had been unofficially confirmed but before steps had been taken for the actual creation of the Cherbourg army, the department complained to the Convention that it now had a general, but no men for him to lead.

91. A. D. Calvados, L10125 (documents pertaining to federalism). This carton contains two letters, among other documents, the first of which, dated July 5, was anonymous and unaddressed. The second letter, sent by Lenormand to Caen, paraphrased the information contained in the first, except that Lenormand embellished the descriptions somewhat. Dufour, in addition to being pockmarked and toothless, became skinny, ugly, and dirty. And Lenormand had somehow learned that Le Cinque was not only big but also married and jealous!

troops began their march at 11:00 A.M. on July 13 and within a short distance encountered the Parisian lines. According to Puisaye's report, he sent out a herald and trumpet to deliver a message, and the Parisians opened fire. Vaultier, who had volunteered for the Caen contingent, recorded a different version of the first encounter. In his account, the troops lay bivouacked in a field near the château of Brécourt when a round of fire whistled through the trees over their heads. Only the apples suffered.

Which version one chooses to accept is of little consequence. Puisaye's bestows more honor on himself and his troops; Vaultier's adds a touch of comedy. They agree, however, on the events that followed. A few more cannon shots rang out before both sides turned on their heels and beat a hasty retreat, the Calvados volunteers once again in the vanguard! Puisaye claimed that he tried to rally his troops to retake Pacy-sur-Eure but that only the 6th Battalion responded, hardly enough for a counterattack. The troops retreated to Evreux, but Puisaye despaired of holding even that position. Wishing to avoid bloodshed and pillage, he ordered a retreat to Lisieux. Only on reaching Lisieux, on July 17, did Puisaye learn that the Mayenne battalion and the Ille-et-Vilaine troops had been willing to stand and fight. The Breton soldiers, in fact, expressed considerable disgust at the lack of discipline among the Norman volunteers. Yet one can understand the reaction of the volunteers, who had repeatedly been told that they were on their way to the capital to "fraternize" with the Parisians. Apparently only the generals and the Calvados civil commissioners realized that some kind of battle was likely to occur. And when the battle came, one participant recalled, Bougon-Longrais in particular, along with Puisaye, favored a full retreat.[92]

The July 17 issue of the *Bulletin des Autorités Constituées* described the Vernon fiasco as "one of those accidents so common at the beginning of a campaign." Although leaders of the force had thought it prudent to retreat to Lisieux, they would undoubtedly soon be back in Evreux.[93] Such was not to be the case. General Wimpffen met the retreating force in Lisieux and immediately conferred with the Calvados civil commissioners. On July 18, he sent a letter to the general assembly in Caen conveying the commissioners' sentiments that a policy of conciliation and negotiation should now

92. Vaultier, *Souvenirs*, 22–25; *Brochures Normandes: Caen sous la Révolution*, B. M. Caen, Rés. Fn. Br. C315–368 (Puisaye's report to the general assembly in Caen); René Norbert Sauvage (ed.), *Le Fédéralisme en Normandie: Journal du quartier-maître du 6ᵉ bataillon bis des volontaires du Calvados* (Caen, 1909), 61–67.
93. A. C. Caen, I37 (*Bulletin des autorités constituées*, no. 9).

be pursued. The Breton battalions' clearly stated intention to return to their departments may have assisted the commissioners in reaching that conclusion. Wimpffen, for his part, felt that the Central Committee of Resistance to Oppression should make the final decision, but he reaffirmed his commitment to defend the region with all the means at his disposal.[94]

Wimpffen's ambivalence throughout the revolt was undeniably an important reason for its ultimate failure. The general had been enthusiastic at the start—when called to Paris by the minister of war on June 23, he had replied that he would come to the capital only at the head of sixty thousand Normans. But his actions as commander of the federalist forces did not match his rhetoric. Vaultier blamed Wimpffen's procrastination for the poor turnout of volunteers at the July 7 ceremony, and it is hard to understand why the general did not go himself to Evreux to take charge of the troops. Perhaps he recognized the hopelessness of their cause. After the force had retreated to Lisieux, Wimpffen still made little effort to salvage the situation. Instead, he proposed to the fugitive deputies that they negotiate with England and perhaps seek refuge there. Louvet and several other deputies had felt all along that Wimpffen's sympathies lay with the royalists, probably an accurate appraisal.[95]

In Caen, a reassessment of the situation now took place. Two undated procès-verbaux suggest that support for the revolt within the Jacobin club had dissipated by this date. As early as mid-June, the Jacobin club, at that time presided over by the district administrator Henri Michel Saillenfest, had warned the departmental administration of the danger that the Parisians might misconstrue the intentions of the "fédérés" marching to Paris. The club suggested that a circular be prepared to make clear that the Norman volunteers wished only to fraternize with their Parisian brothers, a gesture that the general assembly did indeed make shortly thereafter.[96]

By July, open dissension had erupted within the club regarding the role of the departmental force. Four sheets of handwritten minutes are all we have to reveal the attitudes of club members during this period, but they are illuminating. These notes record the proceedings of two Jacobin club meetings during the first week of July. At the first meeting, a member raised the

94. A. D. Calvados, L10136 (letter of July 18, 1793); Vaultier, Souvenirs, 26–27.
95. See the Bulletin des autorités constituées, no. 1, B. M. Caen, Rés. Fn. B402, for Wimpffen's letter to Paris; and Vaultier, Souvenirs, 33–41, for excerpts from Louvet's memoirs.
96. A. D. Calvados, L10134 (letter of June 16, 1793).

complaint that in recent days, decisions had been taken that ran counter to the views of a majority of the members. The minutes do not identify those decisions; but in response to the complaint, the club voted to nullify the actions of the previous day and henceforth to hold at least three *public* meetings per week. The minutes give the impression that those public meetings would reevaluate club positions taken in recent weeks.

The next day, a noisy club meeting resumed this discussion, with Louis Caille and Chaix-d'Estanges now in attendance. Chaix accused Charles Pierre Marie Aubin, the current club secretary, of having urged people to boycott the march on Paris. Aubin defended himself, arguing that an armed march on Paris would be the equivalent of fratricide. But Chaix and Caille carried the day. The meeting deteriorated into recriminations against Marat and the Mountain, but not before an oath of loyalty to the revolt had been sworn, with those refusing the oath to be expelled from the club.[97]

The Jacobin club made no public declaration when the revolt began to disintegrate later in July (at least, no record of one exists), but it is clear that two factions had developed within the club: one group opposed to the march on Paris, led by Aubin, François Outin, Jacques Caroger, and Louis Guillaume Harfort, all of whom would be named local officials after the revolt collapsed, and another group, dominant in June and early July, led by Louis Caille and Chaix-d'Estanges.

On July 19, volunteers arrived in Caen from the town of Vire, joining the Finistère battalion that had arrived earlier in the week. But this was not enough to counter the serious misgivings that now began to plague even the two insurrectionary assemblies. On July 20, the Central Committee proposed that primary assemblies be called to consider the new constitution. Perhaps the committee members hoped that the people would reject it, but only weeks before, the committee had forbidden even the publication of this document. The Calvados general assembly hesitated to call primary assemblies and decided instead to consult the Caen sections as to whether the sections should discuss the constitution or reject it out of hand. Delegates from the general assembly addressed the sections on the following day, in each case taking great pains to emphasize that the assembly had always acted on the express wishes of the people. One cannot avoid the impression that the administrators were belatedly trying to remove responsibility from their

97. A. C. Caen, I275 (Société Populaire).

own shoulders. Indeed, the general assembly requested copies of the sections' *procès-verbaux* in order to show that it had only acted on behalf of its constituency.

The sections of Caen no longer unanimously supported the insurrection, as they had on June 8. Three of the five sections quickly voted an end to their state of insurrection and demanded distribution of the constitution. The section Civisme went so far as to recall its delegates to the general assembly. The two sections that decided to maintain their resistance were the section Union, dominated by the eloquent Chaix-d'Estanges, now president of the general assembly; and the section Liberté, the wealthiest section in Caen, which housed within its limits the majority of Caen's merchants and *haute-bourgeoisie*. Benard's letter to Lévêque had suggested that support for the insurrection was seriously breaking down as early as the first week of July, but these votes marked the first overt opposition to the march on Paris among the sections of Caen.[98]

On the days on which the sections deliberated, July 20 and 21, the *procureur* and the mayor of Caen, DeVic and Le Goupil Duclos, urged the municipal council to consider the new constitution. Both delivered impassioned speeches defending the pure intentions of those who had at first supported revolt but arguing that the time had come for unity and that the new constitution would provide a rallying point for all Frenchmen.[99]

Despite these voices of moderation and conciliation, no consensus could be reached in the general assembly. It tabled Le Goupil's proposal that a mediator be sent to Paris, as well as a motion for the release of Romme and Prieur, who had been held in isolation in the Château since June 13. The general assembly's resolve to maintain its insurrectionary stance may have been weakened, however, by the increasingly precarious grain supply in the Caen market. On July 23, armed soldiers removed from the meeting hall an unruly crowd demanding grain, and the assembly prudently closed the market for that day. The people of Caen, so long passive in the face of exhortations to revolt, were now growing restive.

By this time, volunteers from the departmental force were returning to town, bringing stories of a Parisian army intent on pillaging Caen and guillotining 1,400 people (the precise figure no doubt lent some veracity to this tale). On July 24, Wimpffen appeared before the assembly to discuss the

98. A. C. Caen, I45 (Rétractations de l'insurrection, juillet 1793).
99. A. C. Caen, D2.

situation. After hearing the general, several members proposed that the city be declared in a state of siege, with Wimpffen in charge of preparing a reasonable defense. The motion passed, and tents for the troops began to go up on the plain of Ivry, straddling the road to Paris.

Happily, this new hysteria proved short-lived. On that same day, the Central Committee issued orders to the Breton battalions for an immediate departure to Rennes, where the committee would reconvene. In addition, local authorities in Caen one by one retracted their support of the insurrection. The minister of the interior, Garat, had just sent a decree promising clemency to those administrators who retracted their declarations of insurrection within three days. The first to do so were the Caen district officials, claiming that they did not seek to profit by the amnesty but hoped to avert the disastrous consequences of a siege. The municipal councillors soon followed suit, putting their signatures to a statement almost identical to the mayor's speech of July 21.

The next day, July 25, the general assembly summoned both the municipal and district councils. Finding itself isolated and exposed by virtue of those councils' retractions, the assembly denounced them for their cowardly and traitorous acts. Council members defended themselves in various ways. Le Goupil Duclos ignominiously suggested that the municipality had retracted because of "the insidious pressure and influence of the district," which had not even consulted Louis Caille! Two district administrators offered only feeble excuses, but the assembly could do little to punish them. Both Caille and Chaix-d'Estanges gave accounts of their conduct and received the approbation of those present, after which the assembly moved that the sections of Caen be convoked to freely decide on a course of action.[100]

There is no record of the sections' deliberations, but on July 26, both the general assembly and the united administrative and judicial corps of Calvados issued formal retractions of their insurrectionary declarations. Both statements stressed that the resistance to Paris and the Convention had been the mandate of the people, that the people's concern had been for the liberty and unity of the nation, but that since the new constitution promised a sound basis for a free and republican government, the time had come for an end to dissension. Only twenty signatures appear on the general assembly's retraction, evidence that many of the nearly fifty delegates who had arrived in late June had long since returned to their homes. Fifty-five judges and ad-

100. A. D. Calvados, L189, L160ter, L387, and L10135; A. C. Caen, D2.

ministrators signed a separate retraction. The Caen district officials signed only their own statement.[101]

With this, the federalist revolt in Calvados came to an end. The Central Committee of Resistance to Oppression and the Breton battalions left for Rennes. The fugitive Girondin deputies, disguised as volunteers, accompanied them. On July 29, Romme and Prieur emerged from the Château, Romme having completed during his detention the revolutionary calendar, perhaps the most lasting product of the revolt. Several of the compromised local officials went into hiding in the Calvados countryside. For most of the people of Caen, however, nothing remained but to wait for the representatives on mission and their "army of pacification."

The lack of popular support for a protest directed against Paris and the Montagnard Convention doomed the revolt in Calvados to failure from the beginning. That reality plagued the federalist movement not only in Caen but in Bordeaux and Marseille as well. Departmental administrators instigated the revolt in Calvados and remained its staunchest partisans throughout June and July. A departmental official, René Lenormand, led the mission to Paris in early June. Departmental officials dominated the general assembly during the crucial weeks in which the revolt developed. And when the focus of the revolt shifted to Evreux, Calvados departmental administrators took full responsibility for the coordination of the volunteer forces and the preparation of a march on Paris.

In many ways, the revolt in Calvados was an exercise in deception and self-delusion. Samuel Chatry helped to instigate resistance with a speech that he insisted be delivered anonymously. Section assemblies convened late at night on June 8, and the crucial general meeting of June 9 began at 4:00 A.M., a most inhospitable hour. Those who favored the declaration of insurrection and the arrest of Romme and Prieur shouted down the reasoned objections of Tirel and Fleury, threatening them with arrest as traitors. Others who would later oppose the revolt, such as Antoine DeVic and Mayor Le Goupil Duclos, were absent from that meeting. Leaders of the revolt led volunteers for the departmental force to believe that they marched to Paris only to fraternize with the Parisians, a replay of the 1790 festival in which *fédérés* from the provinces gathered in the capital to celebrate the fall of the Bastille. The

101. A. D. Calvados, L189, L160ter.

first shots fired on July 13 disabused the volunteers of that naive notion, and the revolt promptly crumbled.

The failure of the revolt, then, can largely be explained by its lack of popular support. A secondary factor was its complete disorganization. The ostensible leader of the march on Paris, General Wimpffen—a reluctant commander at best—would probably have been more comfortable in a plot to restore the monarchy than in a movement to defend a moderate republic. Lenormand, Lévêque, and Bougon-Longrais possessed little military acumen and were ill prepared to cope with the problems of supply, morale, and discipline that beset the rebel troops. It is notable, though, that local leaders, and not the fugitive Girondin deputies, took responsibility for leading the march to Paris. This underscores the regional grievances that constituted such a large part of the motivation for this insurrection.

But why, if popular support was weak, did resistance in Caen progress as far as it did? This question can best be answered by a brief comparison of the situation in Limoges with that in Caen. The Haute-Vienne administrators, too, showed an inclination in early June to join with other departments in protesting the proscription of the Girondin deputies. The factors that turned them away from revolt simply did not exist in Caen. The Montagnards had no influential advocate in Caen comparable to Bishop Gay-Vernon in Limoges. The bishop, and Xavier Audouin as well, bombarded Limoges with letters assuring the people that Paris remained calm and that May 31 had been a victory for liberty and equality. Bonnet de Meautry, the Calvados deputy who sat with the Montagnards, did not enjoy a broad base of support in his home town and, moreover, did not correspond diligently with his constituents. Instead, it was Lomont, Doulcet, and de Cussy, supporters of the Girondins, who kept the people of Caen informed of developments in Paris and exhorted them to rise in protest.

As already noted, the letters of Gay-Vernon alone would not have turned the Haute-Vienne away from the federalist movement. The strength of the Limoges Jacobin club, along with the activism of the municipal council, guaranteed that the bishop's reports would not fall on deaf ears. The Jacobin club in Caen had long since broken ties with the Paris Jacobins and no longer represented a potent force in Caen politics. In any case, the club followed the leadership of Louis Caille, who, by virtue of his eloquence and his ties to the deputies Fauchet and Barbaroux, prevailed in July over dissident voices within the club. Those who spoke against the march to Paris—Aubin,

Outin, and Caroger—could boast of no ties to national figures, nor did they hold official positions. As for the other popular group in Caen, the Carabot club, we know little about its membership. At no time in 1793, however, did the club appear in an adversarial relationship to local authorities, and it supported the revolt from start to finish. Evidence suggests that the Caen municipal and district councils did not enthusiastically support the revolt, but both appeared intimidated by departmental officials (as well as by Caille and Chaix-d'Estanges), even when it became clear that the revolt had failed. In sum, no organized group, either official or popular, opposed the decisions of the Calvados departmental administration.

The Vendée revolt, which may have deterred Haute-Vienne administrators from joining in resistance to Paris, could be more easily ignored by officials in Calvados. To Calvados, the Vendéan rebels did not pose an immediate threat. They did threaten the Haute-Vienne, whose source of grain stood jeopardized as the rebels moved south toward Poitiers. The Haute-Vienne sent roughly two thousand soldiers to battle the counterrevolution in the west, whereas the sole Calvados battalion sent to the Vendée returned in June, disgusted by the lack of discipline displayed by the Parisian "brigands" and prepared to join the volunteers in Evreux.

Finally, the demands of the Central Committee of Resistance to Oppression make it clear that more was at stake in June, 1793, than the proscription of the Girondin deputies. The Haute-Vienne stood dependent on the central government for grain supplies and hospital funds. Calvados and the Breton departments, by contrast, had blockaded Paris, attempting to deprive the capital of grain. They denounced the domination of Paris in national affairs and complained about inequitable taxes and inflationary *assignats*. By joining the federalist revolt, Calvados asserted its regional independence and protested the excesses of centralized government.

Five

Repression and Reorganization

Repression of the federalist revolts marked the beginning of the Terror in revolutionary France. The severity of repression varied from department to department, just as the revolutionary tribunals, in the long term, dispensed their cruel justice in selective fashion. In Lyon, where resistance to the Convention continued until October, the representatives on mission Jean Marie Collot d'Herbois and Joseph Fouché oversaw the execution of nearly 2,000 people between November, 1793, and April, 1794. The Revolutionary Commission in Toulon sentenced 282 people to death from December, 1793, through January, 1794, and roughly 800 people were shot without trial after the royalist revolt in that city collapsed. Repression also struck hard in the Finistère (destination of the Girondin deputies who fled Caen in late July), with departmental administrators the principal victims of the guillotine. For the most part, however, the repression was moderate, and few federalists paid for their mistakes with their lives. In Bordeaux, despite the Military Commission's reputation for vindictiveness, reprisals for federalist actions proved restrained. Just over 300 people died on the guillotine, and while many of these were wealthy lawyers, merchants, and professionals, the Military Commission did not single out leaders of the revolt for vengeance. Even fewer were executed in Marseille, where local Jacobins spared a number of wealthy merchants eventually brought to justice by representatives on mission. The Revolutionary Tribunal in Marseille sentenced

286 people to death between August, 1793, and April, 1794. Nowhere, however, did the repression of federalism adopt as mild a tone as in Caen. Only two federalists were executed, neither of them solely for his role in the revolt, and most escaped even the imprisonment suffered by a number of Calvados officials.[1]

In the late summer and fall of 1793, the necessity of rallying the protesting departments to the National Convention was as important a task as punishing those who had rebelled. For this reason, the Committee of Public Safety adopted the attitude that the citizenry was largely blameless for its reluctant participation in the revolt: administrators had intentionally misled those who joined departmental forces in Caen, Bordeaux, and Marseille. The new constitution would demonstrate to all Frenchmen that the Convention continued to deliberate freely, no longer plagued by the factionalism and bickering that had troubled its sessions before May 31. Punishment would be reserved for those administrators who had neglected their responsibilities and exceeded their authority by calling for revolt. The Convention gave even those officials an opportunity to retract their insurrectionary declarations, and those who did so at an early date were often allowed to retain their positions. Representatives on mission dismissed others and ordered the arrest of some. But very few came to trial before revolutionary tribunals.

Punishment and replacement of individual officials soon gave way to more fundamental reorganization. Nationwide, roughly two-thirds of the departmental administrations had protested by letter the proscriptions of June 2, and in those areas where significant resistance had developed, departmental officials had taken the lead. On November 18, 1793 (28 Brumaire II), in order to prevent a recurrence of provincial opposition to the Convention, Jean Nicolas Billaud-Varenne called for a limitation of the powers and political influence of departmental councils. The Convention incorporated this proposal in the law of 14 Frimaire II (December 4, 1793), which suppressed the general councils, presidents, and *procureurs-généraux-syndics*. Only the departmental directories remained intact, with their functions now explic-

---

1. See Donald Greer, *The Incidence of the Terror during the French Revolution* (Cambridge, 1935); R. R. Palmer, *Twelve Who Ruled: The Year of the Terror in the French Revolution* (New York, 1966); Richard M. Brace, *Bordeaux and the Gironde, 1789–1794* (Ithaca, 1947); Alan Forrest, *Society and Politics in Revolutionary Bordeaux* (Oxford, 1975); Aurélien Vivie, *Histoire de la Terreur à Bordeaux* (Bordeaux, 1877); C. Riffaterre, *Le Mouvement antijacobin et antiparisien à Lyon et dans le Rhône-et-Loire en 1793* (Lyon, 1912); and William Scott, *Terror and Repression in Revolutionary Marseille* (London, 1973).

itly restricted to administrative matters. The new law also suspended local elections, with vacancies to be filled by appointments made by represen- tatives on mission. This same law increased the responsibilities of district councils, which had in general shown themselves to be less "moderate" than departmental administrations and more steadfast in their loyalty to the Na- tional Convention. These councils now assumed responsibility for the enact- ment of all new laws and would report directly to the Committee of Public Safety through appointed *agents nationaux,* not to the departmental direc- tory, as before.[2]

It is the first phase of this reorganization that primarily concerns us here— the dismissal of suspect officials and their replacement by men thought to be more republican in their political convictions. In Calvados, this process ex- tended to virtually the entire departmental administration and the Caen dis- trict and municipal councils. Those officials most active in the revolt went to prison, where they remained for periods ranging from four months to nearly a year. The purge of officials in the Haute-Vienne, on the other hand, was much more selective. The representative on mission Jacques Brival left the Limoges district and municipal councils nearly intact and dismissed only a handful of departmental administrators.

The details of the repression are important not only as a means to identify the federalist administrators and their replacements but also—through in- terrogations, statements, and letters—as a means to examine further the character of the revolt. In their interrogation statements and petitions for clemency, many of those arrested in Caen presented extensive defenses of their actions and outlined what they considered the reasons for the revolt. Most stressed the good intentions of the people of Caen and the misinforma- tion that had led them astray. Also illuminating are the orders issued by the minister of the interior and the Committee of Public Safety and the reports of their agents sent out into the departments.

As with our chronicle of the revolt itself, we begin by examining Limoges, where only a few administrators were purged from office. Representatives on mission arrived in Limoges with little fanfare or advance notice, but as elsewhere in France, they made an impact on the shape of local politics. The National Convention sent Jacques Brival to the Haute-Vienne, specifically

2. Godechot, *Les Institutions de la France,* 282–286.

ordering him to Châteauponsac, le Dorat, Saint-Yrieix, and Limoges but granting him broad discretion with regard to other towns he chose to visit and measures he found necessary to employ. Brival made brief stops in Châteauponsac and Lussac, replacing the entire municipal council in the first and only a few officials in the second. At le Dorat, he replaced two members of the district administration and suspended Jacques Lesterpt (brother of an Haute-Vienne *conventionnel,* Benoist Lesterpt-Beauvais, who had come under suspicion) from his position on the district tribunal.

On August 28, Brival reported to the Committee of Public Safety from Saint-Yrieix, in many respects the primary target of his mission. The Saint-Yrieix district council's letter of June 7, calling for the election of new deputies to the Convention and the dispatch of departmental delegations to Paris, had elicited the disapproval of the departmental administration and earned a denunciation on the floor of the Convention. Now those officials would pay the price for having spoken so freely. Brival suspended the entire district and municipal councils, with the exception of three individuals, as well as the district judges and the municipal *juges de paix.* In consultation with the local Jacobin club, he replaced these officials with more reputable republicans.

From Saint-Yrieix, Brival went directly to Limoges, where he again faced the need for a selective purging of the administrative and judicial corps. The departmental administration, though it had never actively supported the federalist movement, had wavered briefly, and that weakness required a remedy. Accordingly, Brival dismissed four departmental officials: Joseph Durand de Richemont, president of the administration; Jean Hugonneau-Sauvot, a member of the directory; Charles Cantillon-Tramont; and Pierre Mourier.[3] Of the four, only Durand can be said to have been dismissed because of his conduct in June and July. The Limoges *comité de surveillance* described his conduct during that period thus: "he did not show himself to be a partisan of the Mountain, and his weakness very nearly proved disastrous for the department."[4] In addition to his indecision in June, Durand one year earlier had signed the departmental letter protesting the June 20, 1792, attack on the Tuileries. This apparent sympathy for the king now re-

3. A. N., AF II 168, dossier 1383. This file contains several letters from Brival to the Committee of Public Safety written during August and September, 1793.
4. Fray-Fournier, *Le Département de la Haute-Vienne,* I, 102.

turned to haunt him, and it seems to have been this offense for which the Committee of General Security ordered Durand's arrest and transfer to Paris on March 31, 1794 (11 Germinal II). Durand never came to trial, but he remained in La Force prison until after Thermidor.[5]

Hugonneau-Sauvot had also been implicated in the affair of the June, 1792, departmental letter but at that time had managed to exonerate himself. It seems likely that this affair was once again the source of his problems, for within three months Brival restored Hugonneau to his previous position. There is little evidence to suggest reasons for the dismissal of Cantillon-Tramont and Mourier. Brival gave no explanation for their suspension from office. Cantillon-Tramont's attendance at council meetings had been sporadic, but this was hardly exceptional. In May, 1793, he had led a contingent of volunteers to the Vendée, a demonstration of patriotism that scarcely could justify Brival's action. As for Mourier, his responsibilities for supplying wood to the naval shipyards may have conflicted with his duties as an administrator. It is also possible that personal animosities between these two men and Limoges Jacobins led to their dismissal.

To fill the vacated positions, Brival named Jean Baptiste Gay-Vernon president of the administration and promoted François Hilaire Jevardat-Grandchamp to the directory, thereby rewarding two of the staunchest Montagnard supporters on the departmental council. Beyond this, Brival made few changes. He named replacements for the district administrators Jean Boyer and Alexis Villestivaud, having previously appointed those men to replace dismissed judges. Three new faces soon appeared on the municipal council, but these substitutions were due to the transfer or retirement of councillors. The National Convention directly ordered an additional change in the Haute-Vienne administration—the suspension and arrest of François Mathieu-Lachassagne for impeding recruitment and criminally corresponding with émigrés. Lachassagne spent several months in a Paris prison but returned as a departmental official after Thermidor.[6]

In mid-September, Antoine Joseph Lanot joined Brival on mission to the Haute-Vienne and the Corrèze. The two deputies continued to purify district and municipal councils, but their attention now turned more closely to military recruitment and the suppression of "religious fanaticism." Both

5. A. D. Haute-Vienne, L851 (orders of the Comité de Sûreté Générale).
6. Fray-Fournier, Le Département de la Haute-Vienne, I, 108–109.

tasks went well. In late November, Lanot reported that people were flocking to the Temples of Reason (this may have been an exaggeration) and that each department had furnished two thousand volunteers for the army.[7]

A local incident produced the final displacements in Limoges politics in the summer and fall of 1793. It involved three of the most prominent figures from the early years of the Revolution—Jean Baptiste Pétiniaud de Beaupeyrat, Louis Naurissart, and Pierre Dumas. Dumas had been *procureur-général-syndic* of the department in the 1790–1791 term, had briefly served as president of the Haute-Vienne in November, 1791, and since that time had sat on the departmental council. On July 3, 1793, however, he resigned that post because of his responsibilities as president of the Haute-Vienne Criminal Tribunal (the law of June 14 rendered the two positions incompatible).

Pétiniaud and Naurissart had been at the center of political conflict in Limoges since 1791 and were reputed to be the leaders of the "aristocratic" faction in the town. Charged now with materially aiding émigrés, the two appeared before the Criminal Tribunal in July. Dumas, scrupulously honest by all indications, presided over the preliminary review, which quickly concluded with the dismissal of charges against both Pétiniaud and Naurissart. The two had clearly sent money abroad, but Dumas felt compelled to point out to the jury that the offenses had been committed *before* such correspondence had been outlawed. This acquittal by virtue of legal technicality infuriated Limoges Jacobins, who charged Dumas with favoring aristocrats and the public prosecutor with incompetence. Both men eventually lost their jobs, dismissed in September by Lanot and Brival, and Dumas went to prison late in 1793. The district *comité de surveillance* said of Dumas that though he stood on good terms with Limoges sans-culottes, he had lately fallen under suspicion. Dumas had joined in founding the Limoges Jacobin club and had been an early supporter of the Revolution, "but full of ambition and anxious to please all parties, he had eventually all but deserted the club and was suspected of favoring aristocrats in the exercise of his official duties."[8] The Jacobins eventually came to his defense, however, and Dumas left prison in February, 1794, only to be arrested two months later by order

7. A.N., AF II 171, dossier 1398, pièce 30, Lanot letter of 3 Frimaire II (November 23, 1793) sent to the Committee of Public Safety.
8. A. D. Haute-Vienne, L443.

of the Committee of General Security. Transferred to Paris, Dumas sat in Saint-Lazare prison until November 21, 1794 (1 Frimaire III).[9] The charge that Dumas "favored aristocrats" appears entirely unfounded, particularly with respect to Pétiniaud. The two had been enemies since 1782, when Pétiniaud orchestrated Dumas' expulsion from a local Freemason lodge. In 1790, Pétiniaud had opposed Dumas' election as *procureur-général-syndic* and then his election as president of the Criminal Tribunal. As Dumas later observed in his own defense, he had every reason in the world to convict Pétiniaud but refused to subvert the law.[10]

The mission of the deputies Lanot and Brival produced no drastic changes in the Haute-Vienne. The Limoges municipal and district councils, both of which had actively opposed the federalist tendencies of departmental officials, remained virtually intact, and the district council now enjoyed a certain precedence over the diminished departmental administration. The arrival of Brival and Lanot did, nonetheless, bring a temporary end to the long-running battle between moderates and radicals in Limoges. The elections of 1792 had given the upper hand to the latter, and their advantage was now strengthened. In September, the deputies named a local *comité de surveillance*, which immediately arrested a number of former members of the Amis de la Paix. Few former Amis remained in office in August, 1793, but many were prominent Limoges citizens who were now subjected to close surveillance, even prison, because of their past association with the moderate club. The ascendancy of the Montagnards in Paris thus strengthened the hold of Limoges Jacobins on departmental politics.

In examining the repression in Caen we begin not in August but in mid-June, when the minister of the interior, Joseph Garat, sent his first agents to Normandy and when the Convention first denounced the Calvados federalists. On June 13, 1793, the National Convention issued a decree of accusation against the administrators and other officials in Calvados who had signed the June 9 order for the arrest of the two representatives on mission, Romme and Prieur. In August, this decree would serve as the core of an indictment against seventy-three administrators, judges, and representatives of the Caen

9. Fray-Fournier, *Le Département de la Haute-Vienne*, II, 307–309.
10. See *La Franc-maçonnerie Limousine, son passé, son présent, ses ambitions*, in the Bibliothèque Nationale, 8°H. Pièce 2255.

sections and clubs who had adhered to the June 9 order. Most of these men eventually went to prison, but probably only a handful of officials in Caen knew in June of the decree of accusation. After June 8, the departmental directory refused to register or announce any orders or laws issued by the Convention, and only at the end of July did the Calvados directory lift that ban.

The Convention issued two more decrees directed against the federalist rebels. The first concerned General Félix Wimpffen. On June 26, the Committee of Public Safety received the letter from Wimpffen in which he pledged to come to Paris only at the head of sixty thousand men. Bertrand Barère read this insolent letter to the outraged deputies, and after some debate (there were those who wished to place a price on Wimpffen's head), the Convention voted a decree of accusation against the general and dismissed him as commander of the Army of the Coasts of Cherbourg.

During that same session, Robert Lindet introduced a measure relative to all administrators who had signed insurrectionary orders. Lindet, who had been in Lyon during the first two weeks of June, argued that the majority of citizens and administrators were good republicans, regrettably misled regarding events in Paris and the freedom of the Convention. Now that sufficient time had passed for the facts to become known, however, all administrators who had given orders to arm the people against each other, who had intercepted official correspondence, or who had spread spurious reports regarding the Convention ought to be called on to retract publicly those statements within three days or be declared traitors. The Convention quickly adopted this proposal, with the three-day period to begin on publication of the decree. As Lindet hoped, retractions quickly followed in many departments. In Calvados, the decree did not become publicly known until July 20 or 21, at which time, as we have seen, the Caen district council hastily revoked its adherence to the declarations of June 8 and 9.[11]

These three decrees comprised the official punitive measures directed against the rebels in Calvados. More positive steps were taken as well. Early in June, the Convention prepared an official account of the events of May 31 through June 2, stressing the cooperation of the Central Revolutionary Committee and the people of Paris in the cause of liberty, unity, and the indi-

11. For the text and discussion in the Convention of these three decrees, see *Réimpression de l'Ancien Moniteur,* XVI, 641 (session of June 13, 1793), and 755–757 (session of June 26, 1793).

visibility of the Republic. More importantly, the Convention moved quickly to satisfy the year-long demands for a new constitution. On June 10, Jean-bon Saint-André addressed the deputies: "It is time to prove to the departments that the unity and the indivisibility of the Republic are the fundamental dogmas of the constitution; it is the constitution that will call back to their duties all constituted authorities."[12]

Reports from representatives on mission to the departments reinforced this call time and again. From Brittany, the deputies P. M. Gillet and Antoine Merlin wrote to the Committee of Public Safety on June 12, warning it of the impending general assembly in Rennes and observing that "it would seem simple to us to avert the consequences that might follow such an extraordinary measure, if the Convention turns without delay to the constitution." Robert Lindet, while still on mission in Lyon, wrote succinctly on June 15: "Publish a constitution."[13] The Convention did precisely that. Marie Jean Hérault-Séchelles began his report on the newly drafted articles during the session of June 10, and after two weeks of discussion and revision, the deputies approved the constitution on June 24. Two days later, C. Lacroix (of the Marne) underlined the importance of this document: "When the constitution is presented to the people, they will abandon those who have misled them and will rally around this Palladium of liberty."[14]

To present the constitution to the people in those departments where the local authorities could not be expected to cooperate, the minister of the interior, Garat, commissioned fifty-two agents to travel incognito, distributing copies as they went. He assigned no fewer than seven of these fifty-two agents to Calvados and the surrounding departments.

Another group of agents sent by the minister of the interior was in the field at this time. As early as January, 1793, Garat had expressed dismay at the lack of means for surveillance of the departments and had warned the Executive Council and later the Committee of Public Safety of internal enemies who threatened the Revolution. The Executive Council authorized Garat to assign seventy-two agents, whose mission would be secret, to visit the departments and report back to Paris on political and economic conditions. Although the plan was never fully implemented, Garat named thirty-

---

12. *Ibid.*, 608.
13. Aulard, *Recueil des Actes du Comité de Salut Public*, IV, 532, 575.
14. *Réimpression de l'Ancien Moniteur*, XVI, 756.

six agents in May and June, and two of these "observers" journeyed to Calvados.[15]

One of the first of these agents to be named was Perrin de Sainte-Emmelie, sent in late April to observe the Channel coast. Still on mission when the revolt broke out, Perrin wrote from Valognes (in the Manche) on June 11, reporting to Garat that public rumor blamed the recent conduct of Romme and Prieur for the extreme measures taken by the Calvados authorities. A letter written four days later amended this report, declaring that the actions of the people of Caen grew largely from their resentment that the 14th Military Division headquarters had not been established in their city. One may doubt that the location of the headquarters in Bayeux rather than Caen could have caused such hard feelings. Romme and Prieur's order dissolving the administrative council attached to the 14th Division may well have engendered considerable resentment among local authorities, however. Additional rancor may have been caused by the dismissal from office of several minor officials ordered by the two deputies late in May.[16]

No other secret agents sent reports from Normandy during the month of June. The second observer sent to Calvados, Le Grand, was appointed on June 29 and arrived near Evreux just after the rebel forces had been routed on July 13. Le Grand wrote to Garat on July 16, describing the disorderly retreat of a force that he estimated at two thousand men. He mingled with the soldiers and heard a number of them complain "that they had been deceived by their leaders as to the motives of their gathering and that they would now return to their homes." He considered it unlikely that the rebels would be able to rally their forces. Le Grand followed the volunteers to Lisieux and wrote on July 20 that three hundred more had recently deserted, muttering as they left "that they believed they were going to the *fédération* in Paris, and not to do battle." Wimpffen reportedly still hoped for re-

<hr />

15. Caron, *Rapports des Agents du Ministre de l'Intérieur,* I, iii–xxv. Caron describes these agents as coming from the liberal professions for the most part. That they were sent to gather more than political information is suggested by the fact that each was given copies of Arthur Young's *Voyage en France* and Adam Smith's *Recherche sur la nature et les causes de la richesse des nations* and told to study and be inspired by them. Garat was clearly interested in gathering information on commerce, agriculture, and industry from throughout France, and some of the published reports deal with those subjects.

16. *Ibid.,* II, 303–304; A. D. Calvados, L10024 (departmental administration *procès-verbal,* May 27, 1793). Several Caen citizens protested their dismissal from office at a May 27 departmental council meeting. I found no other reference to these dismissals, suggesting that those affected held minor posts.

inforcements, but Le Grand counted more leaving than arriving and wrote that outside of Caen no support for the revolt could be found in Calvados.[17] This news must have been heartening indeed compared with the pessimistic reports sent to Paris just one week earlier by representatives on mission. On July 3, the Convention had empowered the deputies L. Le Cointre and Pierre Louis Prieur (of the Marne), already in Normandy, to take all measures necessary for the suppression of the rebels in the Eure and Calvados. This authorization proved to be of little value, since authorities in Calvados had kept a close watch on the two deputies and in late June had peacefully escorted them out of the department.[18] On July 4, the Committee of Public Safety received news of the march of forces from Eure and Calvados on Paris and began taking steps to resist that march. The Committee assembled an army composed of Parisian battalions (soon christened the "army of pacification" by the people of Evreux) and on July 9 sent Robert Lindet, a member of the Committee, and Jean Michel DuRoy to the Eure for one last try at averting the confrontation through mediation and conciliation.[19]

The July 13 skirmish at Vernon signaled the failure of these efforts, and early reports to Paris did not make clear the disarray into which the rebel troops were falling. Lindet's brother, Thomas, wrote to him from Paris almost daily, relaying the concern felt in the capital over the situation in Normandy. On July 15, he advised Lindet against pursuing a strategy of conciliation, observing that the Normans had shown their true colors by attacking the Parisians at Vernon, and warned him that to enter Evreux ahead of the army would be both dangerous and unnecessary.[20]

Robert Lindet worried about the liability posed by the Parisian battalions almost as much as he felt reassured by the protection they offered. In an undated letter to Jean Baptiste Noel Bouchotte, the minister of war, he complained: "The composition of our small army is disquieting. The chasseurs have the worst reputation and merit it. We receive serious complaints about them. The hussars are also, by their conduct, a continual source of alarm or indisposition." Lindet reported that the troops mistreated the people of the countryside and spread panic faster than the representatives could inspire

17. Caron, *Rapports des Agents du Ministre de l'Intérieur*, II, 192–95.

18. A. D. Calvados, L189 (Registre des arrêtés du Conseil Général du département du Calvados, 11 août 1792–26 juillet 1793). On June 27, the Calvados general assembly ordered two of its members to accompany Le Cointre and Prieur, then in Vire, out of Calvados.

19. Aulard, *Recueil des Actes du Comité de Salut Public*, V, 165–66.

20. A. D. Calvados, L10122 (Lindet personal papers).

confidence. The arrival in Evreux on July 24 of Xavier Audouin, the erstwhile resident of Limoges who now served as adjunct to the minister of war, helped to resolve this problem. Lindet himself had requested Audouin's presence. The two of them, in conjunction with General Sepher (commander of the Parisian troops), instituted strict regulations forbidding harassment of the countrypeople and managed to restore discipline to the five-thousand-man army.[21]

Despite Thomas Lindet's misgivings, Robert Lindet and his fellow representative on mission, DuRoy, entered Evreux without incident and by July 18 could report that no rebel forces remained in the department of the Eure. Anxious not to lose their temporary advantage by allowing Wimpffen time to regroup his soldiers, Robert Lindet appealed to Paris for an extension of the two representatives' powers so that they might press on into Calvados. This authorization reached Evreux on July 21 along with Pierre Louis Bonnet de Meautry, who had been dispatched by the Committee of Public Safety to assist DuRoy and Lindet in Calvados. The Committee sent Bonnet de Meautry, a Calvados deputy to the Convention and former mayor of Caen, because of his familiarity with the local citizenry.

As the representatives prepared to move on to Lisieux, their primary concern remained the reputation for pillaging and disorder that preceded the "army of pacification." Several of Garat's secret agents, now in Calvados, reported the common fear that the army had been sent to slaughter everyone. Etienne LeHodey wrote to Garat on July 29 that the March 29, 1793, census decree calling for the posting at each house of the names, ages, and so on of all residents had been libeled in Calvados as an order of Marat, issued so that some night all those older than sixty or younger than ten could be killed in their sleep. The agents tried to reassure those they met and, in fact, had some success in allaying the people's fears. One agent, Guillaume Delabarre, visited Lisieux posing as a cattle merchant, an appropriate disguise in that rich grazing region. He met some of the Norman volunteers in the cafés and, after listening to their complaints about the deceptions of their leaders, urged them to support the Convention and abandon Wimpffen. He reported that many did so. The agent Heudier, sixty years old and a native of Calvados, arrived in Caen on July 20, allegedly on matters of business (a plausible story, since he was a wine merchant). He stayed with relatives, which strengthened his cover, and told everyone he met that local admin-

21. A. D. Calvados, L10119 (Lindet correspondence).

istrators had misinformed the public about events in Paris and had prevented messengers from the Convention from reaching them. All of these agents also distributed the new constitution, a measure made doubly important because the Central Committee of Resistance to Oppression (the coordinating body of the assembled protesting departments) had reportedly begun to spread false copies.[22]

The role of Garat's secret agents during this period was a very important one, too seldom noted by historians. At least in Normandy, they quietly and effectively acted as ears and eyes for the representatives on mission, who never could have gained access to the people with whom the agents mingled. These men also disseminated information favorable to the Montagnard Convention, allaying the fears and suspicions of the people they met. They thus functioned successfully (the best among them, anyhow) as intermediaries between officials of the state and the people of the towns and countryside. Without that mediation, the task of the representatives on mission and the "army of pacification" would have proved much more difficult.

After the rout of the federalist forces, the representatives on mission quickly took steps to reorganize their forces, to influence public opinion, and to make clear the purpose of their expedition. They secured an order from the minister of war, Bouchotte, bringing the Cherbourg army and the Parisian volunteers under the sole command of General Sepher, thereby boosting troop morale and reducing dissension between the two general staffs. To counter the propaganda in the newspaper being issued by the authorities gathered in Caen, Lindet obtained a printing press and commenced publication of the *Journal de l'Armée des Côtes de Cherbourg*. The first issue appeared on July 28 in Evreux. The press moved with the troops, and the *Journal* issued its second number in Lisieux on July 30. Its opening paragraph, characteristic of the content of the *Journal* during the weeks that followed, read: "Be reassured, respectable inhabitants of the countryside; we will watch over your tranquility, and your homes will be protected."[23]

22. Caron, *Rapports des Agents du Ministre de l'Intérieur*, I, 231–35, II, 13–15, 209–10 (reports of Delabarre, Heudier, and LeHodey). See A. D. Calvados, L10168 (Comité de Sûreté Générale/Cabinet Noir) for a June 27, 1793, letter written by a Bayeux woman who expressed precisely the fear reported by LeHodey.

23. A. D. Calvados, L10529 (*Journal de l'Armée des Côtes de Cherbourg*, July 30, 1793). The *Journal* was edited by J. J. Derché, who accompanied the "army of pacification" with responsibility for the surveillance and reorganization of local popular societies. Except for a one-month hiatus, during which time the army was occupied in the Vendée, the *Journal* continued publication until the end of December, 1793.

The "army of pacification" arrived in Lisieux the evening of July 28 and found the town calm. All three section assemblies had unanimously adopted the new constitution, and the town turned out a fraternal greeting for the army.[24] Lindet wrote to Paris that the people of Lisieux had only reluctantly supported the revolt under the considerable pressure of departmental authorities. Although they had housed the Caen volunteers on their route to Evreux, few had actively participated in the insurrection. Patriotism in Lisieux remained strong, though republican enthusiasm required revitalization. The most pressing need, however, was to restock the Lisieux grain market, which had been seriously undersupplied since the enactment of the *maximum*. The success of the representatives in securing supplementary grain facilitated their political mission in Evreux, Lisieux, and later Caen.[25]

Encouraging news awaited the representatives in Lisieux regarding the current situation in Caen. Earlier reports of the town's preparations to defend itself gave way to word that Wimpffen had fled, that the administrators had issued retractions, and that Romme and Prieur once again enjoyed their freedom. Cause for concern persisted, however. Lindet doubted the sincerity of the Calvados retractions. Issued only out of fear, they sounded more like an apology or a defense of past actions than an admission of error or guilt. In addition, the rebel administrators had incurred "unbelievable expenses," draining large sums of money from the public treasury. Lindet considered it imperative that an accounting of the records be made and that no false *assignats* be allowed to circulate. He also felt it necessary to replace all local officials, since the people would certainly no longer tolerate their former administrators.[26]

As Lindet, DuRoy, and Bonnet prepared to advance from Lisieux to Caen, so did the people of Caen prepare to receive them. For most of the departmental administrators, this meant a swift, but discreet, departure from Caen. Sixteen of the thirty-seven members were present at the July 26 meet-

---

24. At least the *Journal* of July 30, 1793, reported that the army had been well received. Another account suggests that the reception was not a warm one, but I found no solid evidence to support this view. Lindet, who would have had no reason to deceive or fabricate, consistently spoke well of the Lisieux citizens and their patriotism in his letters to Paris. For the contrary opinion, see Gaston Lavalley, "La Presse en Normandie: Journal de l'Armée des Côtes de Cherbourg," *Mémoires de l'Académie Nationale des Sciences, Arts et Belles-lettres de Caen* (1899), 205–75.

25. A. D. Calvados, L10119 (July 31, 1793, letter to Garat).

26. *Ibid.* (July 29, 1793, letter to Bouchotte; July 31 letter to Audouin; and August 1 letter from the three representatives to the Committee of Public Safety).

ing for the signing of the formal retraction. By the next day, their numbers had dwindled to ten, and only five officials attended a session on July 31. Of the nine members of the departmental directory, only four attended a July 30 meeting, and by August 8, only two remained. Those present called on other administrators to fill the vacancies on the directory, but no one appeared. All five of the directors who had accompanied the departmental force to Evreux returned to Caen to sign the retraction, but only Adrien Thiboult remained at his post as late as July 31. Pierre Jean Lévêque never attended a meeting, Pierre Mesnil attended one, and Hippolyte Bougon-Longrais and René Lenormand attended two apiece. The directory made no conciliatory overtures to the representatives on mission, concerning itself instead with registering the hundreds of decrees from the Convention that had been ignored since May 31.[27]

The Caen district administration had been less compromised by the revolt, and so its officials had little reason to flee. With the exception of Louis Caille and Bernard Lequeru, members who had maintained regular attendance during June and July continued to attend both the district directory and the district council meetings.[28] Seven of the thirteen administrators signed a retraction, dated July 21 and addressed to the Committee of Public Safety, emphasizing the adverse circumstances that had prevented them from actively opposing the insurrection and citing in particular Robert Tirel's futile objections to the arrest of Romme and Prieur. Two district officials, Daniel François Claude L'honorey and Henri Michel Saillenfest, attended the July 21 meeting but did not sign, though L'honorey later signed the general assembly retraction. René Lahaye, the only district administrator other than Caille to play an active role in the revolt, disagreed with his colleagues over other matters and had not attended a meeting since May 29.[29] During the last week of July, the rest of the council devoted its attention to the increasingly difficult problem of supplying Caen with grain.

27. A. D. Calvados, L165 (Registre des procès-verbaux du Directoire du Département à Caen, 16 mars 1793–10 septembre 1793).
28. A. D. Calvados, L387 (Registre servant à la transcription des procès-verbaux des délibérations du Conseil Général du district de Caen, 15 janvier 1793–20 avril 1795), and L382 (Transcriptions des procès-verbaux des délibérations du Directoire du district de Caen, 15 mars 1793–3 février 1794). Louis Caille went into hiding for obvious reasons. Lequeru, however, played no public role in the revolt and may have quit attending meetings for personal reasons. He had resigned as council president in mid-May in order to deal with family business. He quit attending directory meetings after July 29, without any explanation, but continued to attend general council sessions.
29. A. D. Calvados, L387.

No perceptible change occurred in the pattern of attendance at municipal council meetings in late July, although the council did not record who was present between July 20 and August 27. On the latter date, attendance was normal, with a majority of council members present. On July 25, the municipal council had sent a letter to the representatives on mission along with its retraction. Like the district administration, it stressed that the will of the people had forced it to adhere to the insurrectionary measures of the general assembly, an error that by then had become all too clear. The three representatives responded on July 28 with a carefully worded letter addressed to the municipality. Adopting a reassuring tone, they described their mission as the peaceful restoration of order and liberty among the people of Caen. A public letter to the citizens of Caen followed three days later, explaining that the "army of pacification" must come to Caen in order to prove to the people that the Republic had raised its army not to massacre but rather to fraternize, to restore liberty, and to erase traces of the recent aberration in Calvados. These letters produced the desired effect, and on July 31, the municipal council sent four of its members to Lisieux to pledge its cooperation to the representatives. The municipality offered to greet the deputies with a festive celebration, but Lindet declined, explaining that it would be inappropriate to accept such a welcome from a town that had so recently arrested and imprisoned two of his colleagues.[30]

Officials in Caen were clearly anxious to forget the past two months and to return as discreetly as possible to "business as usual." The municipal council postponed the release of Romme and Prieur from the Château for several days, hoping that public agitation would subside. Finally released on July 29, Romme reported to the Convention one week later that the council had initially suggested that they be released at night, through a back entrance, in order to avoid attracting a crowd. The two deputies objected emphatically, insisting that only a public exit could begin to atone for the public outrage committed against the National Convention. Their objections prevailed, and they left the Château to the sound of saluting cannons before the assembled National Guard and a cheering crowd of citizens.[31]

Upon their release, Romme and Prieur immediately wrote to their col-

30. A. C. Caen, D2 (Délibérations du Corps municipal et du Conseil Général de la Commune, 4 janvier 1792–11 Germinal an II), and I43 (Mission Lindet, Oudot, DuRoy, Bonnet, juillet 1793–an V).

31. Réimpression de l'Ancien Moniteur, XVII, 937 (August 6, 1793).

leagues in Lisieux, urging them to come to Caen as soon as possible. Their letter reported that Caen was quiet and predicted a friendly reception for the three deputies. They cautioned, however, that the town remained in a state of shock: "The people appear cold and passive; the municipality shows itself well. Several members of the Department have the air of being greatly afraid." [32]

Thus advised, Lindet, DuRoy, and Bonnet made the short journey from Lisieux to Caen on August 3, one day behind the "army of pacification." They arrived in Caen still unsure of the precise extent of their authority and responsibilities. The Committee of Public Safety had instructed them to restore order in Calvados and presumably to arrest the guilty. Not until August 6 did the Convention issue a decree authorizing the replacement of departmental administrators, as well as the Caen district and municipal councils. It also called for the demolition of the dungeon in the Château and the dissolution of the Carabot club. Although official notification of this decree did not reach Caen until August 9, Lindet and DuRoy began to consult "local citizens known for their patriotism" regarding the appointment of new administrators shortly after their arrival. [33]

The success of all other measures depended on the ability of the representatives on mission to find adequate grain supplies for the local markets. Curiously, the departmental administration had appealed to the minister of the interior for food supplies late in June, despite its revolt against the central government and the food boycott directed against Paris. One can scarcely believe that the administrators expected a favorable reply. It seems likely that the Committee of Public Safety and the minister of the interior took all possible measures during the revolt (as they did in the cases of Bordeaux and Marseille) to deprive Calvados of grain supplies from Le Havre and Rouen, as a tactic aimed at undermining the insurrection. Several times in July authorities in Caen had been forced to release military supplies to the hungry people in order to prevent pillaging of the granaries. Those stores were now almost exhausted, and armed searches for caches in the surrounding countryside met with only infrequent reward.

In two letters to the Committee of Public Safety, dated August 8 and 9, Lindet, DuRoy, and Bonnet reported that Caen, Lisieux, Bayeux, and Falaise

32. A. D. Calvados, L10119 (letter of July 30, 1793).
33. A. D. Calvados, L165; and A. C. Caen, I46 (Répression, etc., juillet 1793–Pluviôse an II).

all lacked bread. They charged hoarders and monopolizers with depriving the population of what had been an abundant harvest in 1792 and issued proclamations to the countryside threatening fines and imprisonment to farmers who refused to deliver available grain. This brought some grain to the markets, but the representatives had to turn their efforts elsewhere as well. On August 18, Lindet and DuRoy announced to the municipal council that they had procured eight hundred quintals of rye, eight hundred quintals of wheat, and six hundred quintals of flour, which now awaited shipment in Le Havre. This provided temporary relief, enough for approximately ten days, but the supply in Caen remained precariously low well into September.[34]

As they had done in Evreux and Lisieux, the deputies met with the Jacobin club and held public meetings in churches in an attempt to rally patriotism and revive public spirit. Lindet defended the Convention before these gatherings and denied the existence in Paris of any "disorganizing party, known by the name of maratists and anarchists." He even praised Marat; and on August 7, he published a pamphlet detailing why he had voted on June 2 for the arrest of the twenty-nine deputies, citing their conduct since that date as ample proof of their guilt. These efforts produced only a moderate effect. The *Journal de l'Armée* continued to complain of public apathy and low attendance at Jacobin club meetings.

Even the most ambitious attempt to heal the wounds of federalism met with only partial success. In conjunction with the municipality, the representatives on mission planned a public fete to celebrate the anniversary of the August 10 *journée,* which one year earlier had toppled the monarchy. The fete included a parade, music, and dancing, and the "army of pacification" mingled with the citizens of Caen in a festive atmosphere. Workers had erected a stage on the *prairie,* and there the mayor and others addressed the crowd and exchanged fraternal embraces with DuRoy and Bonnet. In the midst of the celebration, however, plans went awry. Gilet, the municipal employee in charge of preparations, had been pressed for time and had cut corners by painting over an old banner used at previous public affairs. Unfortunately, it rained on the festival (not unusual in Caen even in August), and those present watched in dismay as the newly painted letters disappeared, revealing the slogan, "Vive la Nation, la Loi, et le Roi!" The municipal

34. A. C. Caen, D2; and A.N., AF II 168, dossier 1380. See Perrot, *Genèse d'une ville moderne,* I, 188, for an estimate of Caen grain consumption in 1793.

council strongly reprimanded Gilet and sent an explanation, along with profuse apologies, to Lindet and the others.[35]

More problems grew out of the ceremonies that day. The three representatives were not working well together. Bonnet's family lived in Caen, and the former mayor, despite his political radicalism, still had friends in town. DuRoy, from the Eure, had visited Calvados in March on a recruitment mission with Bonnet and also had acquaintances in Caen. The two of them had been sent to accompany Lindet for precisely that reason—their familiarity with local officials would help reassure the understandably apprehensive citizenry. But these assets at the same time presented a liability. DuRoy and Bonnet were not neutral observers and could not dispassionately place responsibility on the shoulders of the apparent leaders of the revolt. This produced tension among the three; and on August 8, after arguing with DuRoy, Lindet wrote to Paris requesting his own recall.[36] In this instance, Bonnet acted as an intermediary, sending his own report of the quarrel to the Committee of Public Safety and suggesting that Lindet's request be ignored. He described Lindet as a difficult man to work with—very sensitive and often resentful of remonstrance—but he was a hard worker, very capable, and Bonnet felt it would be a great mistake to transfer Lindet just as he was mastering the local situation. The three temporarily resolved their differences, and the next day Lindet withdrew his request.[37]

Following the August 10 celebration, however, Bonnet, too, argued with Lindet. Lindet sent a lengthy report to Paris on August 27, outlining the problems of the preceding two weeks. Two of Garat's agents, after discreet investigation, had identified several of the leaders of the revolt. These included Louis Caille ("orateur pathologiste"), Bougon-Longrais ("grand diseur de riens"), Chaix-d'Estanges ("prêtre dans toute l'acceptation du terme"), René Lenormand, Lévêque, Barnabé Cauvin (a departmental administrator), and Mauger.[38] Lindet added to these most of the departmental and district administrators, a number of judges, several members of the municipality, and all of the commissioners who had gone to Paris or who had later been sent to other departments. The result was a list of forty-five to fifty

35. A. C. Caen, D2.
36. A.N., AF II 168, dossier 1375, pièce 26.
37. A.N., AF II 169, dossier 1380, pièce 8.
38. Caron, *Rapports des Agents du Ministre de l'Intérieur,* II, 20, 212 (reports of Heudier and LeHodey). The characterizations in parentheses are those of LeHodey.

whom he believed should be arrested. If nothing else, the 1,300,000 *livres* still missing from the treasury mandated that the guilty be punished.

Lindet presented his list at a meeting with Bonnet, General Sepher, and several other army officers. DuRoy was out of town at the time. Afterwards Bonnet spoke privately to Lindet, objecting that his wife would never speak to him again if they ordered all those arrests! The administrators were not guilty, he claimed, only misled. Local officials had fraternally embraced Bonnet and DuRoy on August 10, in the belief that all had been forgotten. The deputies would be accused of perfidy if they arrested these officials now, and Bonnet would not support such an order.

Bonnet further observed that a single representative on mission could not issue orders. He would willingly sign orders against citizens of the neighboring department of the Manche and finally agreed to the arrest of Cauvin. But he refused to sign an order for the arrest of Samuel Chatry, who had been a member of the committee of insurrection and editor of the Calvados newspaper in July. Although Lindet would assume personal responsibility for the necessary, unpleasant measures, he reached the conclusion that neither Bonnet nor DuRoy would be of any assistance to him in that task. Thus a stalemate had developed.[39]

Not until early September was this dilemma resolved. On September 7, the deputy Charles François Oudot arrived in Caen, apparently as a replacement for both Bonnet and DuRoy. Together, he and Lindet began to arrest those most compromised by the events of June and July. However, the month-long delay increased the difficulty of this task. Many of the administrators had fled the area or gone into hiding, particularly those departmental and district officials who did not live in Caen. Louis Caille, for example, was never apprehended, and René Lenormand hid until after Thermidor near Lénaudières in the Calvados countryside. Lindet did manage to make a few arrests during August. Those taken included the district administrator Lahaye, arrested for having led the party that seized Romme and Prieur in Bayeux; Jean Baptiste Leclerc, acting departmental president during July and August; Barnabé Cauvin; Jean Michel Barbot, the Carabot president; and Gohier de Jumilly, the curé of Saint-Jean, who had played a prominent role in leading volunteers to Evreux.[40]

Arrests increased in September, but it is impossible in many cases to estab-

39. A.N., AF II 168, dossier 1381, pièce 4.
40. A. D. Calvados, L10117 (Bouret and Frémanger mission).

lish the exact date of imprisonment.[41] In the end, the number of men arrested for their alleged participation in the revolt reached approximately forty-five, Lindet's original estimate. Most of these were administrators, including fourteen of the sixteen municipal officers (the mayor and *procureur* among them). Gabriel Fossey avoided arrest because he had resigned on May 29; Richard de Jort not only retained his freedom but was appointed by Lindet to the new municipal council. Of the thirteen district administrators, five went to prison, roughly the number that had continued to meet during the revolt. Notably absent were Bernard Lequeru, who convinced Lindet of his nonparticipation, and Thomas Violette, who had remained at his post until the representatives on mission arrived. Noting Lindet's surprise at finding him in his office, Violette had reportedly remarked, "Didn't someone have to stay to turn over the records and the keys?" Perhaps Violette's courage earned the respect of the deputy and averted his arrest. Thirteen departmental officials joined these nineteen in the Carmelites prison—again, the majority of those who had remained at their post during the revolt. The remaining prisoners included judges, municipal *notables,* and leading club members such as Chaix-d'Estanges and Barbot. Despite Lindet's intention to arrest all those who had acted as commissioners to Paris or other departments, most of them escaped imprisonment.

Lindet and Oudot remained in Caen until October 30 or 31 (9 or 10 Brumaire), replaced shortly by the representative on mission Jacques Léonard Laplanche, a former priest from Nevers whose Jacobin reputation preceded him to Caen. Laplanche lived up to expectations. As his first official duty, he raised a force of 1,200 men that departed in early November to battle the Vendée rebels. Esnault noted in his diary that those who had previously marched to Evreux were among the most eager to enroll.[42] Indeed, a group of prisoners arrested by Lindet, including Chaix-d'Estanges, Le Goupil Duclos, Leclerc, and Barbot, sought to prove their patriotism to Laplanche

41. The list of those arrested by Lindet and Laplanche (who arrived in Caen in late October) includes the names of only twenty-five people, some of whom were not officials, and for each one gives the date of arrest. It almost certainly overlooks several arrests ordered by Laplanche and may have missed a few ordered by Lindet as well. A more complete list of prisoners was prepared after Thermidor. It contains some three hundred names (only fifty or so arrested for federalism) and gives dates of entry and exit into the Maison des Carmelites. Almost all of these, however, would have been held for an undetermined length of time in the *maison d'arrêt* before transfer to the Carmelites—hence the impossibility of fixing a precise date of arrest. This list is located in *Brochures Normandes: Caen sous la Révolution,* B. M. Caen, Rés. Fn. Br. D156–209.

42. Lesage (Esnault), 114.

by petitioning for their release so that they, too, might join the force and rush to do battle with the enemies of the Republic.[43] Laplanche declined their generous offer. The volunteer force, having lost not a single man, returned one month later; and Laplanche, anticipating his remaining tasks, addressed the Jacobin club: "Here returns this Montagnard representative, the terror of *malveillants* and aristocrats, but at the same time the firm supporter of Republicans and true sans-culottes."[44] Laplanche worked with zeal, replacing suspect or incompetent administrators and arresting a number of former officials who had escaped the reach of Lindet and Oudot.

While the majority of the forty-five or fifty eventually arrested were in jail by the end of December, a handful did not enter prison until March, 1794. After hearing of the release of several municipal officers arrested the previous fall, they turned themselves in, no longer fearful that the guillotine awaited them and apparently convinced that it would be wiser to suffer prison now than to risk harsher punishment later as fugitives from the law. Time proved their judgment correct, for by the end of August, 1794, all had left the confines of the Carmelites prison and returned to their homes.

Two less fortunate Calvados federalists suffered severer punishments for their participation in the revolt, though in each case their later actions served to increase their jeopardy. Bougon-Longrais fled Caen in early September when the inevitability of his arrest became clear. Before fleeing, he wrote to Louis Jean Taveau, a Calvados *conventionnel*, to request the deputy's intercession on his behalf. He suggested that Taveau approach Danton, whose ability and honesty Bougon respected. Bougon proclaimed his own innocence, insisting that he had lent his support to the revolt, reluctantly of course, only after Caille and Chaix-d'Estanges had publicly labeled him a *maratiste*. He later appealed directly to Robert Lindet, again without success. In November, Bougon fell in with a band of Vendéan rebels led by the prince of Talmond. Within two months, Republican troops had apprehended the two. After a quick trial in Rennes, Bougon ascended the scaffold and ended his days on January 5, 1794.[45]

Dom Mauger also met his death on the guillotine. Laplanche issued an order for his arrest in December, but by then, Mauger had long since fled

43. A. D. Calvados, L10131 (Laplanche mission).
44. A. D. Calvados, L10529 (*Journal de l'Armée des Côtes de Cherbourg*, December 9, 1793).
45. See Grall, "La très courte carrière d'un procureur général syndic," 333–34.

Caen, settling in Saint-Hilaire, not far from Rouen. The *agent national* of the district of Yvetot ordered his arrest on March 5, 1794 (15 Ventôse II), after a citizen had denounced Mauger to the local *comité de surveillance.* Local authorities ordered his transfer to Paris, where he appeared before the Revolutionary Tribunal. The court convicted him for his role in the revolt and for his suspicious behavior since that time. Mauger was executed on May 13, 1794 (24 Floréal II).[46]

Bougon's appeals to Taveau and Lindet and the petition of Le Goupil Duclos and the other prisoners to Laplanche were not exceptional gestures. The interrogations and pleas for clemency that followed the arrests fill several cartons in the Calvados archives. The interrogations in particular, conducted by Etienne Hubert, a stern *juge de paix,* reveal a great deal about those questioned and their perceptions of the revolt. All of the eleven individuals for whom interrogation transcripts remain professed their innocence. The administrators insisted that they had acted on behalf of the people and that the people had been misled regarding events in Paris. Hubert questioned nearly everyone about instigators and leaders of the revolt and asked about the origin of letters that reportedly had arrived in Caen in late May and early June. All of those questioned denied any knowledge of ringleaders or conspirators, maintaining that the meetings had been public and the decisions shared. Most claimed ignorance of any letters from Paris. Le Goupil Duclos blamed public newspapers for the widespread misconceptions. Only Le Carpentier, a Caen *notable* and leader in the Jacobin club, mentioned letters from the Calvados deputies to the Convention, noting in particular one from Doulcet that had been printed and distributed.

Nearly all of these prisoners condemned the nine commissioners sent to Paris for their volatile report on June 8. Le Goupil Duclos also blamed the fugitive Girondin deputies for inciting the populace and promoting revolt. Each of the three departmental administrators questioned stressed that the general assembly had eclipsed the authority of the departmental council, leaving them powerless to oppose the insurrection. Many of the eleven took care not to claim that they had actually opposed particular orders. Rather, they contended that they had been powerless to do so. Hubert accused Chaix-d'Estanges of having been a leader of the revolt, but Chaix replied that though he had presided over the general assembly during July, the presi-

46. A.N., W364, dossier 795.

dent was only the passive organ of the assembly, without even the right to express his opinion. Unconvinced by Chaix's argument, Laplanche had him sent to Paris, where he languished in prison until after Thermidor.[47]

Letters requesting clemency also inundated the representatives on mission. Those already in prison claimed to have only erred, not committed a crime, and often recounted their records of public service since 1789 in an effort to demonstrate their patriotism. René Lenormand, while in hiding, published his own *Précis exact des motifs qui ont déterminé l'insurrection du département du Calvados, et des faits qui l'ont accompagnée,* an eight-page pamphlet that recited the events of June and July and emphasized that those who had marched to Evreux had gone to defend liberty and the unity of France.[48] A group of Caen citizens published a similar pamphlet in defense of those arrested.[49] In addition, wives, children, and friends of those arrested sent their pleas to the deputies. Occasionally, entire villages wrote on behalf of their native sons. The inhabitants of Douvres, for example, strongly supported their representatives, Saillenfest, François Exupère Mériel, and Jean Jacques Jardin. Some towns, however, took the opportunity to denounce administrators already arrested for their role in the revolt. The citizens of Audrieu wrote to Romme and Prieur in early August regarding their mayor René Lahaye, who was also a district administrator. Not only did they charge him with fomenting civil war, but they also accused him of extortion and hoarding. The people of Bucèls similarly denounced their mayor, Barnabé Cauvin, for having actively spread the revolt in his capacity as departmental administrator. This accusation contrasted sharply with Cauvin's own profession of innocence at his interrogation.[50]

Long before most of these former administrators had been brought to justice, Lindet had turned to the task of appointing new officials. He and DuRoy took responsibility for this chore, which aroused less contention among the three deputies than did Lindet's desire to imprison the guilty. They consequently completed the first round of appointments by mid-August, long before the majority of arrests. In the case of departmental administrators, the necessity for replacement was obvious. Despite their protestations of innocence, those officials had held positions of authority and

47. A. D. Calvados, L10125 and L10136 (interrogations).
48. A. D. Calvados, F6369 (Nouvelles Acquisitions).
49. A. D. Calvados, F3172; and *Brochures Normandes: Caen sous la Révolution,* B. M. Caen, Rés. Fn. Br. B404[1].
50. A. D. Calvados, L10117, L10122–25 (letters addressed to various representatives on mission).

responsibility, had enjoyed public confidence, and could have guided their constituents away from revolt. In dismissing the district and municipal councils, Lindet and DuRoy acknowledged that actual complicity had not yet been demonstrated but stressed that these officials had shown themselves to be undeserving of public confidence by their passivity and their compliance with the general assembly.

Lindet and DuRoy first announced the appointment of departmental and district officials. In seeming anticipation of the law of 14 Frimaire II (December 4, 1793), they named only directors and not full councils, though they did appoint a *procureur-syndic* and a *procureur-général-syndic*, both suppressed by the later decree and replaced by *agents nationaux*. None of the fourteen men selected had previous administrative experience, even at the municipal level. Nearly all of the departmental directors came from the district of Caen, because of the difficulty of quickly obtaining reliable information on individuals from other districts and the necessity of filling the posts as soon as possible.[51] Five days later, on August 18, Lindet and DuRoy made public a full slate of new municipal officials, including *notables*. As with the other administrations, they chose men new to public office. Many of those named had acted as presidents, secretaries, or *scrutateurs* of the Caen sectional assemblies that had accepted the new constitution at the end of July.[52] Only one appointee, Richard de Jort, had previously served as a municipal officer, and one of the new *notables*, Joseph Pierre Chibourg *le jeune,* had been preceded in office by his father, who had served as a *notable* in 1790.[53]

Unfortunately, the appointment of new officials was not a complete success. The people of Caen had witnessed firsthand the liabilities of holding public office, and many undoubtedly hesitated to expose themselves to such dangers. All but one of the new district directors assumed their new posts, but four of the eight departmental directors never attended a meeting, and a considerable number of municipal officials refused to accept their appointments. Many sent their resignations in writing, most often citing lack of sufficient talent or health problems as the reason for their refusal. Vision-impairing headaches seem to have been a common malady![54]

51. A. D. Calvados, L165 and L387.
52. Transcripts of those assemblies are in A. C. Caen, I44 (Acceptation de l'acte constitutionnel, 1793).
53. A. C. Caen, D2.
54. A. D. Calvados, L10118 (Lindet mission).

Even among those who accepted their appointments, not all were pro-
pitious choices. Some proved simply incompetent; others, politically suspect. Frédéric Vaultier complained in his memoirs that since the revolt had
compromised all good patriots in Caen, Lindet had no choice but to select
officials from among the town's petty-bourgeois royalists, most of them of
mediocre talent.[55] Many were indeed petty-bourgeois, but few seem to have
been royalist—mediocrity, rather, being the most common failing. When the
deputy Laplanche arrived in early November, he immediately announced
that he would change all the administrations, promising to name "honest
shoemakers, tailors, and hatters" to replace the lawyers and other professionals who currently dominated the councils.[56] Laplanche found fewer lawyers in office than he had expected; but in December, after consultation with
the "purified" and once again active Jacobin club, he did replace a number
of officials deemed incompetent or politically unacceptable.[57]

The problem of who would fill public offices persisted in the changing political climate of the year II. Over the next twelve months, four sets of representatives on mission visited Calvados, and each revised in some fashion the
local administrations. Indeed, it becomes difficult to keep track of who held
office at any given time. One thing, however, is clear. Few of those who first
came to office after July, 1793, enjoyed lengthy careers as public officials,
and many of those dismissed in August by Lindet later returned to replace
the men who had once replaced them.

In the long term, the Terror in Calvados proved to be milder even than
that in the Haute-Vienne. The Limoges Criminal Tribunal sentenced thirteen people to death in early 1794, most of them refractory priests, while in
Calvados the Terror claimed only seven victims. Two principal reasons account for the leniency shown to the Caen federalists. The attitude of the representatives on mission to Calvados played a significant role. Both Bonnet
and DuRoy showed reluctance to deal harshly with the local officials. Lindet,
too, demonstrated moderation, despite his determination to see the guilty
punished. He clearly believed that harsh repression would not be the most
effective policy in restoring unity to the troubled Republic. While on mission
to Lyon in early June, Lindet had repeatedly written to the Committee of

55. Vaultier, Souvenirs, 28.
56. A. D. Calvados, L10529 (Journal de l'Armée des Côtes de Cherbourg, November 5,
1793).
57. A. D. Calvados, L10075 (administrative personnel), and L10128 (Laplanche mission).

Public Safety that the town still contained many good republicans and that mediation and negotiation, along with the publication of a constitution, would provide a resolution to the difficulties.[58] That the Committee could not, or would not, follow Lindet's recommendations in dealing with Lyon stands as one of the great tragedies of the Revolution. Lindet adopted a similar attitude in Caen, despite pressure from Paris to take more drastic action. In a letter dated September 9, Xavier Audouin pointed out to Lindet that whereas eight people had just been executed in Rouen for burning a tree of liberty, none had yet been so punished in Caen, where an entire army of rebels had gathered.[59]

Lindet resisted even that entreaty, as we have seen, but local circumstances must also be credited for rendering violent repression an infeasible option in Calvados. No organized radical group existed in Caen to push for harsh punishment or to support it had the representatives on mission chosen to impose it. The Carabots had joined in the revolt, consistent with their role as a client group for the merchant elite and the departmental administration. The Jacobin club had severed its ties with the Paris Jacobins and had grown lethargic since the split. It followed the lead of Louis Caille and Chaix-d'Estanges on those rare occasions when it stirred itself to action. Even as the club revived in the months following the revolt, the only calls for revolutionary justice came from an outsider, J. J. Derché, brought to Caen by Lindet to edit the *Journal de l'Armée des Côtes de Cherbourg*. Men such as Charles Aubin, François Outin, and Jacques Caroger stepped forward to fill positions in the local administrations but showed no desire to persecute the men they replaced.

The repression and reorganization carried out by representatives on mission marked both an end and a beginning in Caen and Limoges. Although the ascendancy of the Girondins had never been complete, their political philosophy was reflected in the relative departmental autonomy that prevailed in the two years before June, 1793. The dangers of that departmental independence for the new republic became apparent in the revolt that challenged the authority of the National Convention after the proscriptions of June 2. The Convention utilized representatives on mission to neutralize those dangers

---

58. Aulard, *Recueil des Actes du Comité de Salut Public*, IV, 497, 509, 522–23, 551.
59. A. D. Calvados, L10126 (representatives on mission).

by eliminating "moderate" elements from local administrations. The law of 14 Frimaire reinforced their efforts by restricting both the size and the responsibilities of departmental administrations, in fact rendering them subordinate to the more dependable district councils in the registration of national laws and decrees. The appointment of *agents nationaux,* attached to local administrations, and the eventual designation of *commissaires du directoire exécutif* commenced the consolidation of a centralized government, a process never entirely halted by either the post-Thermidor Convention or the Directory.

In Limoges, this shift constituted not so much a dramatic end as a confirmation of the local political situation. The departmental administration, extremely cautious and mindful of the law, had been politically dominated since the summer of 1792 by the more radical municipality and the Limoges Jacobin club. These groups welcomed the revolution of May 31 and prevented the departmental council from straying into the federalist camp. Representatives on mission rewarded the loyalty of these groups to the Convention by reinforcing their hold on local politics. Only after Thermidor would that hold be broken.

The Terror was not bloody in Limoges, but local authorities enthusiastically embraced its principles by imprisoning royalists, former nobles, and those suspected of *incivisme,* particularly former adherents of the moderate Limoges club, the Amis de la Paix. This spirit extended beyond local officials and Jacobin club members—most of the people of Limoges shared and supported it. After the deputy Cherrier ordered the disarming of local terrorists in April, 1795, the sections of Limoges vociferously defended them, eventually refusing to vote on the year III constitution until Cherrier had rearmed the terrorists.[60]

In Caen, on the other hand, the months of August and September, 1793, constituted a definite break with the past. None of the local administrations had been strong enough in its loyalty to the Convention to actively oppose the insurrection. Moderates dominated all three councils, and the weak Jacobin club offered no restraint on the actions of elected administrators. Lindet and DuRoy suspended nearly every local official, replacing them with men new to public office, many of whom lacked the talents or experience necessary to fulfill their responsibilities.

60. A. D. Haute-Vienne, L442 (Constitution de l'an III). See also Fray-Fournier, *Le Département de la Haute-Vienne,* II, 144, 315–34.

Lindet suggested that the old officials had misled the people, who would no longer tolerate them in office. Evidence from statements and interrogations made after the revolt tends to confirm this impression. Volunteers for the march to Paris complained that officials had deceived them, leading them to believe that they journeyed to Paris to fraternize and join in another *fédération*. Le Goupil Duclos and others blamed the Calvados commissioners returned from Paris for falsely reporting on the status of the Convention. Even the concerted efforts of the general assembly (dominated by departmental administrators) to establish belatedly the existence of public support for its actions points to the absence of that very support.

But while the people of Caen had not supported the insurrectionary intentions of their administrations, they showed no desire to see them punished for their actions. In late August, a petition circulating in Caen called for a general amnesty and a recall of the decree issued against the rebel administrators. Lindet squelched this project, warning the citizenry that such a petition to Paris would enrage the National Convention and undermine the progress the deputies had achieved thus far.[61]

Nor did the people of Caen show enthusiasm for the instruments of the Terror. In October, Lindet and Oudot called on section assemblies to elect a *comité de salut public*, forerunner of the *comité de surveillance*. The sections responded by choosing men who had played no active role in the Revolution, who were mostly too old or indifferent to care one way or the other. The deputies nullified the elections and appointed a committee themselves, acknowledging that the motivation of the sections had been a desire for peace and quiet after the recent turbulence but warning them against the pitfalls of complacency.[62]

Local attitudes did not change, however. The deputies J. Frémanger and Bouret arrived on mission in late January, 1794, and found the people of Caen barely in step with the Revolution. Torpor and laziness prevailed, they reported, and the paucity of capable patriots to staff district and municipal administrations appalled them. The representatives appealed to Paris for guidance in reconstituting the councils. People in Caen, they explained, fell into four categories: (1) Conspirators who had supported Buzot and the others. Most were in prison, but some had escaped arrest and still lurked

61. *Ville de Caen: Recueil de pièces relatives à la Révolution*, B. M. Caen, Rés. Fn. Br. B583–616 (August 25, 1793, issue of *Journal de l'Armée des Côtes de Cherbourg*).
62. A. D. Calvados, L10124 (repression of federalism).

about. (2) Those misled during the insurrection. Most had since realized their error but now played no role in public life, forced from their posts by revolutionary committees. They remained eager to serve their country, though, and the deputies felt that the greatest reserve of talent and wisdom lay in this group. (3) Good patriots—fewer in number but long on effort, though unfortunately short on talent. These were the men currently in office. (4) Assorted misfits—"les modérés, les insouciants, les intrigants, les égoistes, les faux patriotes, les hommes à circonstance, les caméléons du corps politiques." The bitter enemies of the two middle groups, these types always tried to sow division.[63]

The dilemma that faced Bouret and Frémanger points again to one of the reasons for the mildness of repression in Calvados. No organized Jacobin faction existed in Caen that could step in and capably assume local administrative responsibilities. Bouret and Frémanger wondered if it would not be advisable to restore to office some individuals from the second group, given the shortcomings of those in the third. In retrospect, both their assessment and their recommendation appear particularly astute, but the Committee of Public Safety did not agree. After hearing from Paris, the two deputies made only a few changes in the local administrations. Most of those previously appointed by Lindet, Oudot, and Laplanche remained in office.

Bouret and Frémanger did, however, issue one order that eased the stigma of federalism for the local population. Upon arriving in Caen, the two representatives were swamped by letters from friends and relatives of imprisoned officials, imploring them to grant the prisoners' release. After consultation with the district comité de surveillance and the Jacobin club, they ordered the release of fifty-two prisoners on March 7, 1794 (17 Ventôse II), including all of the municipal officers arrested as federalists. The town's joyous celebration three days later convinced the two deputies that they had made the right decision and had taken an important step toward healing old wounds.[64]

The stigma of federalism was not fully removed in Calvados until after

63. A.N., AF II 175ᴬ, dossier 1435, pièce 45.

64. A.N., AF II 176, dossier 1448, pièce 38; A. C. Caen, I50 (Bouret and Frémanger mission); A. D. Calvados, L1975 (Comité de surveillance générale). In a January letter to Paris, the local comité de surveillance had lamented that the clamor of the people of Caen for the release of the imprisoned federalists was so great that it was impossible to put the affair behind them. They suggested that two representatives on mission be sent to solve the problem. Frémanger and Bouret arrived shortly thereafter.

9 Thermidor (July 27, 1794). By September, 1794, it had virtually disappeared. Representatives on mission released nearly all of those arrested. Many returned to their former positions, and the local administrations once again resembled those of June, 1793. Le Goupil Duclos sat as mayor of Caen, and Pierre Jean Lévêque soon returned to head the departmental directory. Lévêque subsequently served as departmental *commissaire du directoire exécutif* from November, 1795, until 1799.

What, then, do the patterns of repression and reorganization tell us about the federalist insurrection? Both the circumstances of the revolt and the nature of the repression reinforce the impression that the revolt was one of leaders without followers. In Limoges, because of the well-organized radical faction in town, this meant that no revolt developed. In Caen, the lack of popular support guaranteed the failure of the revolt. Representatives on mission and official interrogators searched in August and September for evidence of a conspiracy, but without success. Although reports from Garat's agents suggested that the federalist leaders had misled the populace, there was nothing explicitly devious or conspiratorial about their actions. They genuinely believed that their defense of a moderate republic, and of local autonomy, represented not only their own interests but those of their constituency as well. To a point, they were right—the people's later defense of their "misguided" leaders shows the confidence and trust they felt in their political elite. For the most part, the lower classes of Caen passively followed those leaders and accepted their dominance in local affairs. Only when their leaders called upon them to arm themselves and march against the radical scoundrels in Paris did they refuse to follow. They would not discard their passivity to actively intervene in national politics, particularly in such a risky endeavor.

Two factors emerge as crucial, then, in determining the stances of Caen and Limoges during the federalist revolt. One is the character and identity of the local political elite (the federalists in Caen) and the manner in which they controlled local politics. The other is the role of the popular classes in guiding or influencing the actions of their elected leaders. We now consider just who those leaders were and explore further the activism of the Limoges popular classes compared with the passivism of those in Caen.

Six

Behind the Scenes

A Social Analysis of Local Politics

In examining the years 1789 through 1793 in Caen and Limoges, our emphasis thus far has been on events, personalities, and political chronology. We have seen that the administrators of Caen and Calvados placed themselves firmly in the federalist camp in June, 1793, and that Limoges and the Haute-Vienne, though tentatively at first, supported the Montagnard Convention. Previous chapters have suggested that early events in the Revolution, economic conditions, and personal ties and relationships all played a part in determining the actions of each town during this crucial period. Throughout the Revolution, and particularly during the revolt itself, the Calvados departmental administration played a dominant role in Caen politics, while in Limoges, the Jacobin club and the municipal council restrained the federalist tendencies of the moderate departmental administration.

The crucial question that remains unanswered is Why? Why were the people of Limoges, the *menu peuple,* able to intervene and influence the decisions of their elected officials, while those in Caen were not? This question is not easily answered; but by asking a number of other questions, we may be able to fit the pieces of the puzzle together. First, who were the men that the people of Calvados and the Haute-Vienne elected to represent their political interests and administer their public needs? From what social milieu did they come, what were their occupations, and—for those elected in 1792—what was their political experience? With these questions in mind, we can trace the political evolution of the departmental, district, and municipal councils from 1790 to 1793 in these two departments and towns.

I suggested earlier that the social background of national deputies was less important than the social fabric of the regions they represented, and this holds true at the local level as well. We should not expect to see wealthy merchants occupying every key position in Caen, defending their class interests, or sans-culottes on the Limoges councils defending theirs. We will see, however, that as a group the administrators of Calvados reflected the agricultural and commercial character of their region, while in the Haute-Vienne (the administrative hinterland in Fox's schema), lawyers formed the dominant group on both the departmental and the Limoges district councils. Contrasts appear at the municipal level as well. In Caen, the commercial elite increasingly came to dominate the municipal council; in Limoges, the political uproar of 1792 brought to office a municipal council more radical in its political views and more modest in its social background.

The social composition of the administrative councils is instructive, but those councils did not operate in a vacuum. All the councils met in their respective departmental *chefs-lieux,* Caen and Limoges, and the urban milieu strongly influenced their proceedings. In Caen, in particular, the isolation of poor immigrants in the faubourgs was reflected in the geographical composition of successive municipal councils. The passivity of the lower classes was virtually institutionalized in Caen, where sectional lines appear to have been drawn to enhance the power of the wealthy elite.

All of these factors together—the nature of the local economy, social structures, and urban geography—molded the political arena in these two towns. The correlation between urban geography and political geography in Caen and Limoges is very clear. It is reflected in the composition of the municipal councils, in the interaction between those councils and political clubs, and even in the revolutionary festivals and processions staged in the two towns. The impact of these factors is more generally reflected in the nature of revolutionary politics in Calvados and the Haute-Vienne. We return to the process of revolutionary politics at the end of this chapter, to explore more systematically the interaction between the various councils, between them and the clubs, between the councils and their constituents, and between the local scene and the national scene, and finally to place that inter-action within its social context.

For three years, beginning in late 1790, the departmental councils were the preeminent administrative bodies in provincial France. Created by the Con-stituent Assembly, the departmental administrations immediately assumed responsibility for the difficult transition from the old *généralités* to the new *départements*. This involved the mediation of boundary disputes as well as the exchange of administrative, judicial, and tax records. It was a process that brought the councils into contact not only with their neighbors but with departmental administrators all over France, beginning a tradition of consultation and cooperation that would persist until at least June, 1793. And it stood as a precedent for the exchange of protests and proposals that took place between the departments following the proscription of the Gi-rondin deputies.

The departmental councils were subordinate in every respect to the Na-tional Assembly and the king, and their authority was explicitly restricted to administrative matters (the collection of taxes, the assurance of an adequate food supply, the maintenance of a public police force). In practice, however, that legal restriction was often ignored, and many departmental councils issued statements or lodged protests regarding political issues (military re-cruitment, the fate of the king, the role of Paris in national politics). The National Convention eventually remedied this tendency with the adminis-trative reorganization that followed the collapse of the federalist revolt.[1]

In July, 1790, electoral assemblies met in Calvados and the Haute-Vienne to elect their first departmental councils. As in every other department, they chose thirty-six administrators plus a *procureur-général-syndic,* theoreti-cally the representative of the king with responsibility for ensuring compli-ance with the law. The council was elected to a two-year term with half the members up for reelection every year. In September, 1791, eighteen admin-istrators in each department, chosen by draw, stood for reelection, but in November, 1792, the Convention ordered a complete renewal of the coun-cils in order to purge them of their royalist elements. One year later, the de-partmental administrations were reduced to their eight-member directories.

These yearly elections produced few changes in the social character of the

---

1. Godechot, *Les Institutions de la France,* 98–101.

departmental councils. Voters in both Calvados and the Haute-Vienne consistently named respectable, wealthy men to these positions, principally lawyers and rural landowners. No peasants sat on the councils, and of the two artisan/shopkeepers elected in the Haute-Vienne in 1792, one may in fact have been a merchant.[2] Calvados electors named no artisans to their departmental administration. The nobility fared little better—four nobles sat on the 1790 council in Calvados, and three on the Haute-Vienne council of the same year, with only one member of the second estate on the two subsequent councils in each department.[3] The character of the departmental administrations was distinctly *haut-bourgeois*. This is hardly surprising, since in 1790 and 1791, one had to pay taxes equivalent to ten days' wages to be eligible for election to either a departmental or a district council. After August 10, 1792, that requirement was dropped, as was the distinction between "active" and "passive" citizens.

A closer look at the occupational breakdown of the various councils, however, reveals some definite contrasts between the successive administrations of Calvados and those of the Haute-Vienne. Tables 5 and 6 compare the administrations for the three terms from 1790 through 1793. In both departments, the councils in all three terms included at least as many members from the legal profession as from any other single occupational category. In the Haute-Vienne administration, however, the predominance of the legal profession is particularly striking. Lawyers constituted a majority in every term, and in the 1792–1793 term, their numbers grew to twenty-one—57 percent of the membership. In the Calvados administration, the number of men with legal training declined from its 1790–1791 peak of 43 percent to 35 percent in the two following terms.

In both departments, rural landowners played a significant role in the administration, but in the richly agricultural department of Calvados, their presence on the council was more pronounced. In the Haute-Vienne, landowners never constituted more than 20 percent of the council, and in the

2. Pierre Mourier *père*, of Limoges, was identified on the official list of departmental administrators as a *négociant*. A list of Jacobin club members prepared in the year III, however, describes him as a *marchand de bois*, and I have chosen to classify him as such, speculating that in 1792 he might have been tempted to exaggerate his status in order to bring it into line with his new, prestigious position. I have classified *marchands particuliers* as shopkeepers, distinguishing them from *marchands* without designation, whom I have classified as commercial.

3. In addition to local almanacs, I have consulted Louis de la Roque and Edouard de Barthélemy, *Catalogue des Gentilhommes en 1789* (Paris, 1866), I, for this information.

TABLE 5 Occupations of Calvados Departmental Administrators, 1790–1793 (N=37)

	1790–1791	1791–1792	1792–1793
Clergy		1	2
Legal professions	16	13	13
Liberal professions	3	3	3
Commerce	2	4	5
Rural landowning	14	13	6
Artisan/Shopkeeping			
Military	2	1	1
Other[a]			
Unknown		1	7
Nobility[b]	3	1	1

[a] Includes bourgeois, *vivant de son bien, vivant de son revenu.*
[b] Nobility is not treated as an occupation. Those listed as nobles also appear in one of the other categories, most often legal.
Note: Appendix II provides a breakdown of occupational categories.

TABLE 6 Occupations of Haute-Vienne Departmental Administrators, 1790–1793 (N=37)

	1790–1791	1791–1792	1792–1793
Clergy			1
Legal professions	19	19	21
Liberal professions	3	4	4
Commerce	2	2	1
Rural landowning	6	7	3
Artisan/Shopkeeping			2
Military			
Other[a]	4	3	2
Unknown	3	2	3
Nobility[b]	4	1	1

[a] Includes bourgeois, *vivant de son bien, vivant de son revenu.*
[b] Nobility is not treated as an occupation. Those listed as nobles also appear in one of the other categories, most often legal.
Note: Appendix II provides a breakdown of occupational categories.

1792—1793 term, after four consecutive years of bad harvest, they dwindled to 8 percent. Replacing them, to some extent, were men from the liberal professions, who added to their numbers at each election. Professionals and lawyers together accounted for nearly 70 percent of the 1792—1793 administration in the Haute-Vienne.

In Calvados, the apparent decline in landowners from 35 percent in 1791—1792 to 16 percent in 1792—1793 is deceptive. Seven administrators elected in 1792 did not give an occupation, a much higher number than in previous years.[4] Six of these men came from small villages, and it would scarcely be surprising if all six were landowners. Certainly four or five owned land, which would raise the number of landowners on the 1792—1793 council close to its level of previous years.

A final significant trend in the Calvados administrations is the slow, but steady, increase in the number of administrators engaged in commerce. Their numbers are not overwhelming—they never rival the lawyers or landowners—but by 1792, they had reached a level of 14 percent, representing a much stronger force than did merchants on the Haute-Vienne council. In addition, many of the large landowners on the Calvados council were producing grain for the market and would thus have had a shared interest with the merchants of Caen and other towns. In the Haute-Vienne, artisans made at least an entree into departmental politics in the 1792 elections, again a contrast with Calvados, where artisans never achieved departmental office.

In sum, from 1790 through 1793, the legal and liberal professions increasingly dominated the Haute-Vienne administration. Landowners played a modest, and decreasing, role on the Haute-Vienne councils. In Calvados, a rich grain region, rural landowners rivaled lawyers for dominance in the administration, and those two groups could not ignore the increasing strength of the commercial contingent among their colleagues.

This contrasting character of the two administrations is reflected in the *procès-verbaux* of their meetings. The Haute-Vienne council clearly appreciated the limitations to its authority and consistently refused to interpret or modify the law in the course of its daily business. The Haute-Vienne admin-

---

4. Officials elected in 1792 in both departments—particularly on the departmental administration, but on municipal and district councils as well—were much more reticent about revealing their occupations than those elected earlier. Whether this was due to a fear that certain professions had now become suspect (farmers cultivating grain might have had reason to be apprehensive) or to a feeling that one's status as "citizen" was now accepted as more important than one's occupational status is hard to say.

istrators frequently declared themselves incompetent to "rien changer aux dispositions de la loi" in response to petitions regarding parents of émigrés, disputes over *rentes*, and military recruitment. One rarely finds similar reservations expressed in the minutes of the Calvados council, which, less dominated by lawyers, showed a greater willingness to stray from the strict letter of the law in order to consider what it believed was just or fair. In June, 1793, the Haute-Vienne council remained cautious in its actions, ever conscious of its constitutional limitations. By the end of that month, the Calvados administration stood accused before the Convention for exceeding its authority and violating the law.[5]

The geographical distribution of the departmental council members may also have influenced their political character. In Calvados, the electoral assemblies chose six representatives from each of the six districts, with the district of Caen enjoying an additional voice in the person of the *procureur-général-syndic*. The Haute-Vienne, represented in Map 4, followed this pattern for the 1790–1791 term, with six delegates from each district and the *procureur-général-syndic* from Limoges; but in subsequent years, the electoral assembly made no attempt to ensure equal representation. For the 1791–1792 term, four districts, including Limoges, each sent seven representatives to the departmental council, while Saint-Yrieix sent only four and Dorat only five, including the *procureur-général-syndic*. The disproportion became even greater in the 1792–1793 term. The district of Limoges sent ten men to the departmental council, and the two northern districts of Dorat and Bellac sent seven and eight men, respectively. The three remaining districts (Saint-Junien, Saint-Yrieix, and Saint-Léonard) sent four, five, and three men, respectively, totaling only one-third of the council members. Of those three districts, two protested the departmental council's actions in June, 1793. The Saint-Yrieix district council berated the Haute-Vienne administrators for not carrying further their protest of the June 2 proscriptions, while Saint-Junien denounced the department's support of the Côte-d'Or resolution (which called for a united departmental protest of

5. See A. D. Calvados, L189, and A. D. Haute-Vienne, L56–58, for the *procès-verbaux* of departmental council meetings. Lenard Berlanstein makes a similar point in *The Barristers of Toulouse in the Eighteenth Century (1740–1793)* (Baltimore, 1975), 142, 171. See also Philip Dawson, *Provincial Magistrates and Revolutionary Politics in France, 1789–1795* (Cambridge, 1972). It is interesting to note that lawyers did not dominate local political bodies in most of provincial France as they dominated national assemblies. See Lynn A. Hunt, *Politics, Culture, and Class in the French Revolution* (Berkeley, 1984).

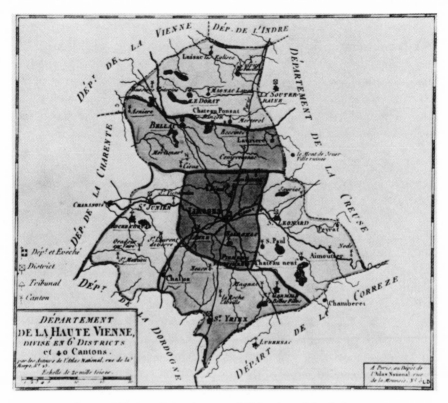

MAP 4. Haute-Vienne Districts and District *Chefs-lieux*

Reprinted, by permission of éditions rené dessagne, from René Morichon (ed.), *Histoire du Limousin et de la Marche* (Limoges, 1975), II, 45.

the factionalism in Paris and declared the departments' readiness to rebel against despotism). What is remarkable here, however, is the predominance of administrators from the district of Limoges, most of them from the town of Limoges itself. They nearly equaled in number the representatives of the three southern districts combined. The town of Limoges, then, exerted a greater influence on its departmental administration than did the town of Caen.

The district councils were in most respects the least consequential of the local administrations during the first four years of the Revolution. The departmental administration could overturn any decision made by the district councils, clearly rendering the latter subordinate to the former. The district councils did enjoy the advantage of closer contact with their constituents—an advantage curtailed, however, by the existence of communal councils, which intervened between the people and the district offices. When representing demands or grievances of the people, districts generally acted as intermediaries between municipalities and the departmental council. Thus, the district councils occupied an ambiguous middle position, restricted in their actions by the superior authority of the departmental administration and removed one step from the voters they represented.[6]

I have not studied in detail the councils of all six districts in these two departments, but only those of the districts of Caen and Limoges. Beyond sending an occasional member on to the departmental administration, the councils of the outlying districts had little impact on departmental affairs. In times of crisis, however, the departmental authorities often met in union with the district and municipal councils of the departmental *chef-lieu*. The Caen and Limoges district officials did exercise a continuing influence on local affairs, and during the crucial months of June and July, 1793, the Haute-Vienne and Calvados administrations invited the two district councils to deliberate with them.

As we have seen, the Caen district council as a body was not influential until the end of the revolt, when it was the first to retract its support of the insurrection. Several individual administrators, however, played very active roles. For instance, Louis Caille, the *procureur-syndic*, advocated revolt

6. Godechot, *Les Institutions de la France*, 101–103. Godechot notes that in some departments, the district councils acted with considerable independence, sometimes directly rivaling the departmental administration. This was never the case in Calvados or the Haute-Vienne, despite occasional conflicts between departmental and district authorities.

against the Convention more aggressively than any other official. Robert Tirel, on the other hand, spoke out in protest of the decision to arrest Romme and Prieur. In Limoges, the district council joined with the municipal council in steering the departmental administration away from the federalist movement. A closer look at the two district councils may help to explain their divergent conduct at this crucial time.

The number of districts varied from one department to the next, but both the Haute-Vienne and Calvados were divided into six. Each district elected a council composed of twelve men plus a *procureur-syndic*, the counterpart at the district level of the *procureur-général-syndic*. The schedule of elections followed that of the departmental administrations, with district electoral assemblies naming the first councils in July, 1790. Half the council members stood for reelection in September, 1791, and in November, 1792, the councils were renewed in their entirety.

The occupational composition of the Caen and Limoges district councils mirrors the patterns in the respective departmental administrations, as shown in Tables 7 and 8. In Caen, rural landowners formed the strongest contingent during all three terms from 1790 through 1793, constituting from 30 to 46 percent of the total. As in the Calvados departmental council, their apparent decline from the 1791–1792 term to the 1792–1793 term might be diminished by the one official whose occupation is unknown.[7] Lawyers consistently maintained a strong presence on the district council, declining only by one in the 1792 elections, when their numbers are equaled by men from the liberal professions. Professionals exercised a proportionally greater influence at this level than they did on the departmental administration. These three groups taken together—rural landowners, lawyers, and professionals—never constituted less than 77 percent of the council members. Their predominance came at the expense of the commercial community, which managed to elect only one merchant to the Caen district council. This absence of commercial men on the district council is significant, especially given their increasing strength at the departmental level and their dominance, as we shall soon see, on the Caen municipal council.

In Limoges, the situation was nearly the reverse. Rural landowners on the district council never numbered more than three, representing approxi-

7. Like the majority of departmental officials whose occupations I could not determine, Jean Jacques Bernard Lequeru, president of the 1792–93 district council, came from a small village (Ayran, ten to fifteen miles southeast of Caen).

TABLE 7 Occupations of Caen District Administrators,
1790–1793 (N=13)

	1790–1791	1791–1792	1792–1793
Clergy	1		
Legal professions	4	4	3
Liberal professions	2	2	3
Commerce	1	1	
Rural landowning	5	6	4
Artisan/Shopkeeping			1
Military			
Other[a]			1
Unknown			1
Nobility[b]		1	

[a] Includes bourgeois, *vivant de son bien, vivant de son revenu.*
[b] Nobility is not treated as an occupation. Those listed as nobles also appear in one of the other categories, most often legal.
Note: Appendix II provides a breakdown of occupational categories.

TABLE 8 Occupations of Limoges District Administrators,
1790–1793 (N=13)

	1790–1791	1791–1792	1792–1793
Clergy			
Legal professions	5	6	4
Liberal professions			1
Commerce	2		1
Rural landowning	2	3	3
Artisan/Shopkeeping			2
Military	3	2	
Other[a]	1	2	2
Unknown			
Nobility[b]	2	2	1

[a] Includes bourgeois, *vivant de son bien, vivant de son revenu.*
[b] Nobility is not treated as an occupation. Those listed as nobles also appear in one of the other categories, most often legal.
Note: Appendix II provides a breakdown of occupational categories.

mately 23 percent of the total. Lawyers dominated the council throughout the period, composing nearly 50 percent of the 1791–1792 administration, though declining to roughly 30 percent the following year. The occupational picture here resembles that of the Haute-Vienne departmental administration, except for the virtual absence of professionals. Men from the liberal professions, a significant force among the departmental officials, did not appear on the Limoges district council until the 1792–1793 term, when one doctor was elected. Military men filled the void left by the professionals on the first two councils, giving way in 1792–1793 to artisans and to men identifying themselves simply as bourgeois.

Comparing the two districts, we see a situation similar to that which characterized the two departmental administrations: rural landowners predominant on the Caen district council, lawyers enjoying that position in Limoges. We must once again take note of the overwhelming preponderance of landowners, lawyers, and professionals on the Caen district council. Of the thirty-nine officials elected to the three consecutive councils, only five came from occupations outside these three groups, with the occupation of one additional official unknown. In Limoges, the occupations ranged more broadly, particularly in the 1792–1793 term, when all but two of the eight categories were represented.

Artisans first sat on the councils of both districts in the 1792–1793 term— two in Limoges and one in Caen. The increase in artisanal representation at the district level does not appear large; it is similar to that at the departmental level. Proportionally, however, artisans and shopkeepers enjoyed significantly greater influence on the district councils, which were smaller. That influence was greatest in Limoges. The only artisan elected to the Caen district council, François Jacques Samuel Boiszerard, was a wealthy goldsmith who lived on the rue Saint-Jean, at the heart of the most prosperous parish in Caen. His affinity would have been more with his clientele, the Caen social elite, and other merchants than with the majority of artisans. Jean Baptiste Poncet and Jacques Peyrat, the two shopkeepers elected to the Limoges council, were a *marchand de fer* and *marchand de bois*, respectively, and both lived in the faubourgs of Limoges. They represented a more modest segment of the artisan/shopkeeper community than did Boiszerard in Caen.

Though we come to them last, the municipalities were the first local administrations created by the Constituent Assembly. Motivated by the midsummer outbreak of municipal revolutions in most of the major French towns, the Assembly moved quickly to institutionalize and bring under control this effervescence of political activity.[8] On December 14, 1789, the deputies passed legislation calling for the election of municipal councils in every city, town, and village of France. Each *commune* would also elect a mayor and a *procureur*, who acted as legal adviser to the council. The council itself was composed of two parts: the *officiers*, who along with the *procureur* formed the *corps municipal*, which met on a daily basis to deal with the routine business of municipal administration; and the *notables*, a group twice the size of the *corps municipal*, who together with the *officiers* composed the *conseil général*, convened by the mayor on an irregular basis to address more important matters.[9] The size of the general councils varied according to population. The citizens of Caen elected fifteen *officiers*, including the *procureur*, and thirty *notables*. In Limoges, the council numbered twelve *officiers* and twenty-four *notables*.

Despite their position at the bottom rung of the local administrative hierarchy, the municipal councils, particularly those of the departmental *chefs-lieux*, may have been the most important local administrative bodies. More than either the district or the departmental councils, the municipal councils of the *chefs-lieux* represented a coherent and potent constituency, and they were the only one of the three councils chosen by direct election. During periods of political ferment, the populations of the *chefs-lieux* forcefully expressed their sentiments in both words and action. All three local councils met in the *chef-lieu*, and none could ignore, at times of crisis, the pressures and demands of an often unruly urban population. When grain shortages occurred, both Caen and Limoges received preferential treatment over other hungry towns. Indeed, a number of departmental administrations, including that of Calvados, considered shifting their meetings to other towns to escape popular pressure.

The municipal councils often acted as intermediaries between the urban

8. For an excellent discussion of the municipal revolutions, the patriotic committees that they spawned, and the municipal councils that replaced them, see Lynn A. Hunt, "Committees and Communes: Local Politics and National Revolution in 1789," *Comparative Studies in Society and History*, XVIII (July, 1976), 321–46. For a discussion of local administration in general, see Alfred Cobban, "Local Government during the French Revolution," in Alfred Cobban (ed.), *Aspects of the French Revolution* (New York, 1968), 112–30.

9. Godechot, *Les Institutions de la France*, 105–106. In Caen, after September, 1792, the general council was to meet publicly three times each week. A. C. Caen, D2 (Délibérations du Corps municipal et du Conseil Général de la Commune, 4 janvier 1792–11 Germinal an II), minutes of September 1, 1792.

populace and higher authorities. A council might alternately act as a mouth-piece for the demands of its constituents and as a political thermometer for the departmental administration. If one gauges the success of their efforts by their ability to preserve public order, the municipal councils of Caen and Limoges were reasonably effective, at least until the debacle of the federalist revolt produced a total disruption of Caen daily life. The Caen municipal council must bear at least partial responsibility for this, because of its failure to impress upon the federalist leaders the lack of popular support for the proposed march on Paris. Although the majority of the council members did not actively participate in the revolt, neither did they manifest any concerted opposition to it. The Limoges municipality, on the other hand, made very clear its opposition to any departmental protest or resistance. The council denounced the departmental administration for its support of the May 30 Côte-d'Or resolution and gave a hostile reception to later couriers from Lyon and Bordeaux.

The conduct of the two municipal councils was a major factor in determining the political posture of Calvados and the Haute-Vienne after May 31, far more important than that of the district councils. To understand their contrasting attitudes and actions, we must examine the municipal councils themselves, with an eye not only to the social character of the men in office, and how that changed over time, but also to the social character of their constituencies.

The first municipal councils were elected in February, 1790, to a two-year term. As with the departmental and district administrations, half the members of the general council stood for reelection each year. An *officier* could serve no more than two consecutive terms but could return to the general council as a *notable* for a third term and subsequently be elected as an *officier* again. New elections were held in November or December, 1790, and thereafter occurred at yearly intervals until their suspension in 1793. After the federalist revolt, representatives on mission nominated men to fill vacancies on the councils, usually after consultation with the local Jacobin club and *comité de surveillance*. This system prevailed until after Thermidor.

In Caen, we have five separate councils to consider—February, 1790, November, 1790, 1791, 1792, and 1793, the last being the council named by Lindet and Oudot in August, following the revolt. For Limoges, a sixth council requires analysis. In August, 1792, the departmental administration finally authorized the replacement of Limoges' mayor, Louis Naurissart, who had abandoned his post the previous winter, after the February grain scandal. The municipal council convened section assemblies, which insisted that they be permitted to elect an entirely new municipal council, despite the fact that regularly scheduled elections were barely three months away. The departmental council acquiesced in the demand, and the sections elected a full council. Elections in November brought a few additional changes in the municipal personnel, and this council remained virtually intact until 1794. The representatives on mission Brival and Lanot named only three new *officiers* in September, 1793, two of whom had previously been *notables*.

In this study of the municipal councils, I have chosen to include only the *corps municipal*—the *officiers,* mayor, and *procureur*—both for reasons of manageability and available data and because this part of the council held the greatest responsibility and the greatest power in the management of local affairs.

The occupational composition of the municipal councils in both Caen and Limoges, shown in Tables 9 and 10, departs radically from the patterns of the district and departmental administrations. Not surprisingly, rural landowners do not appear on these councils, with the exception of one on the 1792 council in Limoges, where the lines between city and country were not as firmly drawn as in Caen. More unexpected is the steadily declining influence of men with legal training on both town councils. Whereas lawyers dominated the Haute-Vienne departmental administration and the Limoges district council, they quickly became a minor factor in the Limoges municipality. Five lawyers sat on the February, 1790, council, but their numbers dwindled to three with the next election; and in 1792, only one lawyer, the *procureur,* secured election to the council. Lawyers fared somewhat better in Caen, where their decline began somewhat later. Their numbers peaked at seven (44 percent of the sixteen-member council) with the second election of 1790, dropped by one the following year, and stood at four (25 percent) in 1792. The council appointed by Lindet and Oudot included only one lawyer, the same number that sat on the Limoges councils of 1792 and 1793. This exclusion of lawyers in Caen seems to have been by design. The representative on mission who followed Lindet and Oudot, Jacques Léonard Laplanche, explicitly stated his intention to rid local administrations of "the men in black coats."[10]

10. A. D. Calvados, L10529 (*Journal de l'Armée des Côtes de Cherbourg,* November 5, 1793).

TABLE 9 Occupations of Caen Municipal Officials, 1790–1793 (N=16)

	February, 1790	November, 1790	1791	1792	1793
Clergy	1	1			
Legal professions	4	7	6	4	1
Liberal professions		1	2	1	2
Commerce	4	3	4	3	2
Rural landowning					
Artisan/Shopkeeping	2	2	3	6	6
Military					
Other	4	1	1	2	2
Unknown	1	1			3
Nobility	4	2			

Note: Appendix II provides a breakdown of occupational categories.

TABLE 10 Occupations of Limoges Municipal Officials, 1790–1793 (N=13)

	February, 1790	November, 1790	1791	August, 1792	1792	1793
Clergy	1	1				
Legal professions	5	3	2	2	1	1
Liberal professions	1	2	1	3	2	2
Commerce	4	5	7	5	7	6
Rural landowning					1	
Artisan/Shopkeeping	2	2	2	2	1	3
Military						
Other			1	1	1	1
Unknown						
Nobility	3		1			

Note: Appendix II provides a breakdown of occupational categories.

Merchants and artisans, in contrast to lawyers, increased their influence between 1790 and 1793. Taken together, the electoral success of these two groups traced a similar pattern in Caen and Limoges. Merchants and artisans in Limoges constituted 46 percent of the February, 1790, council; grew steadily to reach 69 percent with the 1791 elections; slipped slightly in 1792; and returned to the 69-percent level in 1793. An equal number, but a smaller proportion, of merchants and artisans sat on the Caen town council. They accounted for 38 percent of the council members during 1790; slipped moderately in the November, 1790, elections; but recovered in the 1791 elections and reached a strength of 56 percent in 1792 before declining by one, to 50 percent, on the council appointed after the revolt.

If we examine merchants and artisans separately, a somewhat different picture appears. Surprisingly, artisans showed greater strength on the Caen municipal council than in Limoges. On the 1790 and 1791 councils, artisanal strength hovered at around 15 percent in both towns. But on the 1792 Caen council, the number of artisans jumped to six (38 percent), while in Limoges the number declined slightly before rebounding in 1793. Conversely, merchants and manufacturers did better in Limoges than in Caen. Merchants never constituted more than 25 percent of the Caen council, whereas in Limoges they surpassed 50 percent in 1791 and remained near that level through the next two years.

One might have expected the patterns to be reversed, for they do not support the traditional interpretation of federalism as a movement of the commercial bourgeoisie. One would not expect a municipal council dominated by artisans in a federalist town or a council dominated by merchants in a Jacobin town. A closer look, however, will help untangle this apparent paradox.

The assignment of occupational categories to local officials in Limoges poses certain difficulties, because of their disconcerting habit of calling themselves *négociants* in one year and *marchands* in another. This was true, for instance, of six of the seven men on the 1792 council who are classified as commercial. It is impossible to know if they exaggerated their status in 1792 by calling themselves *négociants* or were attempting to paint themselves as good sans-culottes in 1793 by listing themselves as *marchands*. This in itself does not pose a problem for purposes of classification—*marchands* are grouped with *négociants* as commercial in any case. Those merchants, however, who further qualified their occupation as *marchand tanneur* or *marchand teinturier*, for example, are here considered shopkeepers and are grouped with the artisans.[11] Some of the merchants on the 1792

---

11. It is difficult to distinguish wholesale merchants from retail merchants and shopkeepers in the documents of the Revolution. Any criteria will be arbitrary to some extent. Distinguishing between *négociants/marchands* (classified as commercial) and *marchands particuliers* (classified as shopkeepers) probably leads to a slight inflation of the number of wholesale merchants. A small merchant might neglect to designate his particular specialty, but a wholesale merchant would not likely list his occupation as *marchand mercier*, for example. In marking a distinction

Limoges council very likely belong in this latter category. Only one of the seven, Joseph Ardant-Masjambost, can definitely be said to have headed a substantial commercial enterprise, based on records from the forced loan of the year IV and the accompanying estimates of family fortunes.[12] None of the seven, with the possible exception of Ardant-Masjambost, belonged to the Limoges commercial elite. Not one of them attended the 1789 assembly of the *juridiction consulaire* for the election of deputies to the Limoges assembly of the third estate, and none was among the Limoges *négociants* asked by the departmental administration to form a grain-purchasing consortium in 1791.[13] To find that commercial elite in public office, one must look to the 1791 municipality, headed by Louis Naurissart. Seven merchants sat on this council, too, but none of them returned on the 1792 council. In addition to Naurissart, the 1791 council included Gabriel Grellet and François Pouyat. Naurissart, Grellet, and François Pouyat's father were all members of the six-man grain consortium formed just before the 1791 elections. Joseph Pétiniaud, another *négociant* on the 1791 council, had been a *juge consul* before 1789. All but Naurissart voted at the 1789 assembly of the *juridiction consulaire*.

Although men engaged in commerce dominated the 1791 and 1792 municipal councils in Limoges, the character of the councils was very different. The 1791 council numbered six former Amis de la Paix (the moderate club that had challenged the Limoges Jacobins in late 1790), including Naurissart, Grellet, Pétiniaud, and Pouyat. In August, 1792, the insistent demands

---

between merchants and shopkeepers and grouping the latter with artisans, I am following the lead of Maurice Agulhon, who makes a similar distinction between merchants and small merchants in *Pénitents et francs-maçons de l'ancienne Provence*, 148–53.

12. A. D. Haute-Vienne, L252 (an IV, forced loan and list of rich). All seven of the merchants appear on these lists. Ardant-Masjambost stands well above the rest on both lists, with a levied "loan" of 3,000 *livres* and an estimated fortune of 190,000 *livres*. Two of the other officiers, Grégoire Louis Boudet and Joseph Brès, were levied contributions of 1,000 *livres*, but their estimated fortunes were considerably less than Masjambost's, at 30,000 and 60,000 *livres*, respectively. Martial Labrousse *père* was levied a loan of 900 *livres*, but this figure may have been revised after his fortune was estimated at only 10,000. Mathieu Nadaud brought up the rear in this group, paying 200 *livres* on an estimated fortune of 9,000. All of these figures pale in comparison with those for Louis Naurissart, probably the richest man in Limoges, who was levied 10,000 *livres* based on an estimated fortune of 800,000. The registers did not indicate which of those listed had paid this special tax. The figures for estimated fortune were based on 1790 currency valuation.

13. A. C. Limoges, AA7 (Assemblée des différents corps de la ville pour nommer des députés à l'Assemblée du Tiers-Etat de la ville de Limoges). The municipal archives of Limoges are split between the Archives Municipales and the Bibliothèque Municipale. These documents are held at the Bibliothèque. A. D. Haute-Vienne, L850 (documents pertaining to Limoges grain supply).

of the Limoges sections forced that council from office prematurely. Jacobin club members dominated the next two councils, totaling eleven of thirteen *officiers* on both the August and November, 1792, councils.

We see, then, that social, economic, and political lines separated the old commercial elite from the merchants represented by the 1792 council. An incident involving the 1791 grain consortium suggests that the social divisions cut deepest. The departmental directory originally named seven *négociants* to coordinate the purchase of grain for Limoges. The seventh was Jean Baptiste Nieaud, mayor of Limoges for the 1790–1791 term and cofounder of the Jacobin club. The others, who referred to Nieaud disparagingly as a *teinturier* (despite his thriving wool trade and a fortune estimated at 500,000 *livres*), refused to work with a man "who had so mismanaged the municipal administration, and whose principles were in complete opposition to their own."[14] They would not accept this "nouveau-riche" with his unimpressive family lineage. Nieaud, who had one month earlier been elected to the departmental council, quietly withdrew from the group. His social affinities lay with the Jacobins, who would one year later dominate local politics.

In Caen, the situation on the 1792 council, with its strong contingent of artisans, is similarly complicated. A comparison of this council with the 1793 municipality (appointed by Lindet and Oudot), which also included six artisans, reveals the danger of accepting occupational categories at face value. The artisans on the 1792 council included an apothecary, a *parfumeur,* and a *bijoutier,* all catering to the social elite in their trades and all living in the wealthier, central districts of Caen. A fourth artisan on the council, David Nicolas, was a *marchand mercier* with close business and social ties to Jean Samuel Paisant, a wealthy *fabricant en blondes* who also sat on the council. Among the six artisans on the postrevolt council we find, to be sure, a *confiseur* and a *marchand papetier,* both with well-to-do clienteles. But we also find, more characteristically, a poor *vinaigrier,* Jean Cachelou, and the printer for the Jacobin club, Pierre Chalopin *fils.* As with the Limoges council, more differences exist between the 1792 and 1793 Caen councils than the tables reveal.

The availability of tax records for both Caen and Limoges lends another dimension to our analysis of the municipal councils. Several factors render meaningless any comparison of the tax payments made in one town or de-

14. A. D. Haute-Vienne, L850. The quotation is my own paraphrasing of a department transcription.

partment with those in another. The tax rate was not uniform nationwide. The Constituent Assembly divided the tax burden among the departments roughly according to the regional distribution of Old Regime taxes. They made no systematic effort to levy the new taxes equitably, and departmental entreaties resulted in adjustments in 1792 and 1793. Both Caen and Limoges received rebates after appealing to the Legislative Assembly. Departmental administrations divided their tax quotas among the districts, which in turn assigned quotas to the *communes,* which were then responsible for levying individual taxes. In addition, each municipality had the option of levying a surtax, not to exceed four *sous* per *livre,* to defray local expenses. Within this system, two equally wealthy men in two different towns, even within the same department, would only by chance have paid identical taxes. Within a town, however, the tax rates were consistent, and so we can employ the tax rolls to gauge separately the social evolution of the Caen and Limoges councils.[15]

The pattern of the *contribution mobilière* paid by members of successive municipal councils followed roughly the same trend in Caen and Limoges. As Tables 11 and 12 show, the mean tax paid by municipal *officiers* in both towns gradually, but steadily, declined. The one exception to this trend—the 1791 Limoges council—corresponds with the political developments of that

15. For this study, I used the rolls of the *contribution mobilière,* a tax I consider preferable for two reasons to the *contribution foncière,* the other principal revolutionary tax. First, the *contribution foncière* taxed property; and many of the elected officials at the municipal level, especially after 1791, did not own property and therefore do not appear on these rolls. Second, many of those who did own property also owned property outside the town—a *maison de campagne* or a *manoir.* Records for these rural cantons have often disappeared, but even when they do exist, the task of scanning them would be enormously time-consuming. The fact that some officials owned land in other departments further complicates the task. The *contribution mobilière,* therefore, offers a much more accessible tax record. And the rolls for Caen and Limoges are exceptionally complete. Of the 158 officials on the eleven municipal councils under consideration, I found tax records for all but 19, just 12 percent.

The Constituent Assembly passed legislation for the *contribution mobilière* in January, 1791. It was not to be a tax on property like the *contribution foncière,* but the deputies clearly realized the inadvisability of attempting to levy a tax on income. They settled on rent as the most visible and most easily verifiable indicator of wealth, and this became the primary base of the *contribution mobilière.* There were other elements to this tax as well. All taxpayers paid a tax equivalent to three days' wages; those with domestic servants paid an additional imposition, as did those who owned horses or mules. Those with large families were taxed at a lower rate, while bachelors paid a higher premium. Day laborers and artisans received a tax break, and citizens who paid a *contribution foncière* could deduct that payment from their *contribution mobilière.* It should be noted that this allowance for deductions would tend to reduce slightly the *contribution mobilière* of the wealthiest taxpayers, who in most cases would also have paid a *contribution foncière.* See Godechot, *Les Institutions de la France,* 136–38.

TABLE 11 *Contribution Mobilière* of Caen Municipal Officials,
1790–1793 (N=16)

	February, 1790	November, 1790	1791	1792	1793
Officials paying:					
0–49 *livres*	1	0	3	9	7
50–149 *livres*	4	3	7	5	3
150–499 *livres*	3	7	4	1	1
500–999 *livres*	6	2	0	0	1
1,000 *livres* and above	2	2	0	0	0
Unknown	0	2	2	1	4
Mean tax (*livres*)	542	493	123	53	97[a]
Median tax (*livres*)	399	261	74	39	38

[a] If we exclude the one council member who paid 560 *livres* tax, the mean tax for 1793 is 54 *livres*.

TABLE 12 *Contribution Mobilière* of Limoges Municipal Officials, 1790–1793 (N=13)

	February, 1790	November, 1790	1791	August, 1792	1792	179.
Officials paying:						
0–49 *livres*	3	4	3	10	10	9
50–99 *livres*	1	2	4	1	2	2
100–249 *livres*	4	5	3	1	0	0
250–499 *livres*	0	0	1	0	0	0
500 *livres* and above	1	1	1	0	0	0
Unknown	4	1	1	1	1	2
Mean tax (*livres*)	124	118	150	43	28	27
Median tax (*livres*)	100	90	75	27	20	18

year. The municipal elections of 1791 marked the temporary political resurgence of the moderate, wealthy bourgeoisie of Limoges. Louis Naurissart, as mayor, headed a municipality composed of the Limoges commercial elite. The 1791 council witnessed the nadir of Jacobin club influence in municipal affairs and the zenith for supporters of the disbanded Amis de la Paix. The tax figures for the 1791 council reflect that political shift.

A second discrepancy in the general pattern of declining taxes—the 1793 Caen council—is explained by a statistical quirk rather than a political shift. The mean for 1793 is distorted by the one *officier* who paid a tax of 560 *livres*. If one excludes this figure from the total, the mean tax paid becomes 54 *livres*, very close to the mean of the previous year. It should also be observed that tax data is missing for four members of this council, more than for any other Caen council. The occupations of three of these men are also unknown; the fourth was an artisan. Three of the four were new to politics in 1793 and disappeared from local politics after the year II. The difficulty in finding tax information for them stems from a lack of positive identification. These men were simply not active long enough in local politics to be positively identified. Had tax information for these men been available, the mean tax shown for 1793 *officiers* in Caen would probably be slightly lower than that for 1792.[16]

For a similar reason, the mean tax paid by the February, 1790, council members in Limoges was probably higher than that indicated in Table 12. Again, no tax information could be found for four men. Of these four, one was a prominent doctor, one was a noble, one was a Pétiniaud (a ubiquitous name on the Limoges rolls) and therefore certainly wealthy, and the fourth was a former *avocat du roi au présidial*. If the tax figures for these four men could be included in the computations, the mean tax shown for that council would rise to at least the level shown for the 1791 council.

If we examine the median tax in each council, we find a more regular and consistent downward trend. The median tax in the 1793 Caen council was slightly lower than that in the 1792 council. In both Caen and Limoges, the highest median tax was paid in the 1790 council, with the sharpest drop coming between 1790 and 1791 in Caen and between 1791 and August, 1792, in Limoges. The median tax does, however, underestimate the wealth

16. The process of positively identifying municipal officials was a difficult one. It was somewhat easier in Limoges, where election results almost always listed the occupations of those elected. I was also aided in Limoges by the roster of Jacobin club members, which listed first names and occupations and often mentioned the offices held by members. In Caen, I was more dependent on jury lists (which I also used in Limoges) and certificates of residence. Both of these sources generally included addresses and occupations. By comparing signatures on these lists with those on the *procès-verbaux* of council meetings, I could be very confident in my identifications. For the 1793 council, this was not always possible, however, since not all members consistently signed the *procès-verbaux* and because a few of those appointed appeared at only one or two meetings. Some, particularly among the *notables*, never accepted their appointment.

of the Naurissart municipality in 1791. The mean tax, I believe, represents more accurately the economic and social character of the Limoges council of 1791.

Looking again at the two tables, one sees that the gradual decline in tax paid is paralleled by a shift in the distribution among the five categories. Although the extremely wealthy never overwhelmingly dominated any council, eight of the sixteen members of the February, 1790, Caen council paid 500 *livres* or more. Year by year in Caen one sees the largest bloc of *officiers* move down one level, until in 1792 nine of the sixteen officials paid less than 50 *livres* tax. In Limoges, the shift was less dramatic—there was never a great number of officials in the higher categories—but in the councils of 1792, one again sees the vast majority of municipal officials paying less than 50 *livres* tax. Taxpayers in the two highest categories are virtually absent from the last three councils in both towns.

The declining trend in taxes, along with the occupational profile of the councils, suggests a broadening of the social base of local politics in Caen and Limoges. In Limoges, the legal elite was increasingly excluded from municipal politics. Lawyers in Caen suffered the same fate, but only after the federalist revolt. In both towns, merchants and artisans combined to dominate the councils from 1791 on, and there appears to have been some shift away from the commercial elite to less prominent and less wealthy merchants, particularly in Limoges. Taxes paid by council members fell dramatically in Limoges in August, 1792, after the discrediting of the Naurissart municipality. In Caen, the first big drop came between 1790 and 1791, probably in part because of the Affair of 84 (the alleged conspiracy of nobles), which occurred just prior to the 1791 elections. The mean and median taxes for the 1792 council show a further significant drop.

Although this broadening of local politics occurred in both towns, the shift was more substantial and came earlier in Limoges, where it appears to have affected the local posture toward the federalist revolt. In Caen, on the other hand, it was the revolt itself (or, more precisely, its repression) that produced a wholesale change in the municipal council.

Highlighting this contrast is the fact that all but one of the *officiers* who served on the 1792 council in Caen had previously sat as a *notable* or *officier*. In Limoges, only four of those elected in 1792 had experience in municipal politics. Thus, whereas there was still considerable continuity between the 1792 Caen council and earlier municipal administrations, the officials elected in Limoges in 1792 were new to municipal politics and had very few ties to the *haut-bourgeois* elite that had dominated Limoges politics during most of the period from 1789 through 1791.

In evaluating the composition of the municipal councils, we can consider several factors not pertinent to the district and departmental councils, such as Freemasonry, Protestantism in Caen, and the impact of Jacobin club membership (which can be more fully gauged at the municipal level than for district and departmental administrations). An earlier chapter discussed the role of Freemason lodges in Caen and Limoges at the end of the Old Regime. The influence of Freemasonry on local politics appears to have declined as the Revolution progressed. In both Caen and Limoges, the number of Masons on the municipal council peaked in 1790—at five, in each case. Thereafter, their numbers diminished. Only one Mason sat on the 1792 Caen council, and only two sat on that of Limoges in the same year. This pattern suggests that the lodges attracted as members men already active in local affairs in the 1780s. Having fallen inactive after 1789, the lodges did not enroll the new men drawn into municipal politics in 1791 and 1792. As progressive as the lodges may have been, their role was taken over after 1790 by the section assemblies and popular societies, associations more in tune with revolutionary ideals. Although the lodges themselves fell dormant after 1789, however, their influence clearly did not. The rivalry and opposition between the two Limoges Freemason lodges seems to have revived in the hostility between the Jacobin club and the Amis de la Paix in 1790 and 1791.

A more intriguing factor in evaluating the nature of Caen politics is the city's sizable Protestant population. No estimate of this group's numbers on the eve of the Revolution exists, but an 1820 report to the Calvados prefecture put the Protestant population in Caen at 1,200.[17] Although Protestants could not openly practice their religion until 1787, there was no persecution of the Protestant population in Caen during the eighteenth century. No long-standing animosity divided the Protestant and Catholic communities, as it did in Nîmes, for example.[18] In fact, a 1788 letter from the Caen mayor and *échevins* to the minister of state referred to Caen Protestants as "that

17. A. D. Calvados, M4886 (Protestant population in Calvados, 1820). The only other large Protestant community in Calvados was in Condé-sur-Noireau, south of Caen, where 300 to 500 Protestants lived. The prefectural report estimated another 689 Protestants in the district of Caen, principally in Douvres.

18. See Hood, "Protestant-Catholic Relations," 245–75.

respectable class of our fellow-citizens" and described them as "a very numerous class, and unquestionably our wealthiest fellow-citizens."[19]

A number of Protestants were prominent in Caen, particularly the merchant families, such as Massieu, Chatry, and Signard d'Ouffières. Protestant families controlled the most lucrative branches of Caen commerce in the late eighteenth century. Jean-Claude Perrot has observed that the willingness of Protestant merchants to secure foreign grain purchases for Caen throughout the eighteenth century earned them the high esteem of the town elite.[20]

Five Protestants sat on the municipal council of February, 1790. Both Chatry brothers, as already noted, were elected mayor of Caen early in the Revolution, though both declined the office. As the Revolution progressed, fewer Protestants appeared on the municipal council (the *officiers* of 1792 included only one), but the Protestant presence at all levels of local government remained important. Samuel Chatry, a Caen *notable* in 1792, was demoted to that position simply because he had already served two consecutive terms as an *officier*, and he remained very active in municipal politics. His brother, Jean Louis Isaac, sat on the departmental council from 1791 through 1793 and was an extremely conscientious administrator. François Jacques Samuel Boiszerard, a municipal officer in 1790, served as a *notable* in 1791 and was promoted to the district council the following year. Pierre Mesnil, a Caen *négociant*, was a member of the patriotic committee in 1789, spent two years on the district council, beginning in 1790, and then joined the departmental directory for the 1792–1793 term. Gabriel de Cussy, of course, represented Caen in the Constituent Assembly and two years later became a Calvados delegate to the National Convention. All of these men knew each other—they witnessed each other's marriages and family baptisms—and most played an active role in the federalist revolt.[21] The ties within the Protestant community clearly did not dissolve as the Revolution

19. Sophronyme Beaujour, *Essai sur l'histoire de l'Eglise Réformée de Caen* (Caen, 1877), 490.

20. Perrot, *Genèse d'une ville moderne*, I, 212, 465. Perrot notes Signard d'Ouffières in particular as an active grain broker after 1750 and credits the Massieu family with relieving the town in 1789. Jean André Signard d'Ouffières and Jacques Samuel Michel Massieu sat on the February, 1790, municipal council.

21. In 1787, Louis XVI declared a policy of tolerance for non-Catholics, granting them the right to officially register births, marriages, and deaths, even those that had transpired in previous years. It is in these registers, primarily, that I found the names and relationships of Caen Protestants. They are contained in A. D. Calvados, I40–41 (Eglise de Caen; Etat civil). The earliest recorded act was dated 1739.

began, but to suggest that Caen's participation in the federalist revolt represented some sort of Protestant conspiracy would be unwarranted. Protestantism did, however, act as a cohesive force within the Caen commercial elite, many of whom actively participated in local politics, and also constituted a link between that commercial elite and their coreligionists among the artisans and shopkeepers of Caen.

The role of the Caen and Limoges Jacobin clubs in municipal politics was undeniably one of the most important factors during the early years of the Revolution, and the contrast between the two towns is a sharp one. The limited sources available suggest that the Caen Jacobins were not a dominant force in local politics, particularly after February, 1792, and the number of Jacobin club members on the municipal councils reflects this.[22] Jacobin club members apparently dominated none of the Caen municipal councils. On the February, 1790, council, there were no known Jacobins, and only one club member sat on the next council. The peak of Jacobin influence came in 1791, when the *officiers* elected included three Jacobins. The confrontation between the club and the departmental administration in February, 1792, over the installation of the Criminal Tribunal split the Jacobin club, and its sway over public affairs declined thereafter. Only one Jacobin club member sat on the 1792 municipal council.

These figures probably slightly underestimate Jacobin strength in Caen because of the incompleteness of the records. Claude Fauchet's arrival in 1791 clearly boosted club membership, and Esnault complained in his diary of the excessive influence of the Jacobin club during that year.[23] But the events of early 1792 undercut Jacobin prestige, and the formation of the Carabot club further challenged the club's position in Caen. We lack membership rolls for the Carabots, but every indication is that this club functioned in a client relationship to the departmental administration, requisitioning grain, searching the mail, and leading the volunteers to Evreux. The Carabot president during much of the revolt, Jean Michel Barbot, often served as a messenger for municipal officials and worked as a clerk at the

22. A. D. Haute-Vienne, L813, contains a complete list of the Limoges Jacobin club membership from the year III. No such list exists for the Caen club, but the Caen Bibliothèque Municipale collection of papers from the Revolution includes a fair number of Jacobin club letters and declarations, along with a few scattered *procès-verbaux,* from which I obtained the names of some club members. A few additional names turned up through incidental references in various archival documents. A. C. Caen, I275, contains papers directly relating to the Jacobin club.

23. Lesage (Esnault), 51–74.

Tribunal of Commerce, where Samuel Chatry sat as president in 1793. The Carabots, then, appear never to have constituted an independent source of popular political pressure, which the Caen Jacobin club had at one time represented.

One might expect that after the collapse of the revolt the Jacobin club enjoyed a resurgence. But despite the efforts of the representatives on mission and other Paris Jacobins who accompanied the "army of pacification," the people of Caen showed a strong reluctance to return to the club. Even as late as December, 1793, the *Journal de l'Armée* complained about the disappointing turnout at club meetings.[24] Attendance picked up in subsequent months, but the Jacobin club appears never again to have been a truly vital force in Caen politics.

The situation in Limoges was quite the reverse. Four future Jacobins sat on the February, 1790, council (the club was not formed until late that year), and the next council included nine Jacobin club members. In 1791, men associated with the Amis de la Paix made a concerted effort to regain control of municipal politics, and the number of Jacobins on the council fell to four. But on each of the next three councils—August, 1792; 1792; and 1793—eleven of the thirteen *officiers* were Jacobin club members, a reflection of the extremely important role played by the Limoges Jacobins in local affairs. Not only did large numbers of club members sit on each local administrative council in 1793, but the club acted as a watchdog over elected officials and effectively represented the views of the Limoges popular classes.

The striking contrast in Jacobin strength on the municipal councils prevailed at the district and departmental levels as well. Available evidence shows sixteen Jacobin club members on the Haute-Vienne council for the 1792–1793 term, compared with just nine in Calvados. On the 1792–1793 Limoges district council, eight of thirteen administrators belonged to the Jacobin club, while in Caen the number of Jacobins on the district council appears never to have exceeded two.

One final observation can be made with respect to all three administrations in these departments. Electors in Calvados invariably showed a greater aversion for Old Regime officials than did Haute-Vienne electors. This contrasting attitude toward men associated with the royal bureaucracy is consistent with the posture of the two departments during the federalist revolt.

24. A. D. Calvados, L10529 (*Journal de l'Armée des Côtes de Cherbourg*).

The demands issued by the Norman federalists embodied their strong objections to the expanding powers of the National Convention (particularly the Committee of Public Safety) and its emissaries to the departments, the representatives on mission. The federalists similarly denounced the excessive influence of Paris on national politics. What one sees here is a continuing antipathy among the Caen (and Calvados) elite toward the encroachment of the centralizing state, an antipathy that was equally apparent during the waning years of the Old Regime. Limoges and the Haute-Vienne, largely because of harsh economic realities, never manifested a comparable resistance to the central government.

The relative social homogeneity of the departmental and district councils in these two departments points to the importance of municipal politics in explaining the divergence in the political postures of Calvados and the Haute-Vienne in 1793. The character of the municipal councils fluctuated much more than that of either of the other two councils, and one sees the introduction of a "popular" element into Limoges politics reflected both in the municipal *officiers* elected in 1792 and in the increasing influence of the Jacobin club. Revolutionary politics was particularly vital in the urban setting, and this relatively simple observation suggests two things. First, the urban setting itself exerted a substantial influence on revolutionary politics. Second, politics is a process, not a static phenomenon. Exploring the social dynamics of politics will be more enlightening than examining the social background of political actors alone. Therefore, we must place the revolutionaries of Caen and Limoges in their contexts by considering the political geography of the two towns and the nature of the political arena in Calvados and the Haute-Vienne.

For electoral and judicial purposes, both Caen and Limoges were divided into sections in late 1790. Municipal authorities created five sections in Caen and four in Limoges, all roughly equal in population, though differing in total area.[25] Maps 5 and 6 show the sections of the two towns.

I have located the address, at least the section, for nearly all of the *officiers*

---

25. A. C. Caen, L315 (Division de la Ville en cinq sections, 1790). I found no papers relating to the creation of sections in the rather more disorganized Limoges municipal archives. However, the boundaries of the four sections have been roughly traced on a 1785 map of Limoges that I obtained from the departmental archives. This map is also included in Paul Ducourtieux, *Limoges d'après ses anciens plans* (Limoges, 1884).

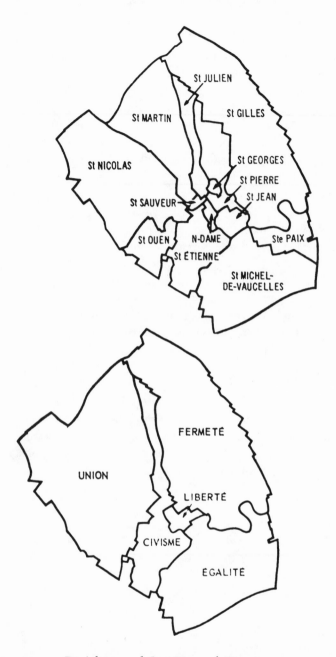

MAP 5. Parishes and Sections of Caen

Reprinted, by permission, from Jean-Claude Perrot, *Genèse d'une ville moderne: Caen au XVIIIe siecle* (Paris, 1975), I, 43.

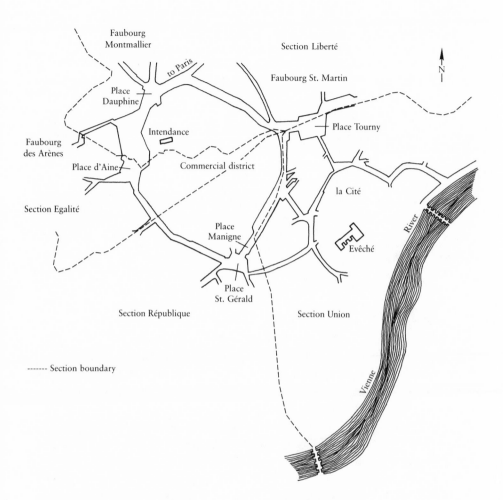

MAP 6. Limoges, 1793

Colleen Baker

TABLE 13 Sectional Representation in Caen and Limoges, 1790–1793

Caen municipal councils (N=16)

	February, 1790	November, 1790	1791	1792	1793	Total
Union	0	0	2	2	1	5
Civisme	3	6	8	7	4	28
Fermeté	5	4	2	5	5	21
Liberté	8	6	3	1	3	21
Egalité	0	0	1	1	1	3
Unknown	0	0	0	0	2	2

Limoges municipal councils (N=13)

	February, 1790	November, 1790	1791	August, 1792	1792	1793	Total
Union	0	0	0	2	1	0	3
République	6	5	6	6	5	6	34
Egalité	3	5	3	2	5	4	22
Liberté	1	3	3	3	2	2	14
Unknown	3	0	1	0	0	1	5

in both towns from 1790 through 1793. A glance at Table 13 shows that the sections were not evenly represented on the municipal councils. In Caen, sections Union and Egalité were virtually unrepresented. Nearly 90 *officiers* came from the town's three central sections. Within that bloc, section Liberté dominated the 1790 councils, with the edge thereafter shifting to section Civisme, until the 1793 reorganization balanced the situation somewhat.

This distribution becomes meaningful when related to the social character of Caen's urban geography, a task made possible by two sources: Jean-Claude Perrot's masterful study of Caen during the eighteenth century, *Genèse d'une ville moderne;* and the revolutionary tax rolls for the Caen sections. Section Liberté, dominant in the 1790 Caen municipal councils, included the Place de la Liberté (formerly Place Royale), where many of Caen's wealthiest merchants lived. It contained most of the parish Saint-Jean, the oldest part of Caen, where the nobility and rich bourgeois had their *hôtels* and also where most Caen Protestants lived. The Affair of 84, in November, 1791, began with a confrontation at the church Saint-Jean. On the rolls of the *contribution mobilière*, section Liberté paid 151,000 *livres*, an average of 114 *livres* per entry, both figures at least 50 percent higher than those of any other section. Adding this to earlier evidence, we would expect section Liberté to have been dominant during the first years of the Revolution, and indeed it was.

Section Civisme's ascendancy in the 1791 elections coincides with the socioeconomic evolution of the municipal council. Within this section's boundaries lay the parishes Saint-Etienne, Saint-Sauveur, Notre Dame, and part of Saint-Pierre, the heart of the commercial and artisanal district of Caen. The residents of section Civisme paid 97,000 *livres* into the *contribution mobilière*, an average of 59 *livres* per entry. The difference between this and the section Liberté average tax closely parallels the drop in the mean tax paid by municipal council members between 1790 and 1791, the year in which Civisme replaced Liberté as the dominant section on the council.

The character of these two districts and the relationship between them had undergone considerable change in the quarter-century before the Revolution. The parish Saint-Jean (section Liberté) had once been more purely the domain of the nobility and wealthy bourgeois (in the Old Regime sense of the term). The prosperous commercial enterprises of Caen had grown up in the parishes Notre Dame and Saint-Pierre (section Civisme), but since 1768, many of the big banking and commercial houses had shifted from that area to the less congested Place Royale and Ile Saint-Jean.[26] In the 1790s, section Civisme was not as wealthy as it once had been, but there remained strong ties between the retail merchants of that district and the *négociants* of section Liberté, as exemplified by the close relationship on the 1792 council between the *fabricant* Samuel Paisant, of section Liberté, and the *marchand mercier* David Nicolas, of section Civisme. The common interests of these two groups considerably outweighed their differences. The shift in political influence after 1791 from section Liberté to section Civisme represented a rejection of the nobility and bourgeois *rentiers* of the parish Saint-Jean, who were associated with the Affair of 84, rather than a reaction against the commercial elite of Caen.

Section Fermeté, the third Caen section that was well represented on the municipal councils, is more difficult to characterize socially. Unlike Liberté and Civisme, section Fermeté extended into the faubourgs, and it embraced within its boundaries one of the poorest areas of Caen, the parish Saint-

26. Perrot, *Genèse d'une ville moderne*, I, 526.

Gilles.[27] But it also included a sizable part of the parish Saint-Pierre, as well as an area around the Château that, as in most eighteenth-century French towns, housed many of the town's lawyers. The section as a whole paid 60,000 *livres* into the *contribution mobilière,* an average of 43 *livres* per entry. The Fermeté *officiers*—the vast majority of whom were lawyers and artisans—came from the part of the section near the center of town, and not from the parish Saint-Gilles.

The last two sections, Union and Egalité, together sent only eight *officiers* to the five municipal councils we have considered. Section Union lay entirely in the faubourg l'Abbé, beyond the Abbaye-aux-Hommes, and included another of Caen's poorest neighborhoods, the parish Saint-Nicolas. The taxpayers of section Union paid only 38,000 *livres* to the *contribution mobilière,* the lowest total among the five sections, for an average of 34 *livres* per entry. Section Egalité consisted primarily of the faubourg Vaucelles, made up of the parishes Vaucelles and Saint-Paix. This was the third of Caen's poorest districts and even in 1789 was considered the most "revolutionary" of the town's neighborhoods. Its border with the parish Saint-Jean may have contributed to this reputation among the Caen elite. The Orne River separated the two, with Vaucelles on one side and the military garrison protecting Saint-Jean on the other. During the tense days of grain shortage in 1789, the military governor simply leveled his cannons across the bridge. The fearsome reputation of Vaucelles may have inspired the municipal authorities in 1790 to include a sliver of the parish Saint-Jean in section Egalité. This insurance against the rabble somehow securing election proved effective— those few *officiers* who did come from Egalité lived on the Saint-Jean side of the river. Section Egalité as a whole paid 53,000 *livres* into the *contribution mobilière,* 40 *livres* per entry, just slightly more than the residents of section Union. The difference is probably due to the inclusion of that small corner of the parish Saint-Jean.

This pattern of sectional representation takes on more meaning when related to immigration into Caen in the late eighteenth century. As already described, by 1770 the central district of Caen had reached its maximum population density. After that date, immigrants tended to settle in the faubourgs, forming a ring of relatively poor neighborhoods around the old city. Perrot notes that during this same period, "the financial segregation of the quarters was accentuated; the most capitalistic activities anchored them-

27. *Ibid.,* II, 926.

selves at the heart of the city."[28] It was precisely those central sections that dominated Caen politics after 1789. As we have seen, the people of the faubourgs had very little voice on the Caen municipal councils during the Revolution. Even in the year II, they were largely absent from the council, though they appeared somewhat more frequently among the *notables.*

In Limoges, the situation was quite different, and the discrepancies in sectional representation on the council are explained by other factors. There was no clear social demarcation between Limoges neighborhoods on the eve of the Revolution, nor was there such a significant break between the heart of the city and the faubourgs. Moreover, section boundaries in Limoges radiated out from the center so that all the sections, except Union, contained both part of the central districts and part of the faubourgs.

In Limoges, then, the pattern of sectional representation does not reflect the evolution in the municipal council's composition. As Table 13 shows, men from section République consistently outnumbered those from other sections on the council. République included slightly more of the central town than the other sections and also encompassed much of the commercial area, though it did not monopolize it. The bustling row of shops along the rue du Clocher lay in section Egalité, which shared the commercial district with République and consistently sent a strong contingent to the council. Section Liberté lagged behind these two in its representation, for two possible reasons. It included the faubourgs Montmallier and Saint-Martin, both more sparsely populated than the other faubourgs. Furthermore, most of Limoges' lawyers lived in section Liberté, and as we have seen, they fell out of favor with the voters after 1790. Section Union came in a weak last in sectional representation, but its position is easily explained. Union consisted almost entirely of la Cité, the ecclesiastical part of town, which was only incorporated into Limoges in November, 1791. Not surprisingly, the newcomers were not quickly assimilated into Limoges politics.[29]

This striking contrast in the political geography of Caen and Limoges was reflected in the public celebrations held in each town during the Revolution. Mona Ozouf has made a detailed study of the revolutionary fetes of Caen

28. *Ibid.,* 526. Tax rolls for the sections are in A. D. Calvados, L584–646.

29. Unfortunately, the rolls of the Limoges *contribution mobilière* are not organized by section, and so I have been unable to carry out the kind of sectional comparison by taxes that I did for Caen. Furthermore, Daudet is not as thorough or as insightful about Limoges as Perrot is about Caen. I do, however, feel quite confident about the sharp contrast in the extent of social differentiation by neighborhood in the two towns.

and found that most patriotic processions during the Revolution bypassed the faubourgs of Caen. Fewer than one-third of the thirty-four processions traced by Ozouf entered the faubourgs at all. Of these, four were agricultural fetes, three occurred during the year II, and four others were military parades of the National Guard, very probably sent out to the faubourgs by municipal authorities as a salutary show of force. In contrast to the processions of the Old Regime, which nearly always finished at the heart of the parish Saint-Jean (the noble *quartier*), those of the Revolution generally headed to the Place de la Liberté, that square fronted by the homes of wealthy merchants. As if to pay further tribute to commerce as the lifeblood of the town, the municipal council shifted its meeting place early in the Revolution from the Abbaye-aux-Hommes to the church of the Eudistes, on the west side of the Place de la Liberté. The most common route of the revolutionary fetes linked the Place de la Liberté to the Place Saint-Pierre, traversing the two dominant sections in Caen municipal politics and linking the artisanal district to the residential neighborhood of the *haute-bourgeoisie*. These revolutionary fetes not only reflected the primacy of the central districts in Caen political life but helped to establish and strengthen that primacy.[30]

In Limoges, the pattern of revolutionary processions was quite different. Rather than being planned by the departmental administration or the municipal council, as early as 1791 the fetes were generally organized by the Jacobin club. The parades and celebrations in Limoges had a more spontaneous flavor than those in Caen. Citizens in attendance at public ceremonies often concluded the affairs with unplanned marches through the streets of Limoges. In contrast to the fetes in Caen, confined most often to the central districts, the processions in Limoges generally stretched out to embrace the faubourgs as well. Thus, one sees an almost perfect symmetry between the urban geography of municipal politics in Caen and Limoges and the fetes that gave revolutionary politics its public expression.[31]

We shift our attention now from the local elites themselves to the political arena in which they interacted. How did politics operate in Caen and Li-

---

30. Mona Ozouf, "Innovations et traditions dans les itinéraires des fêtes révolutionnaires: l'exemple de Caen," *Ethnologie Française*, VII (January, 1977), 45–74; Mona Ozouf, *La Fête révolutionnaire, 1789–1799* (Paris, 1976), especially 163–76; M. A. Campion, *Les Fêtes Nationales à Caen sous la Révolution* (Caen, 1877).

31. Alfred Fray-Fournier, *Les Fêtes Nationales et les Cérémonies Civiques dans la Haute-Vienne pendant la Révolution* (Limoges, 1902).

moges during the first four years of the Revolution? The two *chefs-lieux* are of primary interest here. Unlike departments such as the Seine-Inférieure—where Le Havre rivaled Rouen—or the Bouches-du-Rhône—where Marseille overshadowed Aix-en-Provence—Caen and Limoges were the unchallenged, supreme towns in their departments. The administrations, courts, and popular societies that functioned in those towns dominated departmental politics. By examining their interactions, we will see how some of the factors analyzed earlier in this chapter came into play. The situation in 1792 and 1793 is of greatest significance to us, but we must consider it in context and not isolate it from the developments of earlier years.

Let us first consider the administrative corps. The Constituent Assembly had established a hierarchy of responsibilities and authority among the local administrations but had generated no explicit policy regarding cooperation and consultation among them. Throughout France, the departmental administrations tended to meet with the district and municipal councils of the department *chefs-lieux* at times of crisis, and we have seen that both the Haute-Vienne and Calvados administrations did so during June, 1793. But practice during normal times varied, as it did between these two departments.

There appears to have been much closer contact among the three administrations in the Haute-Vienne than among those in Calvados. Early in 1793, upon observing that the National Guard commander, the district president, and the Limoges mayor frequently attended departmental meetings, the council formally invited the three to attend all its meetings.[32] The departmental administration held public meetings approximately every five days, and by May, 1793, even the departmental directory had opened its meetings to the public.[33]

The Calvados administration was neither as accessible to its constituents nor as solicitous of the subordinate councils. There is no evidence that departmental meetings were ever open to the public, though delegations from the clubs and sections of Caen often gained admission to deliver particular requests. Nor is there any indication that representatives of the municipal

32. A. D. Haute-Vienne, L57 (departmental administration minutes, February 3, 1793).

33. A. D. Haute-Vienne, L57 and L72 (departmental directory minutes). Jacobin clubs nationwide mounted a lobbying campaign in 1790–91, calling on the Constituent Assembly to pass legislation requiring that all elected bodies hold public meetings. No such legislation appeared; but in Limoges, the pressure of the Jacobin club undoubtedly influenced the departmental administration in its decision to hold public meetings. Kennedy, *The Jacobin Clubs in the French Revolution*, 215.

and district councils regularly attended departmental meetings. Indeed, in spring, 1793, the district and the department clashed over departmental army recruitment policy, with the district council insisting that the departmental directory had exceeded its authority by changing recruitment procedures. Most communication among the three administrations appears to have passed through the offices of their *procureurs*.[34]

There were, of course, less formal ties among the three councils. In Calvados, Jean Louis Isaac Chatry was one of the most diligent departmental administrators during the 1791–1793 terms, and his brother, Samuel, participated on every municipal council in Caen from 1789 through 1793. In the Haute-Vienne, Jean Baptiste Nieaud moved in 1791 from his post as mayor of Limoges to a seat on the departmental administration, where he remained through 1793. Nearly all of the departmental councils included former district or municipal officials. But if we focus on the 1792–1793 term, we see the following: The Calvados departmental administration included three members who had served on the Caen district council and three who had been municipal officials in Caen since 1789. The Haute-Vienne administration included only one former Limoges district official, but seven of the ten departmental administrators who lived in the district of Limoges had at one time been Limoges municipal officials. The contrast between the district councils was less marked. Two of the Caen district administrators in the 1792–1793 term had previously been Caen municipal officials, whereas in Limoges, three of the district administrators had previously served on the municipal council.

When we consider all aspects of this analysis together, the contrast between the two departments is striking. The district of Caen sent seven representatives to the Calvados departmental council, while the district of Limoges placed ten members on the Haute-Vienne council. Of these, only three of the Caen men had previously served on the municipal council, while seven of the ten in the Haute-Vienne had at one time sat on the Limoges municipal council. Taking account also of the closer cooperation among the three Haute-Vienne administrations and the greater accessibility of the Haute-Vienne departmental council, we can conclude that Limoges exer-

---

34. Unfortunately, the minutes of the departmental council meetings have disappeared, so one cannot say with absolute certainty that district and municipal officials were not in attendance. However, none of the available documentation (including municipal and district *procès-verbaux*, miscellaneous departmental records, newspapers, and diaries) suggests that they attended.

cised considerably more influence on its departmental administration than did Caen.

This conclusion appears even more justified when we consider the contrasting roles played by the local popular societies. The Limoges Jacobin club remained a vital and active force throughout this period. By 1793, 43 percent of the Haute-Vienne administrators, 62 percent of the Limoges district administrators, and 85 percent of the Limoges municipal *officiers* were members of the Limoges Jacobin club. These percentages represent more than Jacobin strength in local government. They also demonstrate the extent to which the Jacobin club served as a central political forum, bringing together men from all levels of local administration to discuss the contentious issues of the day. The club met at least weekly, and generally more often, throughout the Revolution, with meetings always open to the public. The Limoges Jacobins maintained regular contact not only with the Paris Jacobins but with clubs in other cities around the country. Discussions focused on local and national issues, ranging from the conduct of public officials to the effectiveness of grain requisitions to reports of political developments elsewhere in France. Members debated very practical matters as well as more lofty ideological issues, such as the fate of Louis XVI. Local disputes and broader political controversies no longer needed to be resolved in confrontations between municipality and district or between club and department. The Jacobin club, by 1792, was a common denominator among all three councils, and club members carried the Jacobin viewpoint back to their respective administrations.[35]

This kind of political forum did not exist in Caen, at least not by 1793. The Jacobin club may have served that function in 1791, but by 1793 it had ceded its role as the most important club in Caen to the Carabots, a group more subservient to departmental administrators. No evidence exists to indicate that the Carabots ever functioned as an independent forum for discussion and debate. Nothing suggests more succinctly the difference between the political philosophy of the Carabots and that of the Limoges Jacobins than their mottoes. The Carabot banner admonished those who looked its way, "l'Exécution de la Loi ou la Mort," while the Limoges Jacobins called out to those who would listen, "Vivre Libre ou Mourir." The

35. Michael Kennedy stresses the fact that provincial Jacobin clubs "were nerve centers for the distribution of news and propaganda." Kennedy, *The Jacobin Clubs in the French Revolution*, 54.

mottoes reflect as well the divergent perspectives of Caen and Limoges during those critical months of 1793.

The contrast between local politics in Caen and Limoges seems to parallel the opposition described by Soboul at the national level between moderates favoring "representative democracy" and radicals championing "agent democracy." In Caen, that battle was won by the moderates controlling the departmental administration, who insisted on an orderly political arena in which people would show the prosper respect for and confidence in their elected representatives. In Limoges, the more radical "agent democracy" triumphed. The people of Limoges repeatedly intervened in the political arena, both through the Jacobin club and by spontaneous action, most notably during the grain incident of February, 1792, and again the next summer, when the sections of Limoges recalled their elected "agents," the Naurissart municipal council. Clearly, debates over important issues proceeded in a very different fashion in these two towns.

The shape of local politics affected not only the definition and resolution of local issues and concerns but also the relationship between each town and national affairs. Three different networks of communication unified the country during the Revolution. The first of these was the administrative network. The National Assembly and the ministries communicated the business of government to departmental, district, and municipal administrations through official channels. The Jacobin clubs constituted a second unifying network. The Paris Jacobins reprinted speeches, Jacobin policy statements, and official minutes from the National Assembly to be sent to affiliated societies all over France. The third network, a less coherent one, consisted of the numerous newspapers printed in Paris and sent to subscribers in the provinces. To some extent, there also existed an interdepartmental network of communication, in which departmental administrations and popular societies corresponded with their counterparts in other departments, but this tended to be regional in character and never achieved a truly national dimension. One might also mention personal correspondence, which was certainly important; but this, as we have seen, often traveled through administrative or Jacobin channels. That which did not is only rarely available today for inspection.

Local perceptions of national events naturally depended a great deal on available sources of information. Official communications were more or less a constant factor throughout France, except for the extent to which individual deputies corresponded with the authorities back home. The Jacobin network was more variable, for it depended on the existence in any particular community of an affiliated club. But the reports sent out were generally consistent; they were not tailored to different constituencies. The newspaper network featured the greatest variability, or flexibility. A multiplicity of newspapers offered a diversity of editorial perspectives, and each community's interpretation of national events depended in part on the newspapers available to it.

Limoges and Caen differed with respect to each of these channels of communication. The National Convention sent the same information to both departments, to be sure, but the pattern of communication between national deputies and their constituents was different in the two departments, at least in 1792 and 1793. In Calvados, the *conventionnels* de Cussy, Doulcet, Dumont, and Lomont sent frequent letters to Caen, but almost always to administrators or one of the administrations, most often the departmental council. This solidified the council's position as the supreme arbiter of local affairs. The sole Montagnard deputy on the Calvados delegation, Bonnet, did occasionally write to the Caen Jacobin club, but with limited effect, given the club's waning influence in 1793. When Bonnet visited Caen in March, 1793, he spoke to the club and commented that one could always count on "the good people of Vaucelles and the faubourg l'Abbé."[36] But as we have seen, those people had very little voice in Caen politics. Furthermore, the Caen Jacobin club had split with the Paris Jacobins in September, 1792, thereby eliminating that source of information from the capital. The principal newspaper available in Caen, by virtue of the municipal council's subscription, was Gorsas' *Le Courrier dans les Départements,* which in 1792 and 1793 presented the Girondin viewpoint.

In Limoges, official channels of communication did not dominate the flow of information from the capital as much as they did in Caen. The majority of the Limoges *conventionnels* were Girondin supporters, and they did correspond with the departmental administration. But the Montagnard deputies Bordas and Gay-Vernon frequently wrote to the Limoges Jacobin club, as did the Jacobin Xavier Audouin. Indeed, Gay-Vernon, undoubtedly the most prolific correspondent among the Haute-Vienne deputies, sent nearly all of his letters to the Jacobin club. The strength and vitality of the Limoges

36. Lesage (Esnault), 105.

club and its continued affiliation with the Paris Jacobins enabled it to provide an alternative source of information on national issues. In addition to letters, the club received printed speeches and pronouncements from the Paris club, items that presumably no longer went to Caen after its club had split with the mother society. Finally, there is the question of printed news. We cannot identify all of the newspapers available. However, in December, 1792, the Limoges Jacobins canceled their subscription to the Gorsas paper, which played a prominent role in Caen, in favor of a less moderate journal.

The patterns of political interaction described earlier prevailed during the crisis period of June and July, 1793. In Calvados, the departmental administration dominated the situation. Louis Caille, the district *procureur-syndic,* and Samuel Chatry, the wealthy Caen *négociant,* did play important leadership roles, but otherwise, departmental officials were most active and prominent during the revolt. A district official, Robert Tirel, voiced the most serious objection to the insurrectionary measures and was shouted down. The mayor of Caen, Le Goupil Duclos, missed the crucial early morning meeting of June 9 because he had been told that it would not be held until later in the day. Le Goupil and the rest of the municipal council lent only passive support to the revolt as it developed. The Carabots, following the departmental lead, provided the core of the expeditionary force to Evreux and carried the call to arms to the populace. The people of Caen responded by ignoring the authorities and refusing to enroll in the volunteer force.

From the start, the sections expressed their skepticism of reports from the capital by insisting that a delegation visit Paris to verify the situation. The delegation, led by Louis Caille and the departmental president René Lenormand, returned to give an alarming report, later decried by Le Goupil as misleading and inflammatory. It did, however, convince the section assemblies of the need for drastic action. Thereafter, the departmental council, now absorbed by the general assembly, did all it could to control the flow of information from Paris by prohibiting the circulation of any decree issued by the Convention. Despite these efforts, the Caen sections finally compelled the general assembly to abandon the revolt, which had collapsed owing to the lack of any popular support.

In the Haute-Vienne, the revolt collapsed before it could start, largely because of the more open nature of Limoges politics. The departmental administration showed an initial inclination to support the protest against Paris by its adoption of the Côte-d'Or resolution, but it could not dominate the situation as the Calvados departmental council did. It was precisely during this period that Jacobin club meetings were most animated and most heavily attended.[37] The Limoges municipal council and the Jacobin club immediately objected to the departmental action, and when messengers arrived from Lyon and the Jura, the municipal council intercepted and denounced them before they could state their mission to the administration. The departmental council had little choice but to repudiate their entreaties. Alarming reports did come from the moderate Haute-Vienne deputies in Paris, but these were countered by reassuring letters from Bordas and Gay-Vernon. On the heels of their letters came reports from the Paris Jacobins and the National Convention indicating that the Revolution had once again been defended and that calm had returned to the capital.

We have seen, then, that both the makeup of the local administrations and the way they interacted (with each other, with their constituents, and with national deputies) had a major impact on the political stances of Calvados and the Haute-Vienne in June, 1793. In Calvados, the departmental administration dominated the political arena. The Caen commercial elite played a strong role in that administration, which also included many market-oriented rural landowners. In 1792, the departmental council managed to undercut the influence of the Caen Jacobins and encouraged the growth of another club, the Carabots, which stood in a client relationship to the administration. The Caen municipal council, representing primarily the Caen commercial community, also deferred to or supported the departmental administration in nearly all important matters.

A very different situation prevailed in the Haute-Vienne. Landowners and merchants constituted only 11 percent of the 1792–1793 departmental council, which was dominated instead by lawyers and professionals. The Haute-Vienne administration did not monopolize local politics, as did the Calvados council. The town of Limoges exercised considerable influence on the departmental administration, by virtue of both the seven citizens of Limoges who sat on the council and the vigilance of the Jacobin club and the municipal council. The Limoges commercial elite was unable to maintain control of municipal affairs. That elite itself stood divided, as first evidenced by the 1782 splintering within the Freemason lodge and made very plain by

37. Fray-Fournier, *Le Club des Jacobins*, xxvi.

the revolutionary conflict between Jacobins and Amis de la Paix. Large-scale merchants dominated the Naurissart municipality, but in August, 1792, Limoges voters rejected those men. Small-scale merchants and artisans, most of them club members, subsequently controlled the Limoges council.

The popular classes of Limoges thus exerted greater influence on local politics (both through the Jacobin club and through the municipal council) than did the *menu peuple* of Caen, who remained relatively inert during the Revolution. This was a crucial factor in June, 1793, for while the popular classes of Caen did not actively support the federalist revolt, they possessed no organized medium through which to express their opposition. As we have seen, it was concerted popular opposition, voiced by the Limoges municipal council and the Jacobin club, that steered the Haute-Vienne away from the federalist movement.

The vitality of popular politics in Limoges and the lack of it in Caen emerge, then, as the chief immediate factors determining the towns' political stances in June, 1793. This raises a fundamental question. Why could the popular classes of Limoges mobilize and effectively apply pressure to their elected officials, while the people of Caen could not?

Several factors have already been suggested. The pattern of immigration into Caen in the eighteenth century left recent immigrants isolated in the faubourgs, not fully assimilated into Caen's urban life. This contributed to their passivity during the Revolution. So did the nature of the Caen economy. The overwhelming importance of commerce in Caen left the town's artisan community and commercial workers dependent on the commercial elite of Caen. This patron-client relationship manifested itself in Caen politics, most prominently in the creation of the Carabot club in 1793. The leniency of the punishment meted out to federalist leaders by Lindet and Laplanche is further evidence of the importance of the commercial elite, both to the Caen economy and to Caen politics.[38]

In Limoges, the situation was different. The artisans and workers of Limoges were not isolated in the faubourgs but instead lived nearly side by side with their social and economic betters. They could not be so easily excluded

38. For a thorough and interesting discussion of patron-client relationships and their impact on political behavior, see Ronald Aminzade, "Breaking the Chains of Dependency: From Patronage to Class Politics, Toulouse, France, 1830–1872," *Journal of Urban History*, III (August, 1977), 485–506; and Ronald Aminzade, *Class, Politics, and Early Industrial Capitalism: A Study of Mid-Nineteenth-Century Toulouse, France* (Albany, 1981), especially 47–68.

from Limoges political life. In addition, while commerce was important to the Limoges economy, it was not dominant. Textiles, the construction trades, and the fledgling porcelain industry all employed a considerable number of workers. The consecutive poor harvests also played their role. Although wholesale merchants such as Pétiniaud de Beaupeyrat and Naurissart may have been thanked for provisioning the city in 1789, the continuing poor harvests and high prices created an antagonism between the Limoges popular classes and the merchants who seemed to be profiting by their misfortune. This helps to explain the outburst of February, 1792, when the grain crisis forced Naurissart to flee. But other factors, related to the economy and the social structure of the two towns, must explain the consistent activism of the Limoges Jacobin club and the passivity of the people of Caen.

Sustained political activism on the part of the lower classes in Limoges required both opportunity and capability. Opportunity presented itself when the split divided the Limoges elite, creating a situation in which rival factions turned to the *menu peuple* for support in their struggle for political dominance. The persistent grain problem kept the public mood in Limoges at a heightened pitch, providing the political motivation for the popular classes. This is not to say that the popular classes controlled Limoges politics; but so long as they had allies in Paris (in the Paris Jacobin club and the Montagnard deputies of the Haute-Vienne), they could not be ignored. In Caen, no such opportunity for the popular classes existed, because the commercial elite was much more homogeneous and cohesive. Common economic interests linked landowners and merchants (witness the numerous petitions calling for improvements in the Orne River channel), Protestants and Catholics, wholesale merchants and shopkeepers. Far from appealing to the *menu peuple* for support, the Caen political elite did all it could to control popular political activity, and no serious grain problem existed to incite popular unrest.

Similarly, the capability for political activism among the lower classes was much stronger in Limoges than in Caen. In part, this was due to the social geography of the two towns, already discussed. But patterns of sociability more generally, I would argue, were a crucial factor here. Not only were the lower classes of Caen dispersed in the faubourgs, they had no popular associations to build on as a base for organizing revolutionary clubs. In Limoges, by contrast, nearly every adult male belonged to a penitent confraternity at the end of the Old Regime, and the organizational structures of those groups carried over to the Jacobin club during the Revolution. Far beyond occasionally rioting in protest of grain prices, then, the Limoges popular classes were capable of sustained political expression that manifested itself at the ballot box in the municipal elections of 1792 and in the political forum of the Limoges Jacobin club. In 1793, it was this that restrained the Haute-Vienne departmental administration from joining the federalist revolt.

Conclusion

No single factor can adequately explain the federalist revolt in 1793. The proscription of twenty-nine Girondin deputies triggered resistance in many departments, but the underlying reasons for the pattern of revolt run much deeper than the political affiliations between proscribed deputies and their constituencies. These ties were not unimportant, but the correlation between federalist departments and proscribed deputies is a weak one. Only twelve of the twenty-nine came from departments that engaged in prolonged resistance to the Montagnard Convention, and five of these came from one department, the Gironde. Six of the thirteen departments that actively revolted against the Montagnard Convention were not represented by a single proscribed deputy, while several departments represented by proscribed deputies made little or no protest. Among the deputies excluded on June 2 were two representatives each from the Meurthe and the Orne, departments that protested the May 31 revolution only by letter. Another two deputies, A. B. Chambon and B. F. Lidon, came from the Corrèze, a department that firmly rejected all entreaties to join in resistance. The Eure-et-Loir also supported the Montagnard victory, despite the fact that Brissot, Lesage, and Pétion all represented that department in the Convention.[1]

1. The proscribed deputies and their departments are as follows: Barbaroux (Bouches-du-Rhône); Bergoeing (Gironde); Bertrand L'Hodiesnière (Orne); Birotteau (Pyrénées-Orientales); Boilleau (Yonne); Brissot (Eure-et-Loir); Buzot (Eure); Chambon (Corrèze); Dufriche-Valazé

Although the provincial revolt in June, 1793, cannot be understood as a simple reaction to the proscription of the Girondin deputies, it must be understood as integrally related to the political struggle in Paris that finally produced the May 31 revolution. At the heart of the Girondin/Montagnard split was a debate between two opposing visions of democracy, the liberal representative democracy favored by the Girondins and the more popular participatory democracy championed by the Montagnards and the Parisian sans-culottes. Albert Soboul has labeled this opposition a conflict between "representative democracy" and "agent democracy."[2]

This conflict over what form the new French republic would take was hardly confined to the national political arena. The debate that raged in the streets, clubs, and assembly halls of Paris in the spring of 1793 had been waged and resolved in the provinces during the previous months and years. Clearly, this was the case in both Caen and Limoges, where the character of local politics had already been determined by the summer of 1792. This is not to say that the shape of local politics had anywhere been cast in stone by 1792. The turbulent years that followed brought changes in political structures and practices in many of the departments of France. But the political forms that prevailed in the departments in June, 1793, did play a major role in determining provincial response to the May 31 revolution. And the inability of the federalist departments to overturn the victory of the Montagnards may have been a crucial blow to the immediate prospects for liberal democracy in France. Certainly, the years following 9 Thermidor, when moderates who had supported the Girondins returned to power in Paris and the departments, were an exercise in failure for liberal representative democracy, a failure caused in large part by the divisions and bitterness sown in 1793 and the year II.[3]

The federalist revolt is important to our understanding of the Revolution not only because it was a crucial turning point but because it demonstrates the links between national and local politics in this period. The two inter-

---

(Orne); Gardien (Indre-et-Loire); Gensonné (Gironde); Gomaire (Finistère); Gorsas (Seine-et-Oise); Grangeneuve (Gironde); Guadet (Gironde); Henry-Larivière (Calvados); Kervélégan (Finistère); Lanjuinais (Ille-et-Vilaine); Lasource (Tarn); Lehardi (Morbihan); Lesage (Eure-et-Loir); Lidon (Corrèze); Louvet (Loiret); Mollevaut (Meurthe); Pétion (Eure-et-Loir); Rabaut Saint-Etienne (Aube); Salles (Meurthe); Vergniaud (Gironde); Viger (Maine-et-Loire).

2. Soboul, The Sans-culottes, 106–18.

3. For a discussion of why liberal democracy failed under the Directory, see Lynn A. Hunt, David Lansky, and Paul Hanson, "The Failure of the Liberal Republic in France, 1795–99: The Road to Brumaire," Journal of Modern History, LI (December, 1979), 734–59.

acted continually, and while historians have long belabored the predominant influence of Paris on French national culture and politics, it is important to remember that the provinces, or departments, also influenced the national drama unfolding in Paris. The deputies who voted on the fate of the king, and who later voted to proscribe twenty-nine of their colleagues, were products of local politics. The overwhelming majority had experience as municipal, district, or departmental administrators.[4]

To take but two examples, let us consider the cases of Gustave Doulcet de Pontécoulant and Léonard Gay-Vernon. Doulcet had been president of the Calvados departmental administration in the 1791–1792 term, during the turbulent affair of the Criminal Tribunal. In the midst of that affair, Doulcet denounced the Caen Jacobin club for its unruly intervention in public affairs. He insisted on the need for orderly and informed deliberation by the elected representatives of the people. Doulcet carried that attitude to the National Convention, where he joined the Girondin deputies in their support for representative democracy. In this, he epitomized the general character of Caen and Calvados politics.

Léonard Gay-Vernon went from the municipal council of la Cité, subsequently absorbed by Limoges, to the Legislative Assembly and then to the National Convention. He participated in the founding of the Limoges Jacobin club and maintained an active affiliation with the club after his departure to Paris. Gay-Vernon encouraged the club in its political activism, both in local and national affairs. He had an extreme disregard for individuals and insisted on the accountability of elected deputies, not only to the people who elected them but to all the people. In the Convention, Gay-Vernon sat with the Montagnards and supported their vision of participatory democracy. Although he may not have expressed the views of most Haute-Vienne administrators, he did represent the broad, popular character of Limoges municipal politics.

Doulcet and Gay-Vernon not only illustrate one way in which local politics affected national politics but also point out the difficulty encountered by historians seeking a social basis for the political division between Girondins and Montagnards. Both Doulcet and Gay-Vernon came from noble families. True, Gay-Vernon belonged to a petty noble family, while Doulcet came from a prominent family with a centuries-long lineage. But in a statistical study of the deputies in the National Convention, both would be entered in

4. See Patrick, *The Men of the First French Republic*.

the category labeled "nobility." Overall, one finds very little social distinction between the Girondin deputies and their Montagnard opponents—both came essentially from the upper ranks of the third estate and the liberal nobility.[5]

For this reason, one cannot seek an explanation for the political divisions in Paris solely in the social backgrounds of elected deputies. More important to consider is the social fabric of the regions they represented. This is not a deterministic argument that Calvados produced Girondins while the Haute-Vienne produced Montagnards—that is clearly not the case. But while other deputies than Doulcet and Gay-Vernon might have been chosen as examples above, the noble Montagnard Bonnet de Meautry from Calvados and the Girondin lawyer Lesterpt-Beauvais from the Haute-Vienne were neither the most influential nor the most representative deputies of their departments. Thus, it is crucial to consider national politics and local politics together, to find the links and continuities between the two.

That those links and continuities existed, particularly in the spring of 1793, is relatively clear. The political issues then confronting the nation had confronted local officials in 1791 and 1792, at least in Caen and Limoges. Most of the deputies in Paris in 1793 had moved up through the ranks of local administration. Local clubs and administrative councils inundated the National Convention with letters and petitions throughout the winter and spring of 1793 calling for a constitution and an end to factionalism. Returning the favor, national deputies often lent support by way of letter to their allies on the local scene.

This study has shed light on each of these areas of interaction between local and national politics. It has also established and explored the political contrasts between Caen and Limoges and their relationship to national issues. More difficult is establishing the underlying social and economic forces that produced those political contrasts and divisions. And more difficult still is constructing a logical and consistent interpretive framework that will make those underlying forces coherent. The conceptual model proposed by Edward Fox, positing a political dichotomy between the agricultural hinterland and the commercial periphery, does provide such a framework.

The contrasting economies of Caen and Limoges correspond well to the typology of French towns proposed by Fox. Fox disputes the notion that the growth of commercial towns and the rise of the monarchy were part

5. Chaumié, "Les Girondins et les Cents Jours," 329–65.

of the same process. Instead, he marks a distinction between commercial towns and trade towns (which also served as administrative centers), arguing that the monarchy was built on the latter, with commercial towns never fully integrated into the bureaucratic state.[6]

Caen and Limoges clearly do not constitute the "ideal type" of either variety of town, but it would be fair to classify Caen as commercial and Limoges as a trade, or administrative, town. Although Caen lay in a rich agricultural plain (Fox contrasts the commercial economy with the agricultural economy of administrative towns), commerce spurred the town's growth in the eighteenth century, and the commercial elite of Caen dominated local affairs on the eve of the Revolution. Moreover, the agriculture of Calvados was largely commercial, not subsistence, in character. The Limousin, by contrast, was predominantly a region of subsistence agriculture, and Limoges fits the mold of an administrative town very well. Representatives of the monarchy dominated Limoges politics and provided the impetus for local development. Limoges did engage in trade, some of it at long distance, but wholesale commerce did not play the important role that it did in Caen.

This classification of the two towns corresponds with their political orientation at the end of the Old Regime and during the Revolution. Caen, the commercial town, resisted the encroachments of the state bureaucracy and looked toward other commercial communities and its own agricultural hinterland as the sources of its prosperity. The Caen municipal council quarreled with the royal intendants in the 1780s, and during the 1792–1793 term, the Calvados administration berated the National Convention for neglecting to provide for the defense of its coast, so vital to both the safety and the economy of the department. Limoges, the administrative town, named its grand boulevards for the royal intendants who built them. The Limousin depended on the monarchy for help in maintaining its roads and for grain to feed its people. After 1789, the Haute-Vienne again looked to Paris for funds to rebuild the fire-ravaged Manigne quarter in Limoges and to purchase the grain that local harvests had failed to produce. The Haute-Vienne sent two thousand volunteers to assist the Republic in its battle against the Vendéan rebels, who in 1793 threatened areas that supplied the department with the grain it so badly needed.

Fox's argument holds that the economic role, or function, of a town under the Old Regime determined its political posture, at least vis-à-vis the state.

6. Fox, *History in Geographic Perspective*, 33–54.

His discussion of political life in the two types of towns is explicit. Commercial oligarchies governed the former, generally through compromise and negotiation; hierarchy characterized the administrative towns, with an agent of the crown in the dominant position.[7]

This analysis is reasonably compatible with the situation in both Caen and Limoges under the Old Regime. The local elite in Caen resented the interference of royal officials, while in Limoges the intendant assumed the role of the dominant, and generally accepted, political and administrative figure. After 1789, however, it is Limoges that appears to have been more politically democratic than Caen. In Calvados, the duly elected administrative bodies, particularly the departmental administration, dominated local politics. In the Haute-Vienne, on the other hand, the Limoges municipal council, and more significantly the Limoges Jacobin club, acted as restraints on the moderate (even federalist) inclinations of departmental officials and managed to maintain an active political forum.

Does this constitute a flaw in Fox's thesis? Superficially, it would seem to, but the argument needs only to be refined, not discarded. Fox himself cautions against equating negotiation-minded commercial communities with "democratic" government. Narrow oligarchies ruled these towns. Indeed, the hierarchical, administrative towns often possessed a broader "democratic" base, because agents of the crown frequently favored the lower classes in their efforts to weaken the influence of the local nobility.[8]

Alexis de Tocqueville, too, addresses the relationship between administrative centralism and democratic government at the local level. He argues that throughout France, municipal government had "degenerated into a petty oligarchy" by the end of the Old Regime. In some towns, the monarchy had allowed the democratic forms of a bygone era to survive (in the election of town councils or the periodic convocation of public assemblies, for example), though it seldom invested those forms with any real power or authority.[9] Although Tocqueville may be overestimating the extent of royal power, particularly at the periphery of the kingdom, his argument does help to amplify Fox's thesis. As the power of the monarchy waned after 1789, the democratic forms that it had fostered quickly took on substance, particu-

7. *Ibid.*, 55, 56.
8. *Ibid.*, 38, 66–68.
9. Tocqueville, *The Old Regime and the French Revolution*, 45–50.

larly in a town like Limoges where no homogeneous elite existed that could capture power for itself. In Caen, on the other hand, the commercial oligarchy (whether petty or not) did succeed in capturing power and in stifling a modest movement toward participatory democracy. As Tocqueville so aptly observed, "what perhaps strikes us most in the mentality and behavior of our eighteenth-century bourgeois is their obvious fear of being assimilated to the mass of the people, from whose control they strained every effort to escape."[10] The Caen elite succeeded in this effort, while that of Limoges did not, and as I argued in the previous chapter, the key to that difference lies in the social and economic structures of the two towns and regions.

If the Fox/Tocqueville schema fits Caen and Limoges nicely, how well does it work in explaining the federalist revolt more generally? Many of the factors that led Caen toward revolt in June, 1793, hold true for the other federalist centers as well. Bordeaux, Lyon, and Marseille were all commercial cities. All four cities had a proud history of regional independence and resistance to royal encroachment. At the most superficial level, then, the federalist revolt conforms to Fox's thesis that the political crisis in 1793 represented a conflict between state centralization and commercial development. A closer look at the federalist centers should amplify the character of that opposition.

In each federalist city, departmental administrators took the lead in calling for resistance to the Montagnard Convention. Nowhere did the movement enjoy much popular support, although in Lyon the population did rally behind federalist administrators after republican armies laid siege to the city. The federalist leaders in Lyon, however, never succeeded in mobilizing support for a march on Paris. In Marseille, too, administrators had difficulty enlisting volunteers for the departmental force, and the movement quickly collapsed when republican troops arrived on the scene. Rebel leaders in Bordeaux managed to create an armed force only after offering a cash bonus to "volunteers," and that force never stepped beyond the departmental boundaries of the Gironde.[11]

How were local administrators able to maintain a posture of resistance to Paris without the backing of their constituents? We have seen that this was

10. *Ibid.*, 93.
11. See Edmonds, "'Federalism' and Urban Revolt in France in 1793," 22–53; and Crook, "Federalism and the French Revolution," 383–97. See also Scott, *Terror and Repression in Revolutionary Marseille;* and Brace, *Bordeaux and the Gironde, 1789–1794.*

achieved in Caen in two ways. First, departmental administrators largely controlled the sources of information from Paris, and they carefully censored declarations from the Montagnard Convention and the Paris Jacobins. Officials in the other federalist cities took similar actions. Second, there existed in Caen no organized, popular opposition to the departmental administration. This was true of Bordeaux, as well, but not of Lyon and Marseille.

In Bordeaux, the Jacobin club had shifted its support to the Girondins sometime after the split between Jacobins and Feuillants in Paris. This is hardly surprising, since the Bordeaux Jacobin club numbered among its founders men such as Vergniaud and Guadet. There did exist in Bordeaux another popular society, the Club National, which supported the Montagnards. The Convention looked to this club in July and August for assistance in undermining the Bordeaux federalists. But the Club National included only a small minority of the city's population and did not present a force strong enough to actively oppose the revolt as it developed. The majority of the people of Bordeaux remained politically passive. Alan Forrest describes a situation in Bordeaux very similar to that in Caen: "Economically, the long tradition of commercial dominance in the life of the city had had the effect of instituting a very stable social structure in which the vast majority of the inhabitants were dependent for their livelihood, directly or indirectly, on the buoyancy of overseas trade. . . . The high immigrant population from other areas, men whose aim in Bordeaux was to attain a decent standard of living rather than to win political privileges, probably also helped to entrench this native conservatism. Apathy remained high and participation low." [12] Caen's commercial tradition was not as long, or as illustrious, as Bordeaux's, but the town's prosperity did depend on commerce, and the large number of recent immigrants in Caen remained politically passive during the Revolution. The social and economic structures of the two towns seem strikingly similar.

Both Lyon and Marseille, despite their predominantly commercial role, also possessed sizable work forces engaged in production. Silk workers and printers in Lyon had frequently opposed the merchants who controlled their industries. Marseille, too, contained a considerable number of workers employed in manufacture, generally living in neighborhoods apart from the commercial population. [13] In both of these cities, an active and organized

12. Forrest, *Society and Politics in Revolutionary Bordeaux,* 175.
13. Scott, *Terror and Repression in Revolutionary Marseille,* 12–17.

radical movement opposed the moderate elements in control of local politics during the early years of the Revolution. By early 1793, the Jacobin clubs of Marseille and Lyon had indeed gained control of municipal politics, only to be defeated by moderates in the weeks before the federalist revolt. The limited success of the federalist movement depended on the neutralization of Jacobin power in both cities.

In Lyon, that neutralization came on the very eve of the May 31 revolution in Paris and was due, in part, to the overzealousness of Lyon Jacobins. In early April, 1793, following Dumouriez's treason and the outbreak of the Vendée revolt, the Rhône-et-Loire formed a committee of public safety, dominated by Lyon Jacobins. The Jacobin club, led by Marie Joseph Chalier, controlled the Lyon municipal council and in late April and May pushed for the creation of a revolutionary army to apprehend hoarders and political suspects. The club achieved this goal, but the moderate departmental administration prevented the creation of a revolutionary tribunal, also advocated by the Jacobin club as a weapon against hoarders. By mid-May, opposition to these radical measures began to develop in the Lyon sectional assemblies, described by C. Riffaterre as poorly attended during this period and controlled by the wealthy bourgeoisie. The sectional assemblies looked to the departmental administration as an ally in their struggle against the Jacobin club. The administration maintained a cautious attitude; but on May 27, Chalier played into the moderates' hands by calling for the execution of sectional leaders. The sections reported this outrage to the representatives on mission A. F. Gauthier and P. C. Nioche and demanded the suspension of the municipal council and the arrest of Chalier. Under intense pressure—in fact, taken prisoner by the sections—the representatives ordered Chalier's arrest on May 30, along with the suspension of the municipal council, thereby neutralizing the Lyon Jacobin club. Sectional assemblies controlled municipal politics for the next four months.[14]

In Marseille, too, the struggle between moderates and radicals took the form of opposition between the sectional assemblies and the Jacobin club. Militant Jacobins (primarily professional men, not merchants) had gained ascendancy in Marseille politics by mid-March, 1793, and had succeeded in establishing a revolutionary tribunal. As in Lyon, the Jacobins alienated many property owners, urban and rural alike, by their advocacy of grain

14. Riffaterre, *Le Mouvement antijacobin et antiparisien*, I, 1–100.

seizures and a forced loan. Moderate opposition to the Jacobin municipality soon coalesced in the Marseille sections.

William Scott suggests that many in Marseille blamed the Jacobins (both the local variety and those in Paris) for the lagging economy in 1793. Trade and local industry were in decline. The deputy Barbaroux, unpopular with Marseille Jacobins, blamed the Convention for failing to take measures to protect trade. Barbaroux had long championed free trade and the commercial interests of Marseille and maintained close ties with many of his constituents. Complaints also circulated in Marseille that the Jacobins had discouraged commercial ventures with their threats of a forced loan, driving the rich merchants into exile.

The Jacobin club itself realized that its extreme program had alienated many people, and it purged some of its radical members in May. The sections, however (as in Lyon, dominated by the wealthy bourgeoisie), obtained the arrest of a number of club leaders on May 18, and by the end of the month, they had secured further limitations on the club's autonomy. Moderates argued that all citizens could adequately express their opinions in open, sectional assemblies and condemned the club for manipulating the municipal administration. The arrest of the Jacobin leaders effectively stymied the Marseille club. Its final defeat came on June 3, when sectional deputies closed its meeting hall.[15]

In all four of the federalist centers, then, the launching of resistance to Paris depended on the effective muzzling of popular opposition within the local population. In Caen and Bordeaux, this proved to be a simple matter, since no organized popular movement had developed in those towns during 1792 and 1793. Moderate elements maintained a firm control over departmental and municipal politics. In Marseille and Lyon, however, the Jacobin clubs challenged the hold of more moderate local administrators, who emerged victorious on the very eve of the May 31 revolution. Those administrators, and their bourgeois supporters, naturally viewed the victory of the Montagnards in Paris as a manifestation at the national level of the Jacobin menace, which they had only just succeeded in quelling at home.

The federalist movement represented in part, then, a continued reaction against popular politics, particularly the agent democracy championed by the Parisian sans-culottes. In all four cities, administrators had succeeded,

15. Scott, *Terror and Repression in Revolutionary Marseille*, 71–107.

with varying degrees of difficulty, in defeating Jacobin efforts to control the local administrations. Those administrators viewed the revolution of May 31 as a violation of national sovereignty by the Parisian crowd, a dangerous attack on the representative democracy that they espoused.

More than the defense of a political ideology, though, the federalist revolts constituted a defense of regional interests, both political and economic. The declaration of grievances and demands issued by the federalists gathered in Caen expressed the general motivations of the movement as a whole. Their demands, though couched in terms that emphasized national unity, clearly implied a desire for increased departmental independence. The Norman and Breton federalists denounced the activities of the Parisian *comités révolutionnaires* and demanded the curtailment of section meetings in the capital. They further demanded the abolition of the Jacobin and Cordelier clubs of Paris.

While the federalist rebels decried the undue influence of Paris on national politics, they also called for a restriction of the National Convention's responsibilities. Officials in all of the federalist centers particularly resented the interference of representatives on mission in local affairs. Administrators in Caen, Lyon, and Marseille complained of the inadequate provisions made by the Convention for the defense of their departments and clashed with representatives on mission over the disposition of military forces. Each of these four cities had quarreled with the royal intendants of the Old Regime. They scarcely wished to see them now replaced by representatives on mission.

The economic demands of the federalists in Caen are also illuminating. Conscious of the need to maintain among the people at least passivity, if not support, federalist leaders issued no demands for repeal of the *maximum*, although it was clearly not popular with the commercial classes. They did, however, call for an investigation of the huge individual fortunes that had grown since August 10, insisted on the financial accountability of the municipality of Paris, and called for a reduction in the number of *assignats*, the circulation of which was widely believed to have fueled inflation and seriously damaged commerce.

The sum of these demands, characteristic of those issued by the other federalist centers, illustrates the very opposition within France that Edward Fox has suggested: a conflict between the centralizing state and the commercial cities of the periphery. The federalists denounced not only the excesses of the

Paris crowd but also the growing power of the National Convention, particularly the Committee of Public Safety. In 1793, certainly in April and May, it appeared that the authority of the Convention would be dependent on the active, and unruly, intervention of the Parisian popular classes, a situation that officials in the federalist centers viewed as extremely threatening. Moreover, the Jacobin regime and the requisites of the war effort promised economic controls that the commercial elite of the federalist cities did not welcome and, indeed, felt compelled to resist.

Clearly, more work must be done before we can conclusively characterize the federalist movement, and the accompanying Girondin/Montagnard conflict, as an opposition between the commercial periphery of France and the administrative hinterland. The case of Rouen stands as a prime example of a nonfederalist but commercial city that requires further research. Rouen's sizable population of wage laborers and the city's important administrative role under the Old Regime may well prove to be key factors in explaining its political posture. More work must also be done on the complicated situations in Lyon and Marseille, and the case of Toulon must be carefully scrutinized before that city is placed either in or out of the federalist camp.

The geography of the federalist revolt, however, does correspond to the geographical distribution of Girondin strength, and the evidence from Caen and the other federalist centers does point to the primacy of the commercial elite in those cities. The federalist revolt should not necessarily be understood as a movement of the commercial bourgeoisie defending its economic interests, to be sure. But this study does suggest that the social fabric and economic structures of a town and region are crucial factors in molding the shape of the local political arena. I am not arguing that economic interests determine political values but rather that social and economic factors explain both the ability of the Limoges popular classes to intervene politically in 1793 and the failure of the Caen popular classes to do likewise. And the manner in which local politics played themselves out in the summer of 1793 had a profound impact on the resolution of the key national political question pointed to by both Tocqueville and Soboul: Who was to participate in the new political system?

In the end, ironically, the success of the Calvados elite in controlling local politics and instituting representative democracy contributed to this group's defeat and loss of power in the summer of 1793. The success of the federalist revolt depended on the support of those people whom the elite had excluded from the political arena. The immediate result was a victory for the agent democracy that the federalists had so long resisted, although that soon degenerated into a virtual Jacobin dictatorship. By 1799, both forms of democracy had proven unmanageable, and it would be another seventy-five years before a democratic republic could again take firm root in France.

Appendix I

Demands of the Central Committee of Resistance to Oppression

I

1. Qu'un Décret Constitutionnel assure au Corps législatif une Garde départementale dans laquelle Paris fournira son contingent.

2. Que les Tribunes soient supprimées, ou du moins soumises à une police tellement sévère, qu'elles n'osent plus influencer, troubler les Délibérations.

3. Que dans le lieu de ses Séances, le Corps législatif ne laisse plus défiler des Bataillons armés; qu'il ne reçoive plus de Pétitions que par écrit; qu'un bon Réglement maintienne entre tous ses Membres le respect que se doivent mutuellement les Représentants de la Nation.

4. Que les Députés mis en état d'arrestation, sur le Décret arraché par violence, soient rendus à leurs fonctions, sauf à soumettre leur conduite aux Tribunaux, quand ils auront été légalement accusés.

5. Qu'un Décret solennel casse les Corps administratifs de Paris et les Autorités anarchiques connues sous le nom de Comités Révolutionnaires.

6. Que la Commune de Paris soit divisée en autant de Municipalités qu'elle a de Tribunaux; que ces Municipalités soient formées incessamment, et qu'il ne puisse y entrer aucun Membre des Administrations actuelles de cette Ville.

7. Que les sections de Paris ne soient plus désormais en permanence.

8. Que le Tribunal révolutionnaire soit supprimé; que la conduite de ses Juges soit rigoureusement examinée.

9. Que la commission des Douze, établie pour découvrir les complots tramés depuis six mois contre la Représentation nationale, soit réintégrée et continue ses recherches. Que les auteurs de ces complots soient enfin légalement punis, quels qu'ils soient.

10. Qu'un Décret ordonne de reprendre l'instruction commencée contre les assassins du 2 septembre, de poursuivre ces hommes de sang, qui depuis six mois ne cessent de provoquer au meurtre, soit par leurs écrits, soit par leurs discours dans les lieux publics et dans les Sociétés populaires.

11. Qu'ils soient punis, ceux qui depuis le 31 mai violent à Paris le secret des lettres, et portent de continuelles atteintes à la liberté de la presse.

12. Qu'un Décret abolisse, sous des peines afflictives, les dénominations aussi dangereuses qu'elles sont ridicules, de *Cordeliers,* de *Jacobins,* que portent les Sociétés dégénérées de Paris.

13. Que les scellés soient mis sur leurs papiers, et sur ceux de la Commune de Paris et de ses Comités révolutionnaires.

14. Qu'on exécute dans cette ville les Loix relatives aux étrangers, aux gens sans aveu.

II

15. Que la Convention divisant enfin les Pouvoirs, se borne à ceux qui appartiennent à une Assemblée législative.

15bis. Que le Comité de salut public soit dépouillé de sa Puissance dictatoriale.

16. Que les Députés envoyés près des armées et dans les Départements, retournent au poste que leur avait assigné la Nation; qu'ils rendent compte des sommes qu'ils ont touchées pour leur mission extraordinaire; que l'on examine la manière dont ils l'ont remplie, et les motifs des arrestations qu'ils ont ordonnées; que leur responsabilité ne soit pas un vain mot.

17. Que l'on donne au Conseil exécutif la vigueur nécessaire pour faire marcher le Gouvernement.

III

18. Qu'une commission formé d'hommes capables et intègres soit chargée d'examiner les comptes des anciens Ministres et de la Commune de Paris; de

rechercher les sources des grandes fortunes qu'on a vu subitement éclore depuis le 10 août; et de rétablir enfin l'ordre dans nos finances.

19. Que l'on informe contre les auteurs des vols faits au Garde-meuble, et des pillages de février.

20. Qu'il ne soit plus rien avancé à la Commune de Paris sur le trésor public; qu'elle paye enfin ses impositions arriérées.

21. Qu'il ne soit plus créé d'assignats; que l'on avise aux moyens de diminuer la masse de ceux qui sont dans la circulation.

22. Que le numérotage, les signatures manuscrites et les endossements des assignats soient rétablis tels qu'ils étaient lors de la première émission.

IV

23. Que la Convention, ayant recouvré sa liberté, son intégrité, soit invitée à donner sous deux mois une Constitution digne de la République Française.

24. Qu'elle indique les Loix qu'elle n'a pas rendues librement.

25. Si la Convention ne croit pas que les haînes qui l'ont jusqu'à présent divisée, lui permettent de s'acquitter désormais des fonctions importantes que le peuple lui a déléguées, qu'elle ait du moins la bonne foi de le déclarer; qu'elle convoque les Assemblées primaires, et que de nouveaux Législateurs puissent bientôt réparer les maux qu'elle a faits à la France.

Article ajoûté

Que la Garde nationale de Paris soit promptement réorganisée, et qu'elle n'ait pour Chefs aucuns des Membres des Administrations et des Comités Révolutionnaires du 31 mai.

Source: B.M. Caen, Fn. B2634.

Appendix II

Occupational Categories of Elected Officials

The following is neither an exhaustive nor a definitive list but rather a compilation of the occupations that I encountered among the elected officials of Calvados and the Haute-Vienne and the categories in which I classified them in this study.

Clergy: chanoine; curé; prêtre; vicaire.

Legal professions: avocat; avoué; homme de loi; juge de paix; lieutenant général au bailliage; notaire; procureur.

Liberal professions: architecte; arpenteur; chirurgien; docteur en médecine; journaliste; maître de musique; médecin; peintre; professeur.

Rural landowners: agriculteur; cultivateur; herbageur; laboureur; propriétaire.

Commerce: banquier; commerçant; capitaine de navire; courtier-maritime; fabricant; manufacturier; marchand; marchand de dentelles; négociant.

Artisans/Shopkeepers: apothicaire; aubergiste; bonnetier; cabaretier; cafétier; cartier; chandellier; chaudronnier; cordonnier; corroyeur; entrepreneur; horloger; imprimeur; marchand de bois; marchand boucher; marchand chapelier; marchand cirier; marchand confiseur; marchand coutelier; marchand épicier; marchand fripier-tapissier; marchand mercier; marchand papetier; marchand parfumeur; marchand pelletier; marchand pharmacien; marchand tanneur; marchand teinturier; marchand vitrier; menuisier; orfèvre; perruquier; quincaillier; sellier; serrurier; tailleur; vinaigrier.

Military: chevalier; commandant de bataillon; garde du corps du Roi; gendarme de la garde; lieutenant.

Other: bourgeois; vivant de son bien; vivant de son revenu.

Bibliography

Unpublished Primary Sources

I completed the major part of the research for this study in departmental archives, particularly the Archives Départementales of Calvados. Series L in the Calvados archives is rich in documentation for the period of the federalist revolt. At the time of my research, however, Series L was still in the process of being classified, so some citations (those with numbers above L10000) may be changed in the future. The Caen municipal archives are presently held in the departmental archives but will soon be moved to their own repository. The Bibliothèque Municipale of Caen contains an extensive collection of varied revolutionary documents, many of them relating to the federalist revolt. The Bibliothèque also possesses a fine collection of Caen maps.

I spent two months in Limoges working in the Archives Départementales of the Haute-Vienne. Again, Series L, which is extremely well catalogued, was the source of most of my information. The Limoges municipal archives are split between the Bibliothèque Municipale (pre-1789 documents) and the municipal archives proper (post-1789 documents). Documents from the revolutionary period are somewhat disorganized, but they did yield some valuable material. The *procès-verbaux* of the Limoges municipal council during the Revolution are located in the Bibliothèque Municipale.

The Archives Nationales also yielded a substantial amount of useful information. Particularly valuable were the series relating to departmental administration, reports to the minister of the interior, and the Committee of Public Safety. In the Bibliothèque Nationale, I consulted the Fonds Maçonniques and a variety of obscure published sources.

The following list of archival sources gives only general references. Detailed citations can be found in the footnotes. In both the bibliography and the footnotes, I have included brief descriptions of archival sources. Where the archival inventory offered a succinct description, I have used that description in French. Otherwise, I have devised my own description in English.

Archives Communales, Caen
AA47: Délibérations des Corps et Corporations de Caen, 1789.
BB99: Délibérations du Comité Général municipal, 1789–90.
D1–3: Délibérations du Corps municipal et du Conseil Général de la Commune, 1790–94.
F4: Tribunal de Commerce, 1790–an VI.
I1–71: Evénements remarquables; representatives on mission.
I72–80: Certificats de résidence.
I275–78: Caen popular societies.
Series I 282–84: Fêtes Nationales.
I315: Division de la ville en cinq sections.
K1–12: Organisation électorale; sectional assemblies.
K13–44: Municipal elections, primary assemblies.
O4: Noms des rues, 1793.

Archives Communales, Limoges
Series I: Evénements remarquables.
Revolutionary tax rolls.

Archives Communales, Limoges (Bibliothèque Municipale)
AA7: Délibérations des Corps et Corporations de Limoges, 1789.
AA8: Cahiers de doléances.
Registre des Délibérations de la Municipalité de la Cité, 1790–92.
Registre des Délibérations de la Municipalité de Limoges, 1790–94.

Archives Départementales, Calvados
Series 2E: Family dossiers.
Series F: Nouvelles Acquisitions.
I40–41: Eglise Réformée.
Series L: Departmental records, revolutionary period.

Archives Départementales, Haute-Vienne
Series G, 13G, 16G: Confréries.
Series L: Departmental records, revolutionary period.

Archives Nationales
AA: Ministre de Justice.
AF II: Comité de Salut Public; reports from representatives on mission.
DXLII: Comité de Salut Public.
DXLIII: Comité de Sûreté Générale.
F^{1b}I: Administrative personnel attached to the central government.
F^{1b}II: Administrative personnel, departmental series.

F^{1c}I: Esprit Public.
F^{1c}III: Esprit Public et élections.
F^{1c}V: Conseils Généraux, departmental series.
F^2: Administration Départementale.
F^3: Administration Communale.
F^7: Police Générale.
F^{12}: Commerce et industrie.
F^{14}: Ponts et chaussées.
W: Tribunal Révolutionnaire.

Bibliothèque Municipale, Caen
Brochures Normandes: Caen sous la Révolution.

Bibliothèque Nationale
FM^2: Fonds Maçonniques.

Published Primary Sources

Documents
Aulard, F. A. *Recueil des Actes du Comité de Salut Public avec la Correspondance officielle des représentants en mission.* Vols. IV–VI of 28 vols. Paris, 1891.
Boiloiseau, Marc, M. Reinhard, and G. Lefebvre, eds. *Procès-verbaux de la Convention nationale: Table analytique.* 3 vols. Paris, 1959–63.
Caron, Pierre. *Rapports des Agents du Ministre de l'Intérieur dans les départements (1793–an II).* 2 vols. Paris, 1913–15.
Delasalle, Paul. *Documents inédits sur le fédéralisme en Normandie.* Le Mans, 1844.
Duvergier, J. B. *Collection complète des Lois, Décrets, Ordonnances, Règlements, Avis du Conseil-d'Etat.* Paris, 1834.
Julien, Jean (de Toulouse). *Rapport fait au nom du Comité de Surveillance et de Sûreté Générale sur les administrations rebelles.* Paris, 1793. B. M. Caen, Rés. Fn. B404^2.

Newspapers
Affiches, Annonces et Avis Divers de la Basse-Normandie, 1789–94. Weekly; biweekly starting in 1791. A.D. Calvados.
Bulletin des autorités constituées, nos. 1–9, June–July, 1793. A.D. Calvados.
Journal de l'Armée des Côtes de Cherbourg, July–December, 1793. A.D. Calvados.
Réimpression de l'Ancien Moniteur, seule histoire authentique inaltérée de la révolution française depuis la réunion des Etats-Généraux jusqu'au consulat, mai 1789–novembre 1799. 32 vols. Paris, 1847–50.

Diaries and Memoirs
Lesage, Georges, ed. *Episodes de la Révolution à Caen racontés par un bourgeois et un homme du peuple.* Caen, 1926.
Vaultier, Frédéric. *Souvenirs de l'insurrection Normande, dite du Fédéralisme, en 1793, avec notes et pièces justificatives par M. Georges Mancel.* Caen, 1858.

Secondary Sources

General

Agulhon, Maurice. *Pénitents et francs-maçons de l'ancienne Provence.* Paris, 1968.

Albert, Madeleine. *Le Fédéralisme dans la Haute-Garonne.* Paris, 1932.

Aminzade, Ronald. "Breaking the Chains of Dependency: From Patronage to Class Politics, Toulouse, France, 1830–1872." *Journal of Urban History,* III (August, 1977), 485–506.

———. *Class, Politics, and Early Industrial Capitalism: A Study of Mid-Nineteenth-Century Toulouse, France.* Albany, 1981.

Andrews, Richard M. "Paris of the Great Revolution: 1789–1796." In *People and Communities in the Western World,* edited by Gene Brucker. Vol. II of 2 vols. Chicago, 1979.

Arbellot, G. "Les Routes de France au XVIIIᵉ siècle." *Annales: Economies, Sociétés, Civilisations,* XXVIII (May–June, 1973), 765–91.

Berlanstein, Lenard. *The Barristers of Toulouse in the Eighteenth Century (1740–1793).* Baltimore, 1975.

Bezucha, Robert J. "The 'Preindustrial' Worker Movement: The Canuts of Lyon." In *Modern European Social History,* edited by Robert J. Bezucha. Lexington, 1972.

Brace, Richard M. *Bordeaux and the Gironde, 1789–1794.* Ithaca, 1947.

Brelot, Jean. "L'Insurrection fédéraliste dans le Jura en 1793 (mars–août 1793)." *Bulletin de la Fédération des Sociétés Savantes de Franche-Comté,* no. 2 (1955), 73–102.

Butet-Hamel. *La Société Populaire de Vire pendant la Révolution.* Paris, 1907.

Calvet, Henri. "Subsistances et fédéralisme." *Annales Historiques de la Révolution Française,* VIII (1931), 229–38.

Cameron, John Burton, Jr. "The Revolution of the Sections in Marseille: Federalism in the Department of the Bouches-du-Rhône in 1793." Ph.D. dissertation, University of North Carolina. Chapel Hill, 1971.

Caron, Pierre. *Manuel pratique pour l'étude de la Révolution française.* Paris, 1947.

Carraz, Roland. "Girondins et Montagnards: le cas chalonnais." In *Actes du Colloque Girondins et Montagnards,* edited by Albert Soboul. Paris, 1980.

Chaumié, Jacqueline. "Les Girondins." In *Actes du Colloque Girondins et Montagnards,* edited by Albert Soboul. Paris, 1980.

———. "Les Girondins et les Cent Jours." *Annales Historiques de la Révolution Française,* XLIII (July–September, 1971), 329–65.

Cobban, Alfred. "Local Government during the French Revolution." In *Aspects of the French Revolution,* edited by Alfred Cobban. New York, 1968.

Crook, M. H. "Federalism and the French Revolution: The Revolt in Toulon in 1793." *History,* LXV (October, 1980), 383–97.

Dawson, Philip. *Provincial Magistrates and Revolutionary Politics in France, 1789–1795.* Cambridge, 1972.

Dollinger, Philippe, Philippe Wolff, and Simone Guenée. *Bibliographie d'histoire des villes de France.* Paris, 1967.

Doyle, William. *Origins of the French Revolution.* Oxford, 1980.

Dubois, Louis. *Histoire de Lisieux.* 2 vols. Lisieux, 1845.

Dubreuil, Léon. "Evreux au temps du fédéralisme." *Révolution Française,* LXXVIII (1925), 244–63, 318–48.

———. "L'Idée régionaliste sous la Révolution." *Annales révolutionnaires,* IX (1917), 596–609, and X (1918), 22–36, 230–45, 469–504.

Edmonds, Bill. "'Federalism' and Urban Revolt in France in 1793." *Journal of Modern History,* LV (March, 1983), 22–53.

Forrest, Alan. *Society and Politics in Revolutionary Bordeaux.* Oxford, 1975.

Fox, Edward Whiting. *History in Geographic Perspective: The Other France.* New York, 1971.

Giraudot, Jean. *Le Département de la Haute-Saône pendant la Révolution.* 2 vols. Vesoul, 1973.

Godechot, Jacques. *The Counter-revolution: Doctrine and Action, 1789–1804.* New York, 1971.

———. *Les Institutions de la France sous la Révolution et l'Empire.* Paris, 1951.

Greer, Donald. *The Incidence of the Terror during the French Revolution.* Cambridge, 1935.

Guibal, Georges. *Le Mouvement fédéraliste en Provence en 1793.* Paris, 1908.

Higonnet, Patrice. "The Social and Cultural Antecedents of Revolutionary Discontinuity: Montagnards and Girondins." *English Historical Review,* C (July, 1985), 513–44.

Hood, James. "Protestant-Catholic Relations and the Roots of the First Popular Counterrevolutionary Movement in France." *Journal of Modern History,* XLIII (June, 1971), 245–75.

———. "Revival and Mutation of Old Rivalries in Revolutionary France." *Past and Present,* LXXXII (February, 1979), 82–115.

Hufton, Olwen. *Bayeux in the Late Eighteenth Century.* London, 1967.

Hunt, Lynn A. "Committees and Communes: Local Politics and National Revolution in 1789." *Comparative Studies in Society and History,* XVIII (July, 1976), 321–46.

———. *Politics, Culture, and Class in the French Revolution.* Berkeley, 1984.

———. *Revolution and Urban Politics in Provincial France.* Stanford, 1978.

Jordan, Daniel P. *The King's Trial: Louis XVI vs. the French Revolution.* Berkeley, 1979.

Kaplow, Jeffrey. *Elbeuf during the Revolutionary Period: History and Social Structure.* Baltimore, 1964.

Kennedy, Michael L. "The Foundation of the Jacobin Clubs and the Development of the Jacobin Club Network, 1789–91." *Journal of Modern History,* LI (December, 1979), 701–33.

———. *The Jacobin Club of Marseille, 1790–1794.* Ithaca, 1973.

———. *The Jacobin Clubs in the French Revolution: The First Years.* Princeton, 1982.

Lallié, Alfred. "Le Fédéralisme dans le département de la Loire-Inférieure." *Revue de la Révolution,* XV (May–August, 1889), 6–24, 357–76, 454–73, and XVI (September–December, 1889), 126–38.

Le Bihan, Alain. *Loges et Chapitres de la Grande Loge et du Grand Orient de France*. Paris, 1967.

Lefebvre, Georges. *The Great Fear of 1789*. Translated by Joan White. New York, 1973.

————. *La Révolution Française*. Paris, 1951.

Le Parquier, E. "Rouen et le Département de la Seine-Inférieure aux mois de juin et juillet 1793." *La Normandie*, II (November, 1895), 321–33, and (December, 1895), 353–63.

Lewis, Gwynne. *The Second Vendée: The Continuity of Counterrevolution in the Department of the Gard, 1789–1815*. Oxford, 1978.

Ligou, Daniel. *Montauban à la fin de l'Ancien Régime et aux débuts de la Révolution, 1787–1794*. Paris, 1959.

Lucas, C. R. *The Structure of the Terror: The Example of Javogues and the Loire*. Oxford, 1973.

Lyons, Martyn. *Revolution in Toulouse: An Essay on Provincial Terrorism*. Berne, 1978.

Marx, Roland. *Recherches sur la vie politique de l'Alsace prérévolutionnaire et révolutionnaire*. Strasbourg, 1966.

Mazauric, Claude. "A Propos de la Manifestation de la Rougemare (11–12 janvier 1793): Royalistes, Modérés et Jacobins à Rouen du 10 août 1792 au printemps 1793." *Cahiers Léopold Delisle*, XV (1966), 43–76.

Merriman, John. *The Agony of the Republic: The Repression of the Left in Revolutionary France, 1848–51*. New Haven, 1978.

Montier, A. "Le Département de l'Eure et ses districts en juin 1793." *Révolution Française*, XXX (1896), 128–55, 198–226.

Nicolle, Paul. *Histoire de Vire pendant la Révolution*. Vire, 1923.

————. "Le Mouvement fédéraliste dans l'Orne en 1793." *Annales Historiques de la Révolution Française*, XIII (1936), 481–512; XIV (1937), 215–33; and XV (1938), 12–33, 289–313, 385–410.

Ozouf, Mona. *La Fête révolutionnaire, 1789–1799*. Paris, 1976.

Palmer, R. R. *Twelve Who Ruled: The Year of the Terror in the French Revolution*. New York, 1966.

Patrick, Alison. *The Men of the First French Republic*. Baltimore, 1972.

Perrot, Jean-Claude. "Rapports sociaux et villes au XVIIIᵉ siècle." *Annales: Economies, Sociétés, Civilisations*, XXIII (1968), 241–67.

Peuchet, Jacques. *Statistique Elémentaire de la France*. Paris, 1805.

Riffaterre, C. *Le Mouvement antijacobin et antiparisien à Lyon et dans le Rhône-et-Loire en 1793*. 2 vols. Lyon, 1912.

Roque, Louis de la, and Edouard de Barthélemy. *Catalogue des Gentilhommes en 1789*. 2 vols. Paris, 1866.

Rudé, George. *The Crowd in the French Revolution*. London, 1959.

Scott, William. *Terror and Repression in Revolutionary Marseille*. London, 1973.

Sewell, William H., Jr. *Work and Revolution in France*. Cambridge, 1980.

Soboul, Albert. *The French Revolution, 1787–1799*. Translated by Alan Forrest and Colin Jones. New York, 1975.

————. *The Sans-culottes.* Translated by Rémy Inglis Hall. Princeton, 1980.

Stone, Daniel. "La Révolte fédéraliste à Rennes." *Annales Historiques de la Révolution Française,* XLIII (1971), 367–87.

Sydenham, M. J. *The Girondins.* London, 1961.

————. "The Republican Revolt of 1793: A Plea for Less Localized Local Studies." *French Historical Studies,* XI (Spring, 1981), 120–38.

Taylor, George V. "Noncapitalist Wealth and the Origins of the French Revolution." *American Historical Review,* LXXII (1967), 469–96.

Tilly, Charles. *The Vendée.* Cambridge, 1964.

Tocqueville, Alexis de. *The Old Regime and the French Revolution.* Translated by Stuart Gilbert. New York, 1955.

Vivie, Aurélien. *Histoire de la Terreur à Bordeaux.* 2 vols. Bordeaux, 1877.

Vovelle, Michel. *La Chute de la Monarchie, 1787–1792.* Paris, 1972.

Wallon, H. *La Révolution du 31 mai et le fédéralisme en 1793.* 2 vols. Paris, 1886.

Walter, Gerard. *Répertoire de l'histoire de la Révolution française. Travaux publiés de 1800 à 1940.* 2 vols. Paris, 1941–51.

Caen

In the study of urban or regional history during the Revolution, a number of local journals are extremely useful. For Caen, the most important are *Annales de Normandie, Bulletin de la Société des Antiquaires de Normandie,* and *Mémoires de l'Académie Nationale des Sciences, Arts et Belles-lettres de Caen.*

Beaujour, Sophronyme. *Essai sur l'histoire de l'Eglise Réformée de Caen.* Caen, 1877.

Bonnel. "Communication au sujet des troubles de 4–5 novembre, 1791." *Bulletin de la Société des Antiquaires de Normandie,* XLIX (1942–45), 487–94.

Bonnet de la Tour, G. "Le fédéralisme normand; la bataille sans larmes (Brécourt, 13 juillet 1793)." *Le Pays d'Argentan,* no. 132 (March, 1964), 3–52.

Campion, M. A. *Les Fêtes Nationales à Caen sous la Révolution.* Caen, 1877.

Carel, Pierre. *Etude sur la commune de Caen.* Caen, 1888.

————. "Note sur les magistrats du bailliage et siège présidial de Caen (1552–1790)." *Bulletin de la Société des Antiquaires de Normandie,* XX (1898), 583–647.

Goodwin, A. "The Federalist Movement in Caen during the French Revolution." *Bulletin of the John Rylands Library,* XLII (March, 1960), 313–43.

Grall, Jeanne. "Le Fédéralisme: Eure et Calvados." *Bulletin de la Société des Antiquaires de Normandie,* LV (1959–60), 133–53.

————. "Les foires de Caen pendant la période révolutionnaire." *Bulletin de la Société des Antiquaires de Normandie,* LVII (1963–64), 525–38.

————. "La France au lendemain du 31 mai 1793." *Bulletin de la Société des Antiquaires de Normandie,* LV (1959–60), 513–24.

————. "L'Oeuvre de Robert Lindet dans le Calvados et le problème des subsistances (août–septembre 1793)." *Bulletin de la Société des Antiquaires de Normandie,* LVI (1961–62), 339–57.

————. "La très courte carrière d'un procureur général syndic, Bougon-Longrais

(1765–1794), procureur général syndic du Calvados." In *Droit privé et institutions régionales: Etudes historiques offertes à Jean Yver.* Paris, 1976. 333–44.

Lavalley, Gaston. "La Presse en Normandie: Journal de l'Armée des Côtes de Cherbourg." *Mémoires de l'Académie Nationale des Sciences, Arts et Belles-lettres de Caen* (1899), 205–75.

Le Bourgignon du Perré, L. *Notes d'un détenu de la maison de réclusion des ci-devant Carmélites de Caen pendant la Terreur.* Evreux, 1903.

Lesage, Georges. *La Fabrication des blondes à Caen.* Caen, 1910.

———, ed. *A Travers le passé du Calvados.* 5 vols. Paris, 1927–41.

Mazière, Alfred. *Le Tribunal Criminel du département du Calvados sous l'Assemblée Législative et la Convention.* Caen, 1902.

Mourlot, Félix. *Le Cahier d'observations et doléances du tiers-état de la ville de Caen en 1789.* Paris, 1912.

———. *La Fin de l'Ancien Régime et les débuts de la Révolution dans la généralité de Caen, 1787–1790.* Paris, 1913.

Ozouf, Mona. "Innovations et traditions dans les itinéraires des fêtes révolutionnaires: l'exemple de Caen," *Ethnologie Française,* VII (January, 1977), 45–74.

Perrot, Jean-Claude. "Documents sur la population du Calvados pendant la Révolution et l'Empire." *Annales de Normandie,* XV (March, 1965), 77–128.

———. *Genèse d'une ville moderne: Caen au XVIIIe siècle.* 2 vols. Paris, 1975.

———. "Introduction à l'emploi des registres fiscaux en histoire sociale; l'exemple de Caen au XVIIIe siècle." *Annales de Normandie,* XVI (March, 1966), 33–65.

Renard, Charles. *Notice sur les Carabots de Caen.* Caen, 1858.

Sauvage, René Norbert. "La Loge maçonnique la Constante Fabert à Caen, en 1785." *Mémoires de l'Académie Nationale des Sciences, Arts et Belles-lettres de Caen* (1918–20), 397–406.

———. *Rapports d'un agent du conseil exécutif sur le Calvados à l'époque du fédéralisme.* Caen, 1908.

———. "Les Souvenirs de J.-B. Renée sur la Révolution à Caen, 1789–93." *Normannia,* VI (1933), 565–606, and VII (1934), 11–39.

———, ed. *Le Fédéralisme en Normandie: Journal du quartier-maître du 6e bataillon bis des volontaires du Calvados.* Caen, 1909.

Sée, Henri. "Notes sur les Foires en France et particulièrement sur les Foires de Caen au XVIIIe siècle." *Revue d'Histoire économique et sociale,* XV (1927), 366–85.

Yver, Jean. "Une Administration municipale 'orageuse' à Caen à la fin de l'Ancien Régime: La Mairie de M. de Vendoeuvre." *Mémoires de l'Académie Nationale des Sciences, Arts et Belles-lettres de Caen* (1931), 241–68.

Limoges

The most useful local journals for Limoges and its region are *Archives Historiques du Limousin* and *Bulletin de la Société Archéologique et Historique du Limousin.*

Daudet, R. *L'Urbanisme à Limoges au XVIIIe siècle.* Limoges, 1939.

Delage, Franck, ed. *Limoges à travers les siècles.* Limoges, 1946.

Demerliac, M. "Une Ténébreuse Affaire à Limoges sous la Terreur." *Bulletin de la Société Archéologique et Historique du Limousin*, LXXX (1943), 116–25.

D'Hollander, Paul. "La Vie Religieuse et la Révolution dans l'Haute-Vienne." Thèse de troisième cycle, l'Université de Limoges.

Ducourtieux, Paul. *Histoire de Limoges*. Limoges, 1925.

———. *Limoges d'après ses anciens plans*. Limoges, 1884.

———. *Limoges: Son histoire, son plan, ses monuments, ses rues*. Limoges, 1917.

La Franc-maçonnerie Limousine, son passé, son présent, ses ambitions. Limoges, 1949.

Fray-Fournier, Alfred. *Le Club des Jacobins de Limoges, 1790–95*. Limoges, 1903.

———. *Le Département de la Haute-Vienne, sa formation territoriale, son administration, sa situation politique pendant la Révolution*. 2 vols. Limoges, 1908.

———. *Les Fêtes Nationales et les Cérémonies Civiques dans la Haute-Vienne pendant la Révolution*. Limoges, 1902.

Granet, P. "Extraits du journal de Génébrias de Goutte-pagnon, 1774–1794." *Archives Historiques du Limousin*, IV (1892), 380–87.

Guibert, Louis. "Anciens registres des paroisses de Limoges." *Bulletin de la Société Archéologique et Historique du Limousin*, XXIX (1881), 73–124.

———. "Les Confréries de Pénitents en France et notamment dans le diocèse de Limoges." *Bulletin de la Société Archéologique et Historique du Limousin*, XXVII (1879), 5–193.

———. *La Dette Beaupeyrat*. Limoges, 1888.

———. "Le Parti Girondin dans la Haute-Vienne." *Revue Historique*, VIII (1878), 10–106.

———, ed. *Registres consulaires de la ville de Limoges, 1774–1790*. 6 vols. Limoges, 1897.

Jouhaud, Léon. *Les Gardes nationaux à Limoges, avant la Convention*. Limoges, 1940.

———. *La Révolution Française en Limousin, pages d'histoire vécue, 1789–1792*. Limoges, 1947.

Juge, J. J. *Changements survenus dans les moeurs des habitants de Limoges, depuis une cinquantaine d'années*. Limoges, 1817.

Leroux, Alfred. "Extraits du registre de la confrérie des tanneurs et corroyeurs de Limoges (1581–1790)." *Archives Historiques du Limousin*, III (1891), 79–89.

———. *Les Sources de l'histoire de la Haute-Vienne pendant la Révolution*. Limoges, 1908.

Morichon, René, ed. *Histoire du Limousin et de la Marche*. 2 vols. Limoges, 1972–75.

Perrier, A. *Une Industrie Limousine: La Porcelaine*. Poitiers, 1937.

Plantadis, Johannès. *L'Agitation autonomiste de Guienne et le mouvement fédéraliste des Girondins en Limousin, 1787–1793*. Tulle, 1908.

Pompon, André. *Les Ouvriers porcelainiers de Limoges*. Paris, 1910.

Stein, Henri. "Gabriel Grellet et la manufacture de porcelaine de Limoges sous la règne de Louis XVI." *Bulletin de la Société Archéologique et Historique du Limousin*, LXXVIII (1939), 62–79.

Tintou, Michel. "Réorganisation de la confrérie du Saint-Sacrement de Saint-Pierre-du-Queyroix, en 1763." *Bulletin de la Société Archéologique et Historique du Limousin,* XCVI (1969), 141–50.

Verynaud, Georges. *Histoire de Limoges.* Limoges, 1973.

Biographical Dictionaries

Boisard, F. *Notices biographiques, littéraires et critiques sur les hommes du Calvados.* Caen, 1848.

Brette, A. *Les Constituants.* Paris, 1897.

Hoefer, Jean Chrétien Ferdinand. *Nouvelle Biographie Générale.* Paris, 1858–78.

Lebreton, Théodore. *Biographie Normande.* Rouen, 1857.

Oursel, N. N. *Nouvelle Biographie Normande.* Paris, 1886.

Robert, Adolphe, Edgar Bourloton, and Gaston Cougny. *Dictionnaire des parlementaires français.* 5 vols. Paris, 1889–91.

Wagner, R. *Calvados et Manche: Dictionnaire biographique Illustré.* Paris, n.d.

Index

Affair of 84, pp. 39–43, 42*n*, 45–46, 67, 220, 221
Agent democracy, 14–15, 228, 236, 245, 247
Agriculture: agricultural hinterland versus commercial periphery, 6–7; in Caen, 16, 17–18, 23; in Limoges, 16–17, 23–24; rural landowners in departmental councils, 191, 193–95, 231; rural landowners in district councils, 199–201; in Calvados, 239
Agulhon, Maurice, 28, 29
Aine, Marius Jean Baptiste Nicolas d', 22
Aisne, 10
Alluaud, François, 22, 27, 29
Amis de la Paix, 27, 29, 54–57, 59–62, 69, 84–85, 165, 186, 207, 210, 213, 216, 232
Ardant-Masjambost, Joseph, 207, 207*n*
Army of pacification, 172, 172*n*, 175
Army of the Coasts of Cherbourg, 131–32, 166
Artisans, 195, 200–201, 205–206, 208, 212, 232
Aubin, Charles Pierre Marie, 153, 157, 185
Audouin, Jean Baptiste, 27, 29
Audouin, Jean Baptiste (Xavier), 27, 29, 96, 99, 107, 109, 115, 157, 170, 185, 229
Auvray de Coursanne, Charles François, 46–47

Balezy, Pierre, 85
Barbaroux, Charles Jean Marie, 50, 92, 102, 122, 130, 140–41, 157, 244
Barbot, Jean Michel, 35, 53, 75, 75*n*, 127, 178, 215–16
Barère, Bertrand, 166
Baudot, 114, 115
Bayeux, Georges, 43, 44, 46–48, 50, 67, 71, 75, 89
Beaumier, 122, 122*n*
Belzunce, Henri de, 34–35, 36, 67
Bergoeing, 140
Billaud-Varenne, Jean Nicolas, 160
Boiszerard, François Jacques Samuel, 201, 214
Bonnet de Meautry, Pierre Louis, 38, 48, 50, 75, 76, 84, 94, 98–99, 150, 157, 170, 172, 175–78, 184, 229, 238
Bordas, Pardoux, 27, 78, 85, 86, 96, 98, 99, 106, 107, 112, 115, 229, 231
Bordeaux: federalist revolt in, 1, 3, 5, 10, 102–106, 111, 156–57, 241–42, 244; correspondence with National Convention, 95, 95*n*; messenger to Haute-Vienne, 112, 115, 203; forces marching toward Paris, 114–15; repression and reorganization in, 158; grain shortage in, 175
Bordeaux Jacobin club, 242
Borie, J., 85, 86
Bouches-du-Rhône, 92, 138, 225

Bouchotte, Jean Baptiste Noel, 169, 171
Boudet, Grégoire Louis, 207n
Bougon-Longrais, Jean Charles Hippolyte,
47–48, 68, 74–75, 94, 120, 132, 136,
137, 146n, 147–48, 149, 150, 151, 157,
173, 177, 180, 181
Bouret, 187–88
Boyer, Jean, 163
Boyer-Fonfrède, Jean Baptiste, 92
Brissot, Jacques Pierre, 80, 88, 102, 112,
235
Brival, Jacques, 161–65, 204
Buzot, François, 102, 140, 141, 188

Cachelou, Jean, 208
Caen: comparison with Limoges, xiii–xiv;
federalist revolt in, 4, 10, 115–58, 241,
242, 244–46; agriculture in, 16, 17–18,
23; economy of, 16–21, 23; population
of, 17, 24, 25–26; textile industry in,
18–19; commerce in, 19–21, 30, 231,
238–40; retail fairs in, 19–20; urbanization of, 20–21; grain shortages in, 23;
immigration into, 24, 25, 222–23, 232,
242; faubourgs in, 25–26, 191, 222–23,
232, 233; ratio of "active" citizens to
population, 25; Freemasonry in, 26,
27–28; popular classes in, 29, 62, 69,
189, 191, 232, 233, 246; attitude toward
central government, 30, 217, 239–40;
local government in, 30; revolutionary
politics in, 31–53, 67–69; storming of
the Château in, 31–32; Protestants in, 32,
213–15; violence in, 34–35, 47, 67, 71;
attitude toward nobility, 36, 38, 68; clergy
and church hierarchy in, 36–39, 67–68;
and Affair of 84, pp. 39–43, 42n, 45–46,
67, 220, 221; installation of Criminal Tribunal, 43–46; local elections in, 62;
newspapers in, 68; bourgeoisie in, 69;
deputies to National Assembly, 80; reaction to Revolution, 81; resistance to conscription for army, 83–84; communication network involving, 88–95, 99, 100,
118–20, 229–31; chronology of federalist revolt in, 103–105; disintegration of
federalist revolt in, 106; declaration of
insurrection, 121–30; lack of popular
support for insurrection, 130, 154,
156–57, 189, 230, 232, 242; fugitive
Girondin deputies in, 140–42, 156, 158,
181; interest in new constitution, 154; retraction of insurrection, 155; repression

and reorganization in, 159, 161, 165–89,
232; arrests during repression, 161,
177–82, 179n; army of pacification in,
172, 175; public fete during repression
and reorganization, 176–77; leadership of
federalist revolt, 177–82; clemency for
those arrested, 181–82, 187, 188–89;
types of people during insurrection,
187–88; influence on departmental administration, 198, 227; tax records for,
208–12, 209n; sections of town, 217–23;
revolutionary fetes in, 223–24; politics in,
224–28, 231–33, 241. See also Calvados
Caen district council: lack of support for
insurrection, 158; retraction of insurrection, 166, 173; appointment of new administrators after federalist revolt, 183,
184; influence of, 198–99; occupational
composition of, 199–201; Jacobin members of, 216; relationship with departmental council, 225–27
Caen Jacobin club: influence of, 41–42,
45–46, 48–51, 215–16, 227, 231; and
the Affair of 84, p. 42; and Criminal
Tribunal, 43–44, 49–50; break with Paris
Jacobins, 50–51, 68, 96, 99, 116, 157,
185, 229; decline of, 51, 69, 99; reaction
to May 31 revolution, 116; Fauchet's influence on, 146n; lack of support for insurrection, 152–53; view of departmental
force, 152–53; during repression and reorganization, 176; weakness of, 186, 188;
communication network associated with,
229
Caen municipal council: occupational composition of, 69, 191, 204–208, 212; correspondence with Paris, 90; De Cussy's
complaints of ill treatment, 92; reaction to
May 31 revolution, 116–17; concerns
about grain supply and military defense,
120–21; consideration of new constitution, 154; and lack of popular support for
insurrection, 158, 203; retraction of insurrection, 174; appointment of new administrators after federalist revolt, 183, 184;
size of, 202; different terms of, 203; taxes
paid by members of, 209–12; sectional
representation in, 217–23; relationship
with departmental council, 225–27; influence of, 231
Caen National Guard: formation of, 36; volunteers and, 36; and the Régiment d'Aunis,
41; and the Affair of 84, p. 42; and Crimi-

nal Tribunal, 43; and Bayeux's death, 47; and resistance to conscription for army, 84; and departmental force, 131, 136; parade of, 139

Cahier de Gerville, 44

Caille, Louis: president of Jacobin club, 42, 43, 45, 46, 49, 116; temporary departure from Jacobin club, 50; and Carabots, 52; as district administrator, 116, 117, 129n, 130; as commissioner to Paris, 123; on provisional insurrectionary committee, 127; volunteer for Calvados departmental force, 129; view of Wimpffen, 131; support for federalist revolt from other departments, 136; representative to Central Committee of Resistance to Oppression, 143; relationship with Fauchet, 146n; in Evreux with departmental force, 148, 150; leadership for federalist revolt, 153, 155, 157, 158, 177, 180, 185, 198–99, 230; in hiding during repression, 173, 173n, 178

Caille le jeune, 136

Calvados: agriculture in, 23, 239; economy of, 30; deputies to National Convention, 50–51, 74–80, 93–94, 98–99; nobility in, 68; population of, 78; taxes paid in, 78, 78n; reaction to attack on Tuileries palace, 81–82; reaction to trial and execution of Louis XVI, 81, 82; resistance to conscription for army, 84; departmental force for National Convention, 90–92, 95, 99; communication network involving, 93, 95, 98–100, 147, 229–31; chronology of federalist revolt in, 103–105; federalist revolt in, 115–58; formation of departmental force, 117, 128–29, 131, 136–40, 146; general assembly during early period of insurrection, 117, 128–40, 143; commissioners to National Convention, 117–23, 117n, 230; arrest of Romme and Prieur, 126, 127, 129, 130–32, 135, 136, 156, 165, 173, 199; objections to declaration of insurrection, 127–28, 156–57; military defense of, 131–32; grain boycott against Paris, 132–35, 133n, 158; broadening support for insurrection, 134–36; departmental force to Paris, 134, 156–58, 187; departmental force to Evreux, 136–39, 147–50, 149n, 182; new constitution and, 137, 153–54, 155, 171; reorganization of general assembly during insurrection, 146–47; departmental administration during insurrection,

147–48; retreat of departmental force, 151–52, 154, 157, 168–69; Jacobins' view of departmental force, 152–53; retraction of insurrection, 155–56; involvement against Vendée revolt, 158; repression and reorganization in, 161–89; fear of Parisian battalions, 169–70; grain shortage in, 175–76; attitude toward central government, 217. See also Caen

Calvados Criminal Tribunal, 43–46, 49–50

Calvados departmental council: leadership for insurrection, 156, 158, 230; retraction of insurrection, 172–73; appointment of new administrators after federalist revolt, 182–83; influence of, 190, 231, 240; occupational composition of, 191, 193–96; organization of, 192–93; geographical distribution of members, 196–98; tendency to exceed its authority, 196; departmental force to Paris, 203; Jacobin members of, 216; relationship with district and municipal councils, 225–27; political experience of, 226

Cantillon-Tramont, Charles, 162, 163

Capdeville, Jean, 149

Carabot club, 51–53, 51n, 69, 75, 84, 125, 130–31, 136–37, 158, 175, 185, 215–16, 227, 230–32

Caroger, Jacques, 153, 158, 185

Cauvin, Barnabé, 120, 128n, 177, 178, 182

Central Committee of Resistance to Oppression, 142–46, 142n, 148, 152, 153, 155, 156, 158, 171, 249–51

Central Revolutionary Committee, 101

Chabrol, Abbé, 71

Chaix-d'Estanges, 39, 43, 43n, 45, 74, 136, 146, 146n, 153–55, 158, 177, 178, 180–82, 185

Chalier, Marie Joseph, 243

Chatry, Jean Louis Isaac, 77, 214, 226

Chatry, Pierre Jacques Samuel l'aîné, 77, 124–25, 127, 130, 143, 148, 156, 178, 214, 216, 226, 230

Cherrier, 186

Cheylus, Bishop, 37, 38–39

Chibourg, Joseph Pierre le jeune, 183

Clergy, 36–39, 39n, 58, 59, 63, 67–68

Club National, 242

Collot d'Herbois, Jean Marie, 159

Commercial interests: agricultural hinterland vs. commercial periphery, 6–7; in Caen, 19–21, 30, 221, 231, 232; in municipal councils, 191, 207–208, 212; in de-

partmental councils, 194–95, 231; in district councils, 199–200; in Limoges, 232–33
Commission of Twelve, 1, 8, 15, 87–88, 92, 97, 101–102, 116, 121, 140
Committee of Public Safety, 144, 145, 160, 161, 166, 167, 169, 170, 175, 184–85, 188, 246
Commune in Paris. *See* Paris Commune
Condorcet, Marie Jean Antoine, 80, 96
Corday, Charlotte, 139*n*
Cordelier club, 144, 245
Corrèze, 91, 108, 112, 113, 114, 163, 235
Côte-d'Or, 10
Côte-d'Or resolution, 106, 107–108, 113, 115, 196, 198, 203, 230
Côtes-du-Nord, 136, 142
Creuse, 112
Criminal Tribunal. *See* Calvados Criminal Tribunal

Danton, Georges Jacques, 88, 92, 93, 180
De Cussy, Gabriel, 32, 75, 76, 89–90, 92, 99, 140, 141, 157, 214, 229
De Lessart, Claude Antoine Valdec, 46
Democracy: representative vs. agent democracy, 14–15, 228, 236, 237, 244–45; Tocqueville's view of, 240–41; agent democracy, 247
Departmental councils, 160, 186, 192, 225. *See also* Calvados departmental council; Haute-Vienne departmental council
Derché, J. J., 185
Déroche, Pierre, 27, 84
Deux-Sèvres, 85, 86
DeVic, Antoine, 116, 142, 154, 156
District councils, 161, 186, 198, 198*n*, 225. *See also* Caen district council; Limoges district council
Doulcet de Pontécoulant, Gustave, 44–46, 49–50, 74, 76, 81–82, 118–19, 122, 129, 157, 181, 229, 237
Dubois Dubais, Louis Thibaut, 75, 76
Dufour, Jean Jacques Victor, 31–32, 35, 41, 130, 139
Duhamel-Levailly, Charles François, 136, 136*n*
Dumas, Pierre, 27, 55–56, 77, 164–65
Dumont, Louis Philippe, 76, 81–82, 90, 229
Dumouriez, General Charles François, 82–83, 92, 109, 243
Durand de Richemont, Joseph, 82, 162–63
DuRoy, Jean Michel, 84, 94, 134, 169, 170, 172, 175–78, 182, 184, 186

Edmonds, Bill, 6, 9*n*
Elbeuf, 19
Esnault, Pierre François Laurent, 31–32, 38, 41–42, 49, 52, 83–84, 130, 179, 215
Eure, 129, 136, 137, 142, 143, 148, 149, 169
Eure-et-Loir, 235

Fauchet, Claude, 39, 45, 48, 49, 68, 74, 75, 76, 146, 146*n*, 157, 215
Faye, Gabriel, 78, 108, 110
Federalist revolt: in the departments, 1–13, 102–106, 241–46; and proscription of Girondin deputies, 1–2, 3, 98, 235, 235*n*; scholarly interpretations of, 2–8; Girondin/Montagnard conflict and, 3–4, 5; Marxist interpretation of, 3, 5, 7–8; in Caen, 4, 10, 115–58, 241, 242, 244–46; royalist nature of, 4; in Bordeaux, 102–106, 241–42, 244; in Lyon, 102–106, 166, 241–43; chronology of, 103–105; disintegration of, 106, 154–56; in Calvados, 115–58; lack of popular support for, 130, 154, 156–57, 189, 230, 232, 242–43; underlying fears and resentments, 143–46; repression and reorganization after, 150–61; underlying factors, 235–36, 244–47; and agent vs. representative democracy, 236, 237, 244–45; demonstration of links between national and local politics, 236–38; in Marseille, 241–44
Feret, Guillaume, 118*n*, 123, 124
Feuillants, 49
Finistère, 92, 136, 138, 142, 143, 149*n*, 153, 158
Fleury, Gilles, 127–28, 128*n*, 156
Foucaud, Jean, 58, 109–10
Fouché, Joseph, 159
Fox, Edward Whiting, 6–7, 10, 14, 15, 238–40, 245–46
Fray-Fournier, Alfred, 57, 69
Freemasonry, 26–28, 213, 231
Frémanger, J., 187–88
French army, 82–85

Garat, Joseph, 122, 123*n*, 132, 149, 155, 165, 167–68, 168*n*, 171, 189
Gauthier, A. F., 243
Gay-Vernon, Jean Baptiste, 62, 68, 79, 88, 97–99, 106–10, 113–15, 157, 163, 229, 231
Gay-Vernon, Léonard, 61, 62–63, 78, 237
Gensonné, Armand, 80

Gervais de la Prise, 38–39, 39n
Gironde, 112, 136, 138, 235, 241
Girondins: proscription of deputies, 1, 3, 4, 8, 9, 15, 98, 102, 109–10, 122, 235; Girondin/Montagnard conflict, 2–3, 5, 8, 88; in National Convention, 2–3, 87, 88, 101; association with federalism, 3–4; social background of, 3; formation of Commission of Twelve, 8; trial of Marat, 8; departmental support for, 10–13; concept of representative government, 15, 236, 237; impeachment of Marat, 87; support for, 98; fugitive deputies in Caen, 100, 140–42, 156, 158, 181; in Caen, 157
Gohier de Jumilly, 39, 178
Gorsas, Antoine Joseph, 35, 68, 96, 102, 128, 140, 141
Gouttes, Abbé, 62
Grellet, Gabriel, 22, 207
Guadet, Marguerite Elie, 87, 102, 140, 141, 242

Hanriot, François, 102
Haute-Vienne: support for Montagnard Convention, 10; economy of, 23, 30; grain shortages in, 23–24, 158; clergy in, 58; deputies to National Convention, 77–80, 98–99; population of, 78; taxes paid in, 78, 78n; reaction to trial and execution of Louis XVI, 81, 82; reaction to attack on Tuileries palace, 82; involvement against Vendée revolt, 85–86, 95–96, 113–14, 158, 163, 179, 239; departmental guard for protection of National Convention, 91; communication network involving, 95–99, 108–109, 229–31; chronology of federalist revolt in, 103–105; support for May 31 revolution, 106–15, 157–58; hospital funds for, 114, 115; preparation for resistance to Bordeaux federalists, 114–15; opposition to insurrection, 156; attitude toward central government, 158, 217; arrests during repression, 163, 164–65; repression and reorganization in, 184. See also Limoges
Haute-Vienne departmental council: loyalty oath and, 91–92; support for Côte-d'Or resolution, 106, 107–108, 113, 115, 196, 198, 203, 230; and Vendée revolt, 107; entreaties from Lyon, Jura, and Bordeaux, 110–12, 113, 115; during repression and reorganization, 161, 162, 165; conscious of constitutional limitations, 186, 195–

96; occupational composition of, 191, 193–96; organization of, 192–93; geographical distribution of members, 196–98; Jacobin members of, 216, 227; decision to hold public meetings, 225n; relationship with district and municipal councils, 225–27; political experience of, 226; influence of, 231
Hébert, Jacques René, 87
Henry-Larivière, Pierre François, 72, 72n, 75, 76, 102, 128, 140
Hérault-Séchelles, Marie Jean, 102, 167
Heudier, 170–71
Hubert, Etienne, 181
Hugonneau-Sauvot, Jean, 162, 163

Ille-et-Vilaine, 111, 138, 142, 143, 148
Indre, 136
Indre-et-Loire, 136
Industry. See Porcelain industry; Textile industry
Insurrectionary Commune in Paris. See Paris Commune

Jacobins and Jacobin clubs, 15, 49, 227, 227n, 228, 229. See also Caen Jacobin club; Limoges Jacobin club; Paris Jacobin club
Jort, Richard de, 178, 183
Julien, Jean, 2
Jura, 110–12, 113, 231

Kervélégan, A. B. F., 92, 140

Lace production, 18–19
Lacroix, C., 167
Lacroix, Michel, 77–78, 108, 110
Laforest family, 21, 22, 85
Lahaye, J. C. G., 140, 140n
Lahaye, René, 173, 178, 182
Lanjuinais, Jean Denis, 122, 140, 140n
Lanot, Antoine Joseph, 163–65, 204
Laplanche, Jacques Léonard, 178–82, 179n, 184, 204, 232
Lasseret, Jean Adrien, 46, 94
Lawyers: in departmental councils, 191, 193–96, 204, 231; in district councils, 191, 204; in local political bodies of provincial France, 196n; in municipal councils, 199–201, 204–205, 212
Le Carpentier, François, 35–36, 127, 181
Leclerc, Jean Baptiste, 125, 128n, 178, 179
Le Cointre, L., 169
Lefebvre, Georges, 3–5, 51n

Le Forestier de Vendoeuvre, 37–38, 67
Legislative Assembly: French Revolution and, 70–72; election of National Convention and, 71; relationship with departmental electoral assemblies, 71–72; and the Paris Commune, 72; publication of voting records of members of, 72, 74; satisfaction with, 79; communications with, 82, 228; dissension in, 88; delegates to, 89
Le Goupil Duclos, Jean, 119, 123, 128, 128n, 139, 141–42, 154–56, 179, 181, 187, 189, 230
Le Grand, 168–69
LeHodey, Etienne, 170
Lenormand, René, 117, 118n, 123, 127, 129, 129n, 136, 147, 149, 150, 150n, 156, 157, 173, 177, 178, 182, 230
Lenormand (president of Carabots), 117n, 119, 125, 130, 136
Lequeru, Bernard, 173, 173n, 178
LeRoy, Lieutenant Colonel, 137, 150
Lesage, Denis Toussaint, 140, 235
Les Amis de la Constitution. See Caen Jacobin club
Lesterpt, Jacques, 162
Lesterpt-Beauvais, Benoist, 78, 110, 162, 238
Lévêque, Pierre Jean, 48, 89, 93–94, 95n, 120, 123, 130, 137, 147–50, 154, 157, 173, 177, 189
Lidon, B. F., 235
Limoges: comparison with Caen, xiii–xiv; agriculture in, 16–17, 23–24; economy of, 16–17, 21–24; textile industry in, 17, 21, 23, 233; porcelain industry in, 21–22, 233; urban renewal and road improvements in, 22; fire in, 23, 53–54, 67, 239; grain shortages in, 23–24, 23n, 53, 67, 233, 239; population of, 25, 26; ratio of "active" citizens to population, 25; faubourgs of, 26, 223; Freemasonry in, 26–27; penitent confraternities in, 28–29, 233–34; attitude toward central government, 30, 217, 239–40; local government in, 30; revolutionary politics in, 53–69; clergy and church hierarchy in, 58, 59, 62–63, 67–68; company of dragoons, 58–60, 61, 62; Royal-Navarre regiment, 59, 60–61, 62; grain delivery by Ganny and Bégougne, 64–67; attitude toward nobility, 68–69; communication network involving, 68, 88, 99, 229–31; violence in, 71; deputies to National Assembly, 80; resistance to conscription for army, 83–84; chronology of federalist revolt in, 103–105; support for May 31 revolution, 106–15, 157–58; preparation to resist Bordeaux federalists, 107, 114–15; new constitution and, 113; repression and reorganization in, 161–65, 184, 186; arrests during repression, 164–65; lack of popular support for insurrection, 189; popular classes in, 189, 232, 233, 246; influence on departmental administration, 198, 226–27; grain consortium in, 207, 208; tax records for, 208–12, 209n; sections of town, 217–20; politics in, 224–28, 231–34, 240–41; revolutionary fetes in, 224; commercial interests in, 232–33; as trade or administrative town, 239–40. See also Haute-Vienne
Limoges district council: during repression and reorganization, 161, 162, 165; occupational composition of, 191, 199–201; influence of, 198, 199; Jacobin members of, 216, 227; relationship with departmental council, 225–27
Limoges Jacobin club: compared with penitent confraternities, 28–29; request for assistance due to fire, 54; growth of, 55; influence of, 56, 69, 157, 186, 190, 227, 227n, 229–30, 231, 234, 240; membership of, 57–58; and company of dragoons, 59, 60; Gay-Vernon's influence on, 62–63, 88, 109, 115; decline of, 64, 210; and grain delivery by Ganny and Bégougne, 66; reaction to attack on Tuileries palace, 82; and resistance to conscription for army, 84–85; taxation of aristocracy, 86; attitude toward Marat, 96–97; communication network associated with, 96, 99, 229–30; relationship with Paris Jacobin club, 96, 97, 99; response to Haute-Vienne delegation's correspondence, 98; reaction to May 31 revolution, 107, 109, 110, 113; preparation for resistance to Bordeaux federalists, 114; membership in municipal council, 208; conflict with Amis de la Paix, 213, 232; role in local politics, 216–17; revolutionary fetes and, 224; pressure for public meetings of departmental council, 225n; objections to Côte-d'Or resolution, 231; establishment of, 237
Limoges municipal council: ban on public assembly, 59; political polarization in,

59–62, 69; and Royal-Navarre regiment, 60–61; moderates in, 63; Jacobin members of, 66–67, 216–17, 227; influence of, 157, 190, 232, 240; during repression and reorganization, 161, 162, 165; occupational composition of, 191, 204–208, 212, 232; size of, 202; different terms of, 203–204; objections to Côte-d'Or resolution, 203, 231; taxes paid by members of, 209–12; sectional representation in, 223; relationship with departmental council, 225–27; denunciation of messengers from Lyon and Jura, 231

Limoges National Guard: and company of dragoons, 58–60, 61; preparation to depart for Poitiers, 86; preparation for resistance to Bordeaux federalists, 114

Lindet, Robert, 75n, 134, 149n, 166, 167, 169–87, 172n, 179n, 203, 204, 208, 232

Lindet, Thomas, 169–70

Linen production, 18

Lisieux, 172, 172n, 175

Loire-Inférieure, 142, 143

Lomont, Claude Jean Baptiste, 48, 50, 75, 76, 88–89, 93–95, 95n, 99, 120, 130, 157, 229

Louis XV, 17

Louis XVI, 37, 38, 70, 72, 80, 81, 82, 89, 227

Louvet, Jean Baptiste, 88, 90, 140, 140n, 152

Lozère, 83, 86

Lyon: federalist revolt in, 1, 4, 6, 10, 102–106, 111, 166, 241–43, 246; artisans and workers in, 62; messenger to Haute-Vienne, 110–12, 113, 115, 203, 231; repression and reorganization in, 150, 184–85

Lyon Jacobin club, 243, 244

Maine-et-Loire, 142, 143

Manche, 126, 136, 142, 142n, 149

Marat, Jean Paul, 8, 15, 39, 71, 87, 88, 90, 92, 93, 96–97, 122, 145, 170, 176

Marie, Antoine Nicolas, 117n, 119–20, 123, 129, 129n, 130

Marne, 10

Marseille: federalist revolt in, 4, 5, 6, 10, 106, 111, 156–57, 241–44, 246; artisans and workers in, 62; repression and reorganization in, 158–59; grain shortage in, 175; role in department, 225

Marseille Jacobin club, 243–44

Marxism, 3, 5, 7–8, 14–15

Mathieu-Lachassagne, François, 108, 163

Mauger, Dom, 118n, 121–24, 146, 148, 177, 180–81

Mayenne, 142, 143, 149

Meillan, 140n

Merchants, 205–207, 206n, 212, 214–15, 232, 233

Mesnil, Pierre, 35, 120, 136, 147, 173, 214

Meurthe, 10, 235

Mollevaut, E., 140

Montagnards: political victory of, 1; in National Convention, 2–3, 88; Girondin/Montagnard conflict, 2–3, 5, 8, 88; social background of, 3; departmental support for, 10–12; and Commission of Twelve, 87; denunciations to, 88, 99; provincial reactions to, 88; from Calvados, 98–99, 157, 229; from Haute-Vienne, 99; from Limoges, 157, 229; support for participatory democracy, 236, 237

Montmorin, Armand Marc, 46

Morbihan, 138, 142, 143, 148–49

Mourier, Pierre, 162, 163

Municipal councils, 161, 201–203, 225. See also Caen municipal council; Limoges municipal council

Nadaud, Mathieu, 207n

Nantes, 10, 83

National Convention: proscription of Girondin deputies, 1–4, 8–12, 15, 98, 102, 109–10, 122, 235; Girondin/Montagnard conflict in, 2–3, 8, 88; proposal for relocation of, 9, 87, 93; writing of new constitution, 9, 71, 80, 82–83, 94, 144, 167; Calvados deputies to, 50–51, 74–80, 93–94, 98–99; election of deputies to, 71, 73–80; Haute-Vienne deputies to, 77–80, 98–99; purge of royalists from departmental administrations, 81–82; conscription for army, 82–85; dissension in, 82, 88, 89, 93, 95, 97, 98, 99; and Commission of Twelve, 87, 101–102, 117; Girondin deputies in, 87, 88, 101; impeachment of Marat, 87; Montagnards in, 87, 88; communications with, 90, 91, 93, 95–98, 108–10, 231; departmental forces for protection of, 90–92, 95, 99; completion of constitution, 113; and hospital funds for Haute-Vienne, 114, 115; Calvados commissioners' trip to, 117–23, 117n; federalist proposal for powers and responsibilities of, 144, 145, 245; attitude toward those involved in federalist revolt, 160, 166; restriction of departmental councils, 160–61, 186, 192; responsibilities of district and municipal councils, 161; order against Calvados federalists, 165–66, 175; use of representatives on mission in departments, 167–68, 185–86; political experience of deputies, 237–38

National Guard. See Caen National Guard; Limoges National Guard; Parisian National Guard

Naurissart, Louis, 57, 59, 63, 64, 66, 67, 164, 203–204, 207, 207n, 210, 228, 232, 233

Newspapers, 68, 96, 147, 171, 181, 185, 228, 229, 230

Nicolas, David, 208, 221

Nieaud, Jean Baptiste, 59, 208, 226

Nîmes, 62, 213

Nioche, P. C., 243

Niort, 86, 95

Orne, 4, 136, 137, 142, 143, 235

Oudot, Charles François, 178–80, 187, 203, 204, 208

Outin, François, 153, 158, 185

Pache, Jean Nicolas, 96, 133, 134, 145

Paisant, Jean Samuel, 208, 221

Paris: May revolution in, 1; Commission of Twelve and, 8; excessive influence of, 8–9, 100, 158, 245–46; assault on Tuileries palace, 70, 72, 81; violence in, 71, 87–88, 89, 92–93; Calvados' reaction to, 81, 90, 119–23; Haute-Vienne delegation's view of, 97–98; moderate view of, 97–98, 99; praise for, 107, 109, 112; gravity of situation in, 120; grain boycott against, 132–35, 133n, 158; criticisms of, 133–34; federalist proposal for role in national politics, 143–44; economic issues concerning, 144, 145; Central Committee of Resistance to Oppression's attitude toward citizens of, 145–46; influence of, 237

Paris Commune, 1, 70–72, 87, 101

Parisian battalions, 169–70, 171

Parisian National Guard, 1

Paris Jacobin club: and May 31 revolution, 1; Caen's break with, 50, 68, 96, 99, 116, 157, 185, 229; relationship with Limoges Jacobin club, 54, 96, 97, 99; publication

of voting records of Legislative Assembly members, 72, 74; view of Marat, 90; Robespierre's address to, 101; federalist proposal for abolition of, 144, 145, 245; communication network associated with, 228, 230, 231

Patrick, Alison, 3, 5, 10, 72, 72n

Penitent confraternities, 28–29, 233–34

Perrin de Sainte-Emmelie, 168

Perrot, Jean-Claude, 17, 19, 20, 25, 214, 220, 222

Pétiniaud, Joseph, 207

Pétiniaud de Beaupeyrat, Jean Baptiste, 23, 23n, 27, 59, 63, 67, 164–65, 233

Pétiniaud de Juriol, 56

Pétion, Jérome, 80, 122, 140, 141, 235

Philippeaux, Pierre, 113

Philippe-Delleville, Jean François, 77

Pius VI, 37

Poitiers, 86, 95

Porcelain industry, 21–22, 233

Prieur, Claude Antoine, 121, 126, 127, 129–32, 135, 154, 156, 165, 168, 172–75, 178, 182, 199

Prieur, Pierre Louis, 169

Protestants, 32, 213–15, 213n, 220

Provence, 4

Puisaye, Colonel Alexandre, 150

Puisaye, General Joseph, 150, 151

Rennes, 4, 136, 142

Representative democracy, 14–15, 228, 236, 245

Rhône-et-Loire, 110–11, 243

Rivaud du Vignaud, François, 78, 108, 110

Robespierre, Maximilien Marie Isidore, 1, 49, 50, 88, 90, 93, 101–102, 116, 122

Roland, Jean Marie, 96

Romme, Charles, 121, 126, 127, 129–32, 135, 154, 156, 165, 168, 172–75, 178, 182, 199

Rouen, 10, 20, 135, 141, 148, 185, 246

Roujoux, L. J., 143

Royal-Navarre regiment, 59, 60–61, 62

Saillenfest, Henri Michel, 152, 173, 182

Saint-André, Jeanbon, 167

Salles, Jean Baptiste, 140

Sans-culottes, 3, 15, 62, 63, 67, 164, 236, 244

Seine-et-Oise, 111

Seine-Inférieure, 122, 135–36, 142, 142n, 147, 225

Sepher, General, 170, 171, 178
Seven Years War, 18, 20, 131
Soboul, Albert, 3–4, 14–15, 70, 228, 236, 246
Société des Amis de la Constitution. *See* Limoges Jacobin club
Société Patriotique et Littéraire, 55, 56
Somme, 136
Soulignac, Jean Baptiste, 78, 79, 108, 110
Sydenham, Michael, 2, 4, 4n, 5

Taveau, Louis Jean, 74, 76, 180, 181
Textile industry, 17–19, 21, 23, 233
Thiboult, Adrien, 129, 129n, 147, 173
Tirel, Robert, 127, 128n, 156, 173, 199, 230
Tocqueville, Alexis de, 7, 30, 240–41, 246
Toulon, 4, 6, 159, 246
Tourny, Louis, 22
Turgot, Anne Robert Jacques, 22

Valady, 140n
Valazé, 102, 122
Vardon, Louis Alexandre Jacques, 76, 122
Vaultier, Frédéric, 34–35, 34n, 51n, 52, 124, 128n, 130, 140, 140n, 141, 149, 149n, 151, 152
Vendée revolt, 83, 85–86, 95–96, 107, 110, 113–15, 133–34, 143, 158, 163, 179, 180, 239, 243
Vergniaud, Pierre Victurnien, 80, 88, 95n, 101–102, 242
Viger, Louis François Sébastien, 87
Violette, Thomas, 178

Wallon, Henri, 4, 9, 9n
War of Austrian Succession, 20, 82–83
Wimpffen, General Félix, 120, 127, 130–32, 139, 149–52, 150n, 154–55, 157, 166, 168–70, 172